National Parks Europe

Activity Series

Also available:
Walk Europe

On the internet:
www.activityseries.com

Aalborg, Aberfoyle, Abisko National Park, Abiskojokk canyon, Abruzzo National Park, Acquacheta waterfall, Adamello Brenta Nature Park, Aeulehåg reserve, Aggtelek National Park, Alba Fucens, Almannagjá, Alpi Marittime Nature Park, Amblève river, Antalya, Aöös gorge, Aosta, Apennines, Aran Islands, Ardennes, Arkengarthdale, Armorica Regional Nature Park, Arno river, Aroktó, Around Copenhagen, Arrée mountains, Ascoli Piceno, Augustodunum, Aulne estuary, Aven Armand, Avpromenaden, Áyios Akhíllios, Áyios Yermanós, Azenhas do Mar, Baltic Sea, Bansko, Baradla, Barranco de las Angustias, Barre des Ecrins, Barstyčiai Stone, Bavarian Alps, Bavarian Forest National Park, Baxenghyll gorge, Ben Macdui, Berchtesgaden National Park, Berettyó river, Bernese Jura, Bés Cornapiana, Besseggen ridge, Betws-y-Coed, Białowieża National Park, Biesbosch National Park, Bieszczady National Park, Birka reserve, Black Mountains, Blue John cavern, Boca do Inferno, Bódva river, Boї-Taüll, Botrange, Boubín, Bragança, Brecon Beacons National Park, Brenne Regional Nature Park, Briançonnais, Bukkelægret route, Bünderitsa valley, Burgenland, Burren National Park, Byland abbey, Césis, Caldey Island, Camaldoli monastery, Campobrun, Cantal mountains, Cappadocia, Caraorman forest, Carnuntum, Casentino Forests National Park, Castell Henllys, Castelsantangelo, Causse du Larzac, Central Balkan National Park, Cévennes National Park, Cézallier, Chagford, Chambave, Champagny-en-Vanoise, Chapel of St Laurentius, Chéran gorge, Chérine nature reserve, Cheviot hills, Chilia, Church of Saint Sebastian, Church of St Fridolin, Claise river, Cleddau river, Clermont-Ferrand, Cleveland hills, Cluozza valley, Coire na Ciste, Col de Tende, Collaito grotto, Combe Martin, Combe-Biosse reserve, Connemara National Park, Conwy castle, Coo-Stavelot, Corkova Uvala, Corno Grande, Corno Piccolo, Courland, Creuse river, Crocknafarragh, Crozon peninsula, Cruz Alta, Cuillin peaks, Czorsztyn Castle, Dalälven, Dan-yr-Ogof caves, Danube Delta, Danube river, Dartmoor National Park, Dartmoor Way, Derinkuyu, Derryveagh mountains, Derwent valley, Dobšinská ice cave, Dodona, Doñana National Park, Dónau-auen National Park, Doolin, Dourbie river, Douro river, Dove valley, Drekkingarhylur, Drimmelen, Duirinish peninsula, Dunajec gorge, Dunkery Beacon, Dunvegan castle, Eckartsau castle, Eiderstedt peninsula, El Pico del Teide, Eiltal reserve, Engadine valley, Entorno Natural Park, Epirus, Errigal, Esch-sur-Sûre, Eschenberg, Esk river, Esparron de Verdon, Esrum Sø, Esztramos Hill, Ettelbruck, Exmoor National Park, Eyam, Falkenstein, Färnebofjärden National Park, Feldberg Lake District, Fertő Hanság Nemzeti Park, Fiesch glacier, Finistère, Finneberg lake, Fischland-Darss-Zingst peninsula, Šibenik, Špindlerův Mlýn, Stagerska province, Šumava National Park, Žehra, Žemaičiū Kalvarija, Žemaitija National Park, Flevoland, Föhr Island, Frederiksborg, Gúdu cliffs, Gaping Gill, Garajonay National Park, Gauja National Park, Gelderland, Giant Mountains, Girolata peninsula, Gjende lake, Glacier Blanc, Glacier de Corbassière, Glendalough valley, Glenmore Forest Park, Glenmore valley, Glenveagh National Park, Gola della Rossa-Frasassi, Golica v Krejdi, Gömör-Torna, Goreme National Park, Gotska Sandön National Park, Grafenau, Gran Sasso, Gran Sasso e Monti della Laga National Park, Grand St Bernard Pass, Grands Causses Regional Nature Park, Graubünden, Gribskov, Grosser Aletschgletscher, Grossglockner, Guadalquivir river, Gutenberg castle, Gysinge, Halastó ponds, Hambleton hills, Hämösöšön lake, Hardangervidda National Park, Hanlaid Peninsula, Harrachov, Harz and Hochharz National Parks, Hautes Chaumes, Hautes Fagnes–Eifel Nature Park, Havel river, Hay-on-Wye, Heathens' Stone, Hexenküche, Hexentanzplatz, High Coast Path, Hochalpenstrasse, Hochkalter mountains, Hoge Veluwe National Park, Hohe Tauern National Park, Hornád river, Hortobágy National Park, Hundafoss, Ilhara valley, Inaccessible Pinnacle, Ingleborough, Isle of Hiddensee, Isle of Rügen, Isle of Skye, Jaagarahu Harbour, Jægersborg deer park, Jánské Lázně, Jasmund National Park, Jelenia Góra, Jervaulx abbey, Jönköping, Jostedalsbreen glacier, Jotunheimen National Park, Jumilhac plateau, Juodkrantė, Jura and Combe-Grède / Chasseral Park, Jura High Route, Jyväskylä, Kackar Mountains National Park, Karkonosze National Park, Karpacz, Karula National Park, Keroharju Trail, Keski-Suomen Maakuntaura route, Ketelhaven, Kielder forest, Killarney National Park, Kirk Yetholm, Kiutaköngäs falla, Klutavaraaka Hill, Klaipėda, Königssee, Kornati National Park, Kranjska Gora, Krap's Ring, Krimml falls, Kristinartindar trail, Krka National Park, Krkonoše National Park, Kuršių Nerija National Park, Kuressaare, Kylemore abbey, Kyrkis, Ligatne, L'Étang de Bellebouche, La Caldera de la Taburiente National Park, La Couvertoirade, La Cumbrecita, La Forêt de l'Envers, La Gomera, La Linnea, La Meta, La Montaña del Fuego, La Roque de los Muchachos, La Vanoise National Park, Lac de Guéry, Ladies' View, Laghestël di Pine, Lago di Ridracoli, Lagorai mountains, Lake Bienne, Lake Campotosto, Lake Chaumeçon, Lake Iso Seitsemisjarvi, Lake Kävsjön, Lake Lipno, Lake Maggiore, Lake Mégáli Préspa, Lake Mikrí Préspa, Lake Myczkowce, Lake Neusiedl, Lake Peipsi, Lake Plateliai, Lake Solinskie, Lake Thingvallavatn, Lake Torneträsk, Lake Vassivière, Länsi-Aure, Lanzarote, Las Cañadas del Teide National Park, Le Chasseral, Le Marche, Le Mercantour National Park, Le Verdon Regional Nature Park, Ledreborg Slot, Les Calanches, Les Ecrins National Park, Les Escoyères, Levoča, Livradois-Forez Regional Nature Park, Llanberis, Llangorse lake, Llyn Tegid, Loch Katrine, Loch Lomond and the Trossachs, Loch Morlich, Logar Sisters Hotel, Logarska Dolina Regional Park, Lon Las Cymru, Lough Barra, Lough Leane, Lough Veagh, Lövö Island, Lower Oder Valley National Park, Lusen, Maaninkajoki, Maas river delta, MacGillycuddy's Reeks, MacLeod's Tables, Majella National Park, Malesco, Mandron glacier, March river, Marbuet, Marloes peninsula, Martel footpath, Massif Central, Massif des Bauges Regional Nature Park, Mastomäki forest, Matalascañas, Matkov Škaf, Matterhorn, Maurienne valley, Mecklenburg Lake District, Melnik, Méobecq abbey, Mesta valley, Middle Orchy, Millevache plateau, Monestero river, Money Chasm, Monodhéndhri, Monserrate Park, Mont Bégo, Monte Amaro, Monte Cinto, Monte Gran Paradiso, Monte Marsicano, Monte Sibilla, Monte Vettore, Montesinho Natural Park, Monti Sibillini National Park, Mörsárdalur valley, Morsárjökull, Morskie Oko, Morvan Regional Nature Park, Moulins de Keroüat, Mount Beuvray, Mount Kehlstein, Mount Njulla, Mount Triglav, Mt Aströka, Mt Botev, Mt Erciyes, Mt Falterona, Mt Gamila, Mt Göllük, Mt Hasan, Mt Kackar, Mt Kamenitsa, Mt Kasprowy Wierch, Mt Kizlar, Mt Musala, Mt Okraglica, Mt Olympos, Mt Penna, Mt Rysy, Mt Śnieżka, Mt Sokolica, Mt Szrenica, Mt Vihren, Muckish, Muckross Lake, Multiharju ridge, Müritz National Park, Murter, Nasa silver-mines, National Park of Aigüestortes-Sant Maurici, National Parks of Germany's Baltic Coast, Natural Park dell'Alpe Veglia e dell'Alpe Devero, Nature reserves in Liechtenstein, Neuchâtel, Neusiedler See—Seewinkel National Park, Neustrelitz, Nidderdale, Niederösterreich, Niedzica Castle, Nieuwe Merwede canal, Nigula Nature Reserve, Nizonne valley, Noguera Pallaresa, Noguera Ribagorzana, Nordeifel Nature Park, North York Moors, Northumberland National Park, Nössentiner/Schwinzer Heide, Nuortti wilderness, Nynäshamn, Oder river, Ofenpass road, Okrešelj basin, Old Man of Storr, Oostvaardersplassen, Öraefajökull glacier, Ossola valleys, Østerdalsisen ice-flow, Ouessant, Oulanka National Park, Our Valley Nature Park, Overijssel, Owencarrow river, Öxara river, Pale di San Martino, Paneveggio–Pale di San Martino Nature Park, Panichishte, Parc Naturel Régional de la Corse, Parque da Pena, Pasterze glacier, Path of Peace, Peak District National Park, Pembrokeshire Coast National Park, Pen-y-Fan, Pen-y-ghent, Pennine Way, Pennines, Perama caves, Périgord-Limousin Regional Nature Park, Piano dei Nivolet, Pieniny National Park, Pirin National Park, Pitkäjäni lake, Piz Quattervals, Pizzo del Diavolo, Plechý, Plitvice National Park, Point of Sleat, Poisoned Glen, Preseli hills, Préspa National Park, Preuilly forest, Primiero valley, Psaràdhes, Puy de Dôme, Pyhä-Häkki National Park, Queen Elizabeth Forest Park, Queyras Regional Nature Park, Raіskoto Prúskalo, Rauris valley, Ravnkilde, Rebild Bakker, Reenadinna wood, Reisdorf–Vianden track, Rhônegletscher, Richard the Lionheart Trail, Rievaulx abbey, Rila National Park, Robertville, Rochechouart, Rold Skov forest, Rotmoos, Route de la Bolette, Route of the Volcanoes, Rozhen monastery, Saaremaa, Saint-Léger-Vauban, Saltfjellet–Svartisen National Park, San Martino di Castrozza, San river, Sankt Andreasberg, Sanlúcar de Barrameda, Sava Bohinjka valley, Savinja river, Scandola Nature Reserve, Scanuppia-Monte Vigolana, Schleswig-Holstein Wadden Sea National Park, Schloss Criewen, Schorels fortress, Schwarzenberg Canal, Sedemte Ezera, Seitseminen National Park, Sévérac Causse, Sf Gheorghe, Sgùrr Alasdair, Sigulda, Sintra-Cascais Natural Park, Sirente-Velino Regional Park, Skaftafell National Park, Skaftafellsjökull, Skakavitsa waterfall, Skekarsboberget, Skokholm, Skomer, Skradin, Skrłatica, Skuleskogen National Park, Slåtterdalsskrevan, Slovenský raj, Sněžka, Snowdon, Snowdonia National Park, Solčava yew, Sonnblick, Soomaa National Park, Spa, Spey river, Spiš, Spišský hrad, Spišské Podhradie, St Bride's Bay, St David's, St Katharinenbrunnen reserve, St Kevin's shrine, Stara Planina, Stettiner Bar, Store Dyrehave woodland, Store Mosse National Park, Struma valley, Stützkow, Sulina, Suomenselkä watershed, Svartifoss, Svorová, Swiss National Park, Szatmár-Bereg wetlands, Taivalköngäs falls, Tankavaara, Tarr Steps, Tatra National Park, Telašćica, Termessos-Gülluk National Park, Tevno Ezero, Thayatal National Park, The Boglands of Southern Estonia, The Brocken, The Cairngorms, The Dark Peak, The Glyders, The White Peak, Thingbæk Kalkminer, Thingvellir National Park, Timanfaya National Park, Tisza river, Tjuonatjåkka mountain, Tobar Mweelin well, Tomintoul, Torfhaus moor, Tour du Morvan, Trás-os-Montes, Tre Cime del Monte Bondone, Trentino Nature Reserves, Trient gorge, Triglav National Park, Trojmezí, Troyanski Monastery, Trzy Korony, Tsantelēina glacier, Tulcea, Twelve Bens, Two Moors Way, Üerts da Diavel, Upper Harz plateau, Upper-Sûre Nature Park, Urbino, Urho Kekkonen National Park, Ustrzyki Górne, Utladalen valley, Uudepanga Bay, Vadvetjåkka National Park, Val d'Isère, Val Grande National Park, Val Pogallo, Val Stabelchod, Val Venegia, Valais canton, Valle d'Aosta and the Gran Paradiso National Park, Valle di Tóvel, Valle Rendena, Vallée des Merveilles, Valley of Desolation, Valley of the Beaver, Västernorrland county, Vatnajökull, Vézelay, Vidda, Víkos-Aöös National Park, Ville-Veille, Vilsandi National Park, Vindolonda, Visovac, Vltava river, Voidhomátis river, Volcans d'Auvergne Regional Nature Park, Vøringfossen falls, Vorpommersche Boddenlandschaft National Park, Vršič pass, Vransko, Vuotso, Wang Chapel, Wattenmeer, Watzmann mountains, Weerribben National Park, Weiswampach lakes, Wernigerode, Whernside, Wicklow Mountains National Park, Wiltz river, Winseler tea factory, Wissower Klinken, Wistman's wood, Wittdün, Wye river, Yaylalar, Yeavering Bell, Yorkshire Dales, Zagóri, Zakopane, Zeeland, Zermatt, Zlarin, Zugspitze, Zuider Zee.

Series editor
Mark Hancox

Editorial team
Stephen Bird, Olivia Dickinson, Emma Gilliland,
Sarah Johnson, Aoibhe O'Shea, Toner Quinn,
Julia Sandford

Information co-ordination
Alison Compton

Design
ENDAT Design

Production
Suzy Gillespie, Mhairi Dawson

• Front cover picture:
La Gomera, Garajonay National Park
Used with the permission of the Spanish Tourist
Office. Photographer – Antonio Garrido.

• Printed by Tipolitografia Petruzzi Corrado of
Perugia, Italy.

© **Copyright 2000**
The ENDAT Group Ltd
Ochil House
Springkerse Business Park
Stirling FK7 7XE
Scotland

ISBN – 0 9536111 6

The publishers have taken every effort to ensure the
accuracy of the information included in this book.
However, the publishers cannot accept responsibility
for any loss, injury or inconvenience arising from the
use of this book.

The publishers would be pleased to receive any
corrections or suggestions for incorporation into future
editions. Updated information will also be listed on
the Activity Series web-site: **www.activityseries.com**

ACTIVITY SERIES

Activity Series guides are different from other travel
books. Intended to be read and enjoyed at the creative
stage of choosing a holiday, each title provides a
stimulating overview of a particular environment or
activity across a wide geographical area.

National Parks Europe offers a snapshot of parks across
the whole continent, from the tropical forests of the
Canaries to the frozen landscapes of northern Finland.

■ Clear and engaging text
Written in a lively style, the text acts as an introduction
to a park covering the landscape, flora and fauna,
outdoor activities, selected walking routes, history,
culture and the best time to go.

■ Vivid pictures
The colour pictures are bold, attractive, dramatic
and intriguing. Each one helps bring the park and
surrounding region to life.

■ Illustrative maps
Each entry has a simple illustrative map that helps
to locate places and features included in the text.
A smaller map places the park within the country.

●	Village / town / city
★	Place of interest
– – – ·	International border
——	Regional boundary
– – – –	National park boundary
· · · · · ·	Walking route
——	River
〰	Lake
⍦	Forest
∨ ∨	Marsh
⋀	Mountain
⌢	Small mountain / big hill
⌒	Hill

■ Contact information
The contact information, both at the start of each section
and at the end of each entry, is the ideal stepping stone
for finding out more about a particular area. Postal,
phone, fax and electronic address details are provided
for park and tourism authorities.

CONTENTS

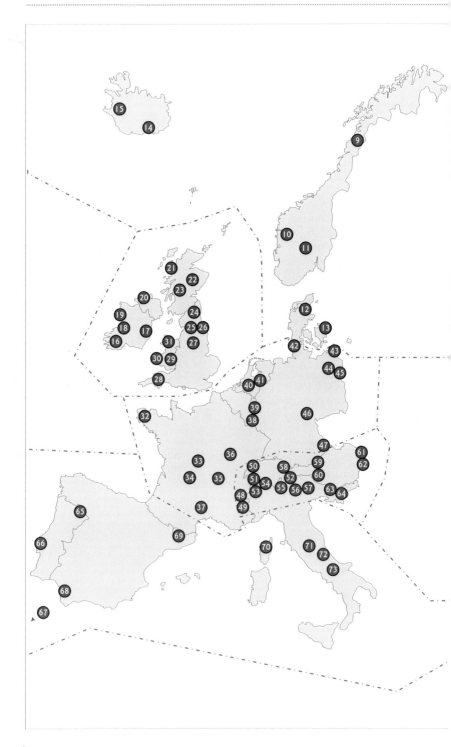

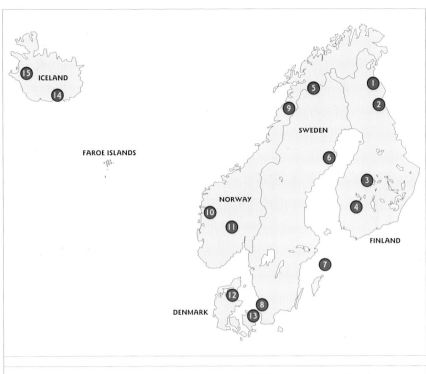

ℹ CONTACT INFORMATION

Danish Tourist Board
55 Sloane Street
London SW1X 9SY
Tel: 020 7259 5959
Fax: 020 7259 5955
E-mail: dtb.london@dt.dk
Web: www.dtb.dt.dk

The Faroe Islands Tourist Board
Gongin
PO Box 118
FO-110 Tórshavn
Faroe Islands
Tel: (00 298) 316055
Fax: (00 298) 310858
E-mail: tourist@tourist.fo
Web: www.tourist.fo

Finnish Tourist Board
30-35 Pall Mall
London SW1Y 5LP
Tel: 020 7839 4048
Fax: 020 7321 0696
E-mail: Mek.Lon@mek.fi
Web: www.mek.fi

Icelandair
172 Tottenham Court Road
London W1P 0LY
Tel: 020 7874 1000
Fax: 020 7387 5711
E-mail: london@icelandair.is
Web: www.icelandair.is

Norwegian Tourist Board
5th Floor, Charles House
5 Regent Street (Lower)
London SW1Y 4LR
Tel: 020 7839 2650
Fax: 020 7839 6014
E-mail: infouk@ntr.no
Web: www.visitnorway.com

**Swedish Travel & Tourism
Council**
11 Montagu Place
London W1H 2AL
Tel: 020 7870 5600 (information)
    01476 578811 (brochures)
Fax: 020 7724 5872
E-mail: info@swetourism.org.uk
Web: www.visit-sweden.com

Urho Kekkonen National Park

Snow cover gives Urho Kekkonen a desolate beauty for much of the year, but the forests, peatlands and fells awaken with the midnight sun, and in autumn display their true colours.

Covering 2,538 sq km, an area the size of Luxembourg, Urho Kekkonen National Park is the second largest park in Finland. It was founded in 1983 to protect one of the few extensive wildernesses left in Europe, and named after Finland's long-serving president Urho Kaleva Kekkonen, who was affectionately known as UKK.

Lapland

Lapland covers most of northern Scandinavia, and accounts for about a third of Finland's total area. The land is generally flat, characterised by gently sloping treeless fells and low sandy hillocks called *tievas*, which are said to be the homes of earth spirits.

Owing to the harsh climate and the acidity of arctic soils, vegetation is scarce. Trees are sparser, shorter and take longer to grow than in the more temperate south. The region is networked by rivers, and the few lakes are frozen for much of the year. When the snow melts, lichen carpets the ground as an indication of the air's extraordinary cleanliness.

Yet, although most of Lapland is north of the Arctic Circle, the

Reindeer are a common sight in the park

changing seasons are clearly marked. *Ruska* is a word used to describe the diverse colours of the autumn foliage, when yellow birch leaves mingle with pale red rowans and green firs, interspersed with scarlet bilberries.

On cold clear nights throughout the winter (from October to March), the Northern Lights spectacularly recreate autumn in the sky with flashes of red, green, yellow and violet. According to legend, the fox's tail touches both snow and sun as he hurries over the plains, and sends coloured sparks up into the heavens.

November to January is the period called *kaamos*, when the sun does not rise above the horizon, and the winter is at its coldest. By contrast, summer is the time of eternal light, when the sun rests behind a hill but does not sleep at night. In Ivalo, the nearest large town to UK National Park, this period lasts for most of June and July and coincides with the warmest time of year, when temperatures average around 16°C.

Urho Kekkonen

The national park is sufficiently large for it to reflect the changing landscape. Northern sections are dominated by barren fell chains, treeless tundra and scree-covered ravines. South of the Saariselkä region, particularly in the Nuortti wilderness, forests are larger and mires more plentiful, with rivers running round low fir-covered hills. To the east are the rarest of the ancient forests, which were once under threat from the timber industry. Western parts of the park are the most accessible, being closer to towns, and have well-marked trails for skiers and hikers to follow.

The park is divided into hiking zones, each with its own regulations concerning camp fires and overnight stays. Camping, however, is not strictly controlled, and forty huts and cabins are sprinkled around the park. In true Finnish style, there are also seven saunas for relaxation.

Wildlife

As well as herds of reindeer, UK National Park is home to a number of rare northern species such as bears, wolverines and otters.

Bird-watchers flock to the far hinterlands in the hope of finding eastern species of unusual birds. Golden eagles, bramblings, Siberian jays, rock ptarmigan and golden plover all nest in the park. Wetland

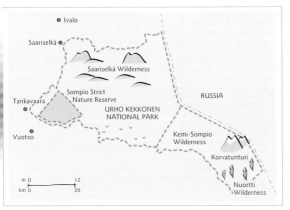

of their traditional way of life. The UK National Park contains grazing, mating and calving areas for reindeer owned by local co-operatives and Sámi farmers. Several Sámi tourist firms feature such attractions as reindeer drives, storytelling evenings, dishes served in traditional tents, handicraft demonstrations and opportunities to participate in seasonal festivities.

Vuotso`, the southernmost Sámi village, is in the south-west corner of Urho Kekkonen. As a reindeer herding centre, it offers a taste of both local Sámi tradition and the historical farm life of later settlers. Two residences of the Eastern Sámi, dating from the 1940s, have been restored in the park itself.

birds, hawks and owls frequent the southern regions. The most common creature, however, is the mosquito, which irritates walkers from mid-June to the first frosts in August. The traditional local remedy is to spread tar over the skin, but most people find it more convenient to come prepared with appropriate creams and sprays.

Saariselkä and Tankavaara

The town of Saariselkä is situated to the north-west of the park. There is a park office here, as well as all the usual attractions of an upmarket skiing resort. The fells surrounding it are between 400 and 700m above sea level, and therefore among the highest in the area. Tankavaara, where Urho Kekkonen's largest visitor centre can be found, is also home to the Gold Village. Its museum is devoted to gold-panning and visitors can try their hand at striking lucky in the rivers nearby – a century ago, both gold and pearls were discovered here.

The Sámi and their culture

There are about 6,000 Lapps, or Sámi as they prefer to be known, in Finnish Lapland. As the only indigenous inhabitants of northern Scandinavia, they have been granted special privileges relating to the preservation

CONTACT INFORMATION

Urho Kekkonen National Park
Koilliskaira Visitor Centre
99695 Tankavaara
Finland
Tel: (00 358) 205 647251
Fax: (00 358) 205 647250
E-mail: ukpuisto@metsa.fi

Finnish Forest and Park Service
Saariselkä Park Office
Honkapolku 3
99830 Saariselkä
Finland
Tel: (00 358) 205 647200
Fax: (00 358) 205 647210

Oulanka National Park

In some places, meadows and sandbanks overlook tranquil rivers, whilst violent rapids hide around the next bend. Elsewhere, peatland wilderness, heaths and coniferous forests stretch for miles.

Oulanka is situated at a climatic crossroads in Eastern Finland, where the distinctive characters of the Arctic Circle to the north, and the warmer lakelands to the south, collide. Perhaps it is not surprising that the Lapps, first settlers of the Oulanka area, were regarded as a rather stationary people. Gaining their livelihood from fishing, hunting and reindeer herding, there was little reason for them to travel far in a such a rich and diverse region as this.

Oulanka is best known for its huge waterfalls, and was established as a national park in 1956 in order to preserve the Kiutaköngäs falls which attract over 40,000 visitors every year. Winters are harsher and snowier than in southern Finland, with temperatures below freezing point from mid-October until the end of April. However, although summers are short, they can also be spectacular – July averages 15°C, with maximum temperatures of 30°C possible in exceptional years.

Nature's bounty

The park's natural diversity is principally a result of climatic factors. During the last Ice Age, in common with most of Finland, the area was shaped by the movement and eventual retreat of a huge glacier which brought with it the seeds of Arctic plants that still grow in the park. Today, the harshness of the Arctic winter is tempered by humid sea-winds brought by the Gulf Stream, encouraging luxuriant vegetation unusual for such a northerly region. Such conditions encourage spruce and pine to thrive on shady or damp rockfaces, while southern plants – wild strawberry, sedges, campions – grow on warm, sunny slopes.

The Oulanka river valley is often said to form a boundary between two areas with different topographies. To the north, groves, mossy spruces, pine swamps and hanging bogs cover the gentle plateau, interspersed with small, wooded islets surrounded by fens. To the south, the backing up of the glacier is indicated by peatland hollows and smaller pools, as well as gravel deposits known as drumlins. The land here has been moulded to a lesser extent by glaciation – at 380m, Kiutavaara Hill is the highest point in the park. The valley itself is only 100m above sea level, with steep banks carved into the gravelly river bed to give it a canyon-like appearance, a deep gorge lined with rugged cliffs.

Kiutaköngäs

The Kiutaköngäs falls are one of the park's main tourist attractions. 600m long, with a horizontal drop of 100m, the surging river crashes dramatically into the deep pool below. The falls were created when the river, running over a confluence of hard quartzite and soft dolomite, eroded the softer rock to form a steep precipice. The striking rusty brown colour of the falls' rocks intensifies its visual effect. Occasionally, boulders still tumble into the water as a reminder of nature's continual processes.

A ladder was installed in 1936 for fish attempting to travel upriver to spawn. Trout are regularly transferred from the pool below the head of the rapids to the area above the falls. Such schemes greatly contribute to the preservation of fish species in the national park.

Other falls in Oulanka include the beautiful Jyrävä with its 10m drop, and the Taivalköngäs where the waters fall into two main channels, with a third, central channel flooded in the spring. The view of the falls is worth the exhilaration of standing on a precarious suspension bridge as it swings with the force of the water and the gusts of the wind.

Man's intervention

The original Lapp settlers were forced to give way to the Finns at the end of the 17th century. Although reindeer herding and hunting continued to be major occupations, these gradually gave way to farming, with cattle fodder gathered from the meadows until the national park was established. Forests were commercially felled from the end of the 19th century up to 1918, when the Russian border was closed, severing the Eastern timber market.

Evidence of past settlers may still be seen in the hay barns, reindeer fences and loggers' cabins scattered around the park. Although reindeer husbandry continues, the emphasis in Oulanka is now upon tourism and science. Oulu University carries out research into the biology, geography and climatology of the region.

Facilities

Hautajärvi Nature Cabin is open daily for most of the year. Its exhibitions feature different bog types, rocks and local history. Oulanka Visitor Centre is near to Kiutaköngäs. The largest campsite can be found nearby, complete with kiosk, overnight cottages and a sauna. Both centres have cafés to refresh exhausted hikers. There are 85km of marked trails, including four nature trails and a large section of the Bear's Ring Trail, which begins at Hautajärvi. The 14km Keroharju Trail crosses the northern half of the park, following a ridge through gentle fenland. The foaming rapids make canoeing a popular pursuit in Oulanka, whilst fishing is permitted with a licence.

ℹ CONTACT INFORMATION

Oulanka Visitor Centre
Liikasenvaarantie 132
FIN-93999 Kuusamo
Finland
Tel: (00 358) 205 646850
Fax: (00 358) 205 646851
E-mail: oulanka@metsa.fi

Forest & Park Service
Torangintaival 2
FIN-93600 Kuusamo
Finland
Tel: (00 358) 205 646800
Fax: (00 358) 205 646801

Kiutaköngäs falls

Pyhä-Häkki National Park

Pyhä-Häkki is distinctly wild in character, offering a rare and potent taste of Finland's dwindling primeval forests.

Pyhä-Häkki is only 12 sq km, but this small area contains some of Finland's most precious virgin forests and fens. Dense groves of spruce mingle with open treeless bogs, deep murky pools and mires dotted with small pines. It is hard to believe that the thriving towns of Saarijärvi and Jyväskylä are only a short distance away.

Peatlands

Peatlands cover about half the total area of the national park. Apart from a small number of artificial drainage ditches, the bogs are untouched by human activity, enabling them to develop and maintain their natural state. Although many fens are deficient in oxygen and nutrients, spruce swamps support several varieties of vegetation, such as birch, mosses, sedge, wavy hairgrass, bilberries, cloudberries and colourful bracket fungi. Pools are often transformed into marshes when floating patches of moss grow over the water, such as on the Rupilampi pool next to Lake Kotajärvi.

Old forests

The forests have been damaged by the fires and storms of several centuries, but continue to regenerate and thrive. The oldest and largest tree in the park is thought to have germinated at the end of the 16th century, and most of the Scots pine stands date back 250 years. Many of the spruce groves, too, are over 200 years old. Trees can therefore be seen in all stages of development, from fragile seedlings to dry, silver-grey pine 'snags' which eventually topple over into the marsh. Massive rotten spruce trunks litter the forest floors.

Spruce thrives in fresh, rich soils, while Scots pines need fewer nutrients to survive. Due to the variety of peatlands the forests grow in clumps at different points around the park. Deciduous birch can be seen on the banks of the eastern streams.

Bird-life

The forests are filled with the noises of typical woodland birds – willow warblers, chaffinches, tits, pipits, cuckoos and owls, as well as less common species such as greater spotted woodpeckers and goshawks. Nesting in the peatlands are greenshanks, meadow pipits, yellow wagtails, snipes and lapwings.

Walking in Pyhä-Häkki

To avoid sinking into a marsh, or stumbling around in the damp and dark of a forest, visitors are advised to stay on the marked paths that weave around the central heaths and deviate to the edge of the Riihineva and Kotaneva fens. Two nature trails indicate points of interest and encompass the major types of forest and marsh. The Central Finland Hiking Route (Keski-Suomen Maakuntaura) passes through the park, along the eastern shore of Lake Kotajärvi. Although camping is prohibited in the park, overnight accommodation is available at nearby campsites.

Jyväskylä

Pyhä-Häkki National Park is about 40km from Jyväskylä, a lively university town and a significant centre for trade and commerce. Capital of the province of Central Finland, it was the home of the famous architect Alvar Aalto, who designed thirty buildings in the town. These include the Administrative and Cultural Centre, the Museum of Central Finland and the Alvar Aalto Museum itself.

[i] CONTACT INFORMATION

Pyhä-Häkki National Park
Adminstered by Seitseminen
  National Park Visitor Centre
Seitseisentie 110
34530 Länsi-Aure
Finland
Tel: (00 358) 20564 5270
E-mail: seitseminen@metsa.fi

PYHÄ-HÄKKI NATIONAL PARK
Riihineva Fen
Kotajärvi
Kotaneva Fen
Rupilampi Pool
Central Finland Hiking Route
Saarijärvi
m 0   0.6
km 0   1.0
Jyväskylä

Ancient trees dominate the national park

 **FINLAND**

Seitseminen National Park

Seitseminen's post-glacial landscape makes it one of the the most famous of Finland's national parks. Its location, close to the city of Tampere, also makes it one of the most popular.

Founded in 1982 and extended to the south-east in 1989, Seitseminen National Park's 42 sq km abounds with the rolling hills, gravel ridges, coniferous forests and lakeside bogs typical of southern Finland.

This distinctive landscape was formed 10,000 years ago. At the end of the last Ice Age, a glacier, which had carved and moulded the land as it travelled south, began to melt. As it retreated, it deposited ridges of gravel to form eskers. The Seitsemisharju and Hirviharju ridges are striking examples of this natural phenomenon.

Lakeland fens

Although more than half the park is peatland, few fens have survived in their original state. The Finnish Forest and Park Protection Service is involved in an ongoing regeneration project filling drainage ditches and thinning planted forests to restore the brown moss fens and Scots pine bogs that are dotted around the park. Most of Seitseminen's thirty small lakes and pools are bounded by bogs, their waters coloured brown with humus. Lake Iso Seitsemisjärvi is gradually being taken over by vegetation, and must be carefully protected to maintain its delicate balance.

Winter adds another dimension to Seitseminen

Coniferous forests

As 90% of Finland's protected forests are found in Lapland, forest protection is a special concern in southern Finland. Two thirds of Seitseminen's forest areas consist of newly planted seedlings and former commercial woodlands. However, the national park is principally renowned for its primeval forests, such as those beside Lake Pitkäjärvi, along the Seitsemisjoki river and in wooded islets on the peatlands. The virgin forest on the Multiharju ridge is composed of huge pines, barkless snags and giant spruces, and has been protected by law since 1910.

Kovero

Man's interaction with nature has played an important role in the development of the Seitseminen area. Most interesting is the Kovero farmhouse, parts of which date back to the 1860s. It has been carefully restored and furnished to give an idea of life on the farm at the turn of the

Seitseminen's rolling landscape of forests, fens and lakes

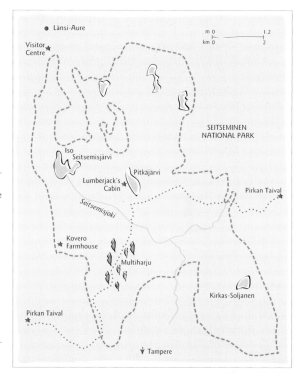

century. Traditional methods of cultivation and animal husbandry have been recreated in order to conserve the native breeds of domestic animal and ancient species of plants that can be found here. As a result, Kovero has become important for research into the development of animal and plant species in managed meadows and grazing grounds. Kovero is open daily between May and October.

Wildlife

Seitseminen is a sanctuary for several endangered species. Its forests are one of the few places in Europe to provide a home for flying squirrels. Visitors also share the park with mountain hares, red foxes, shrews, otters, badgers and moose. The pine marten is such a common sight that it has become Seitseminen's official mascot. Over 140 species of birds have been identified within the park, eighty species of which nest there regularly.

Facilities for visitors

A commitment to environmental education is clear throughout Seitseminen. The main visitor centre is situated in Länsi-Aure. Facilities here include a nature exhibition and auditorium. In addition, visitors can follow four short nature trails which are devoted to the park's main features: hole-nesting animals, eskers, virgin forests and peatlands. Guided tours are available to large groups.

The Pirkan Taival trail crosses the park

An extensive network of cycle paths runs through the park, along with 60km of marked hiking trails including part of the well-known Pirkan Taival route. Although the park is particularly suitable for day trips, there are also six campsites with campfire places and cooking shelters.

Tampere

In 1779, Gustav III, King of Sweden and Finland, climbed the Pispala ridge, said to be the highest gravel ridge in the world and today less than an hour's drive from Seitseminen National Park. He was so taken with the view of the two glistening lakes below that he immediately founded the city of Tampere between them, on the banks of the Tammerkoski falls.

Now the third largest city in Finland, Tampere is home to 182,000 people and is a thriving centre for industry and technical research. The arts also play an important role in the city. Summer visitors can attend the international festivals of music, film

and theatre that are held in Tampere each year. 'Metso', the city library, is a notable example of contemporary architecture, and houses the Moomin Valley Museum where Tove Jansson's famous Moomintrolls have been recreated in tableaux and line drawings. The pine-covered Pyynikki ridge offers a haven of peace amongst all the urban bustle, and the observation tower café is rumoured to serve the best doughnuts in southern Finland.

ℹ CONTACT INFORMATION

Seitseminen National Park Visitor Centre
Seitseisentie 110
34530 Länsi-Aure
Finland
Tel: (00 358) 205 645270
E-mail: seitseminen@metsa.fi

Tampere City Tourist Office
Verkatehtaankatu 2
PO Box 487
33101 Tampere
Finland
Tel: (00 358) 331 466800
Fax: (00 358) 331 466463

 **SWEDEN**

Abisko and Vadvetjåkka National Parks

*With their breathtaking mountain scenery and thriving diversity of birds,
Abisko and Vadvetjåkka National Parks thrill photographers and
ornithologists alike.*

Located at the very top of Lapland,
250km above the Arctic Circle, Abisko
and its neighbour Vadvetjåkka are the
most northerly national parks in
Sweden. Although Abisko is also one
of the most popular Swedish national
parks, it has not been adversely
affected by the comparatively heavy
volume of tourists, with much of the
landscape beyond the marked trails
remaining undisturbed.

A distinguished history

Abisko National Park has long been
regarded as an ideal destination for
both active holidays and scientific
research. As a regular train stops
outside Abisko Tourist Station, it is
easily accessible to those who make
the long journey from southern
Sweden. This stretch of railway dates
back to the late 19th century, and
enabled Abisko Tourist Station to be
opened as early as 1902. Abisko itself
was established in 1909 although it
had already existed as a nature
reserve for several years. The Abisko
Research Station on the outskirts of
the park was built in 1912 and
continues to explore the biology,
geology and meteorology of the area.

When to go

Abisko has one of the lowest rates of
precipitation in the whole of the
country. The shelter provided by the
mountains around the park forms a
'rain shadow' area, resulting in just
330mm of rain per year. As there are
only a few Norwegian islands between
Abisko and the Atlantic Ocean, the
region has a maritime character with
milder winters and colder summers
than would be expected at such a
northerly latitude.

Summer temperatures average a cool
yet comfortable 10°C with the sun
never setting in June. Most visitors
arrive in July and August, but it is in
autumn when the leaves are ablaze
with bronze in the crisp September
air that the park is at its best.

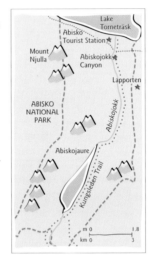

Spectacular scenery

A feature of the park is the splendid
Abiskojokk canyon, down which the
Abiskojokk river flows on its way to
Lake Torneträsk. The river gradually

drops 150m from its highest point in
Abisko, eventually forming a waterfall
as it crashes into the ravine. About
2km long and 20m deep in places, the
canyon's steep sides are striped with
shale. These are nappes formed by
ancient earth movements that also
formed Mount Njulla, a peak of
1,169m that can be reached by cable-
car. The summit yields magnificent
views of Lapporten, Sweden's most
distinctive and most photographed
natural landmark. A glacial U-shaped
valley between the mountains of
Tjuonatjåkka and Nissotjårro, it is
known as 'the gateway to Lapland'.
As most visitors approach Lapland
from the south, a more accurate
description would be 'the gateway to
Abisko', as Lapporten lies outside the
park yet dominates its landscape.

Vibrant vegetation

Abisko's sheltered location and
unusual climate encourages rare and
delicate plants such as the Lapp
orchid, found nowhere else in
Sweden. Rainbows of summer flowers

Abisko Tourist Station is dwarfed by the splendour of Lapporten

burst out in areas made fertile by the limestone bedrock. Mixed birch and pine woodland thrive in the sun-warmed valleys while the slopes of Mount Njulla are clothed in birch forests. The high moors are more barren although spread thinly with willow, heather and mountain flora such as the glacier buttercup.

In places, vegetation is sparse due to a larvae infestation in the 1950s. More than half the birches died and their skeletons still stand as white snags amongst the younger trees. Ironically, the devastation and ready sources of food attracted hole-nesting birds such as the redstart and the lesser spotted woodpecker, now a common sight in the forests.

Bird-life

There are few unusual mammals here, but bird-life is rich in variety. Heaths, marshes and lakes attract all manner of water-loving birds, particularly ducks such as teal and goldeneyes, as well as whimbrels, long-tailed skua, golden plover, greenshank and the rare Temminck's stint. The moors attract buntings, meadow pipit and wheatear, while the forests are home to redwing, bluethroat and warblers. Birds of prey include the rough-legged buzzard, snowy owl and golden eagle.

Activities

Abisko Tourist Station is a good base for an exploration of the region, containing a restaurant, bar, sauna and cabins. Most summer visitors hike the northern stretch of the famous Kungsleden, a 400km trail that begins nearby. Several other paths cross the park and are suitable for day hikes or for longer excursions into the wilderness. In the winter, the station offers several snow-bound activities, such as husky dog rides or telemark skiing, a traditional downhill technique using cross-country skis.

Vadvetjåkka National Park

Vadvetjåkka is less popular than Abisko for two reasons. Firstly, it is located in such an isolated spot that visitors must walk 15km from the road to reach the boundary. Bordering Norway and Lake Torneträsk, it is surrounded by water on three sides, with the fourth a wild terrain of bogs, rocks and steep cliffs. Secondly, although the park is just 35km from Abisko, it receives six times as much rain and heavy snows. Nevertheless, the park boasts a bird-life as varied as Abisko's, and an extensive karst cave system containing two of Sweden's biggest caves, one over 155m deep.

Much of the park is bare mountain, dominated by the precipices of Mount Vadvetjåkka (1,248m), but the limestone bedrock and high rainfall encourage surprisingly lush vegetation for such a northerly region. Meadows and marshes in particular are vibrant with Scandinavian primrose, mountain aven, shrubby speedwell and purple saxifrage. Patches of common bent, a cattle fodder, are evidence of earlier land clearance, while other human influence is demonstrated by pit traps and hay-drying poles near to an old Sami (Lapp) settlement. The unusual geology of the area, with its dramatic canyons and strangely shaped rocks, has long made it a sacred site for the Sami people and much of the cultural landscape is protected by law.

ⓘ CONTACT INFORMATION

Norrbotten County
S-971 86 Luleå
Sweden
Tel: (00 46) 920 96000
Fax: (00 46) 920 228411
E-mail: lansstyrelsen@bd.lst.se

Kiruna Lappland Tourist Bureau
Box 113
S-981 22 Kiruna
Sweden
Tel: (00 46) 980 18880
Fax: (00 46) 980 18286
E-mail: lappland@kiruna.se

Skuleskogen National Park

Skuleskogen is the sort of place that gives geology a good name. With its till-capped peaks and expanses of rocky rubble, dry stone loses some of its ancient remoteness and becomes a fascinating gateway to the past.

Skuleskogen is located to the north of 'The High Coast' area of Sweden, where Västernorrland county's rugged cliffs loom from the cold Baltic Sea. Traditionally an industrial centre, Västernorrland has more recently been acting to safeguard its environment.

Skuleskogen National Park was established in 1984 after a protracted struggle between the authorities and landowners. Its purpose is to preserve a coastal forest landscape. About a third of the park consists of rocky outcrops, boulder fields, stone fells and towering cliffs. Piles of scree and sharp peaks abound, alternating with rock fissures and trenches in the sea. No other area of Sweden can boast such abrupt changes in elevation, or a comparable combination of the harsh and the beautiful.

Rapakivi granite is typical of the high coast region

Land of rotten stone

This scenery, of course, takes an inconceivable number of years to develop. The majority of the bedrock is *rapakivi*, a striking red granite formed about 1.6 billion years ago when shifts in the Earth's crust forced molten magma to cover the region's original surface. Since then, wind, rain, and sea have carved it into hills and ravines. Rapakivi is a Finnish word meaning 'rotten stone', and the coarse granite crumbles easily into crystals and a thin acidic soil. It does, however, erode into regular patterns, most notably forming cliff 'staircases'.

Slåtterdalsskrevan

A vein of a completely different rock runs along the north-east coastline of the park. Diabase is grey-black in colour and, as it produces a fertile soil when eroded, is associated with Skuleskogen's richer areas of vegetation. The park's most famous attraction is Slåtterdalsskrevan, a gorge believed to have been formed by the erosion of another vein of diabase. The ravine is 200m long, 40m deep and just 7m wide.

Meltwater

Other features are very new by comparison, formed as a consequence of glacial retreat. About 9,000 years ago, the entire region was under water, pressed down by the weight of the meltwaters. When the glaciers began to retreat, the land slowly rebounded and continues to do so at the rate of a metre every century.

On the once submerged slopes, moraine deposits vary from the finest of sediments to smooth boulders, which lie in heaps at the bottom of cliffs or form 'Devil's pastures' by collecting in open areas like a huge cobbled road. Other distinctively glacial features include over fifty lakes, some so deep and still that they exude an eerie calmness.

SKULESKOGEN NATIONAL PARK

Stocksjön

Slåtterdalsskrevan

Baltic Sea

m 0   0.6
km 0   1

Human influences

Although the area that is now Skuleskogen has always been wild and uninhabitable, humans have been active in the area for 3,000 years.

Up to eighty graves dating back to the late Bronze Age line the coast. These cairns consist of coffins fashioned from flat slabs and covered with a mound of rocks. Although they are thought to have been constructed over a period of 500 years, few archaeological artefacts have been found in the graves, and as there is no sign of contemporary dwellings, it seems that the bodies were those of sailors or warriors who died at sea.

Since then, the area has been used sporadically for hunting, fishing, reindeer herding and occasional summer grazing meadows. However,

Cottages provide accommodation for visitors

it was not until the second half of the 19th century that humans began to have a real – and devastating – impact on the landscape. The expansion of the sawmill industry led to an insatiable demand for the good quality timber that abounds in Skuleskogen.

The forests were subjected to dimensional cutting, a procedure which is far less sophisticated than it sounds. After the largest trees had been removed, the next biggest were felled and so on until even the stunted pines on barren hilltops had met with the axe. Soon, nearly all the trees were gone. Remarkably, however, the fertile soils have contributed to an almost complete regeneration.

Beard lichen

Skuleskogen is a boundary zone for the distribution of several tree and plant species. It represents, for example, Sweden's northernmost limit for linden, maple and hazel trees, which grow rather like bushes on the southern slopes of the greener hills. There are also delicate grass species, such as fescue and broad-leaved cinna, for which conditions are too harsh any further north.

The most notable plant is the beard lichen whose strange yellow tendrils wrap themselves seductively around old spruce trees. Although it was once widespread in Sweden, it has declined dramatically in recent years and can now only be found in isolated pockets where spruces and the requisite damp climate are available.

Visiting Skuleskogen

About 30km of marked trails form a circuit around the park, although the terrain is often dauntingly steep and only for the physically fit. There is also a nature centre on the park's outskirts, which often holds exhibitions. However, these are the only concessions made to the modern visitor, enabling the park to retain its distinctively untamed character.

$\boxed{i}$ CONTACT INFORMATION

Västernorrland County Forestry Board
Kartongvägen
S-870 33 Docksta
Sweden
Tel: (00 46) 613 40606

Swedish Travel & Tourism
11 Montagu Place
London W1H 2AL
Tel: 020 7870 5600
Fax: 020 7724 5872
Web: www.visit-sweden.com

Slåtterdalsskrevan

Gotska Sandön National Park

Ever changing, yet with a biology as rich as its history,
Gotska Sandön is one of the more unusual of Sweden's national parks.

Situated more than 95km from the mainland, Gotska Sandön is the most isolated island in the Baltic Sea. Its name, loosely translated, means 'kingdom of the sands' and it is formed almost entirely from sand and gravel. The white beaches, encircling the island in their ever-shifting patterns, are reminiscent of the Caribbean. Although the climate is mild, the island is exposed to mighty storms and high tides which alter its foundations and damage its vegetation. One pine thicket is buried in the dunes, symbolising the sense of desolation often associated with Gotska Sandön. Yet far from being inhospitable, it supports a wealth of bird, plant and insect life surprising for somewhere so secluded.

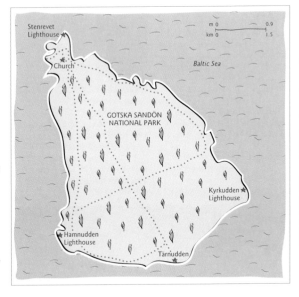

The island's structure

The national park covers an area of about 45 sq km, of which 8.5 sq km are water. Gotska Sandön is the most elevated section of a large sand and gravel reef that stretches for hundreds of kilometres below the sea as a series of concentric circles. The circumference of the island is about 30km and consists of beaches. Rising slightly further inland is a long coastal dune, then a strip of stone rubble and finally a higher and more permanent dune that makes the inner, forested parts of the island seem like a castle surrounded by protective walls. Gotska Sandön's highest point may be only 40m, but this is remarkable for a piece of land that has been repeatedly built up and destroyed by nature.

Human influence

Despite its remoteness, evidence of occupation on Gotska Sandön dates back thousands of years. There are Bronze Age graves on the southern and eastern coasts, while ancient artefacts such as daggers, tools and ornaments have been found all over the island. Since then, many different communities have left their mark. Hunting, farming, sheep herding, logging, tar boiling and shipbuilding have all flourished through the ages, reaching a peak in the early 19th century when one hundred people lived on the island. The old church, the schoolhouse and the remains of other buildings are of cultural interest.

Since Gotska Sandön was purchased by the state in 1860, its only permanent inhabitants have been lighthouse personnel and, more recently, national park employees. Although one of the first national parks, it was not until 1988 that protection was afforded to the entire island and the waters beyond it.

Seagulls at Sankt Annae

Gotska Sandön's sand and gravel landscape is constantly moulded by the elements

An unsavoury past

The shifting shores have long inspired colourful tales of the pirates that once hid here. The most infamous story is that of Petter Gottberg who was found guilty of looting a shipwreck in 1817. He had been the scourge of the seas for twenty years and was responsible for incidents so horrible that his name still provoked fear fifty years after his death. On dark, stormy nights, he would stand on the beach with his lantern and lame horse, scanning the shoreline for shipwrecks. On one occasion, he invited the crew of a stranded ship back to his barn for dinner. When they had eaten and drunk themselves into oblivion, he crept away, locked the door and shot them through the walls. The barn is preserved as a memorial to the men.

A living island

Eternally shifting sands may seem to be poetic and mysterious, but the last 150 years have been a constant battle to prevent the island from slipping away. Sedges, lyme grass and other sturdy species have been planted in the dunes to stabilise the sand.

Although the threat is mainly from strong winds and high tides, the situation has been worsened by the felling of forests and over-zealous grazing practices. It was not until the island's sheep died out that the forest could re-establish itself. About 90% of the island is now pine-covered, the forests carpeted with orchids, ferns, helleborine, heather and mosses. Thickets of deciduous trees such as oak, yew and hazel grow in more established, nutrient-rich areas.

As a result of the island's isolation and lack of fresh water, animal life is limited. In the 17th century, seal hunters came here but today the precious grey seal population is protected in a reserve. The only four-footed creatures are frogs and mountain hares. Seabirds throng the shoreline while, siskins, woodpeckers, doves, wood pigeons, parrot crossbills and spotted flycatchers nest in the pine forests and the leafy groves. They are attracted by an impressive range of insects, about fifteen species of which are not found elsewhere in Scandinavia. Beetles thrive in the pines, notably the giant or longhorn beetle which grows to 7cm or more.

Facilities

Until 1996, foreigners were not allowed to come to Gotska Sandön at all, and even now visitors are strictly limited to a hundred at a time. During the summer, boats run regularly from Nynäshamn (3hrs) on the mainland and from the island of Fårö off Gotland (1hr 45min). As there is no harbour, only specially designed ships can land on Gotska Sandön, so private boats should check with the coastguard before attempting the journey. As the ferries only come three times a week, weather-permitting, visitors stay for at least one night. Accommodation is based on three levels of comfort: campsite, cabins or cottages. Tourists can spend up to seven days on the island before returning to the more stable, yet more predictable, mainland.

ℹ CONTACT INFORMATION

Swedish Travel & Tourism
11 Montagu Place
London W1H 2AL
Tel: 020 7870 5600
Fax: 020 7724 5872
Web: www.visit-sweden.com

Store Mosse National Park

Swedish speakers do not need to be told about the main features of Store Mosse National Park – its name, literally translated, means 'big bog' and it is Sweden's largest marshland area south of Lapland.

Store Mosse is often described as an ocean of bogs, and, resting as it does on a level plateau of gneiss bedrock, the marshes can appear to stretch as far as the eye can see, raised bogs undulating like waves on the surface. The park exudes an eerie primitivism that seems to transcend the pressures of modern life.

An ocean of bogs

Store Mosse National Park

Situated between the towns of Värnamo and Jönköping in the region of Småland, Store Mosse was finally established as a national park in 1982 after years of campaigning from those who recognised its scientific merits.

Bog areas have never been greatly attractive to those wishing to make a living from the environment, but the peat deposits at Store Mosse are 7m thick in some places and traces of 19th century peat digging still remain. It is, however, one of the few places in Sweden to have survived in almost pristine condition. The park now covers 77 sq km, incorporating lakes and mires of considerable ornithological and botanical value, including plants that are rarely found to the south of the Arctic Circle.

Creation of the bogs

It is thought that Store Mosse began to develop its present characteristics thousands of years ago when Fornbolmen, an Ice Age lake which flooded the area, began to dry up.

When the climate became more humid, parts of the lake's exposed sandy bed became waterlogged and starved of oxygen so that dead plant material only partially decomposed. Over the centuries, thick layers of peat gathered on the surface of the water. The raised bogs that dominate the park were formed in this way, gaining all their moisture from precipitation alone. There is certainly no shortage of rain as the Swedish highlands are cool and wet all year.

Variety in the landscape

The second type of mire found in the park is the lowland fen which tends to be more fertile than the raised bogs as it gains part of its moisture from nutrient-rich groundwater. Distinctive peat moss is the dominant form of vegetation, decorating the marshes with a red, yellow, brown or green

One of Sweden's best bird-watching locations

carpet that is thickest in the low, damp hollows. Other plants include heather, bog rosemary, hare's tail cottongrass, cross-leaved heath, sedge and cranberry.

Higher hummocks also support dwarf birches and pines which, despite their great age, lack the nourishment to grow above 2m high. However, thicker pine forests mark the course of winding sandy ridges, believed to have been formed when the wind blew the dried bed of Fornbolmen into loose dunes. Many of these take the form of islands, notably Lövö and Sväno, which are moraine hills composed of sand and gravel and flanked by drifting dunes. Both hills have been used for farming and Lövö once supported four families, but now the island is partially overgrown and only one dwelling remains.

Ornithology

Over 100 species of birds nest in the park, and Lake Kävsjön, with its twin observatories, is one of Sweden's premier bird-watching points. It was partially drained in 1840 for farming purposes, turning the smaller, connected lakes of Häradsösjön and Horssjön into fens. Waders and migrating ducks, however, thrived in these new conditions but numbers began to decline when the land was subsequently abandoned. Grazing and hay gathering are now being reintroduced to maintain the sensitive equilibrium of the habitat.

Wading birds find the area particularly attractive, and visitors include those usually associated with more northerly latitudes such as jacksnipe, greenshank and broad-billed sandpipers. Water birds here include whooper swans, pochards, teal, wigeon, shovellers and spotted crakes.

As well as a large colony of black-headed gulls, the lake is the most important nesting site for cranes in southern Sweden. These huge birds make their nests low in the marshes and can be seen gliding gracefully over the lakes. The rare Slavonian grebe is a summer visitor, recognisable by the golden tufts on its cheeks.

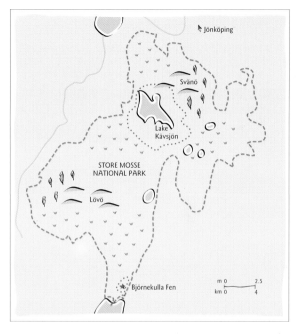

Botany

The marshes teem with insects of all varieties, from flies and mosquitoes to butterflies and moths. Perhaps this explains the profusion of flesh-eating plants such as the sundew and the greater bladderwort, which sucks up aquatic insects as it floats on the surface of a pool. For those who prefer nature to be less dramatic and more beautiful, the rich subsoil of Björnekulla Fen encourages marsh helleborine and the fragrant orchid.

Jönköping

Jönköping is about 40km north of Store Mosse, attractively situated on the southern shore of Lake Vättern. It lies in a region of verdant spruce forest, sloping hills and thousands of lakes and brooks, quite different from the peaty wilderness of the national park. Rich pastures provide a livelihood for the charming farms that speckle the area.

The town of Jönköping itself is notable for housing the only museum in the world that is devoted to the history of the matchstick, the Tändsticksmuseum. Matches were invented in Småland and here visitors can learn about the science behind it.

The arts are also well represented in the form of the town's Museum for Art and Cultural History. This was extended in 1991 using contemporary architecture specifically designed to enhance the collections housed inside. The many differently shaped windows create a rich and varied play of light in the rooms, while the walls are stained in soft shades of white, yellow, green, blue and red. Outside, the garden reflects the spirit of Småland in its use of local trees and coloured stones.

ⓘ CONTACT INFORMATION

Jönköping Tourist Bureau
S-551 89 Jönköping
Sweden
Tel: (00 46) 36 105050
Fax: (00 46) 36 128300

Swedish Travel & Tourism
11 Montagu Place
London W1H 2AL
Tel: 020 7870 5600
Fax: 020 7724 5872
Web: www.visit-sweden.com

Cranes are spring visitors in the park

Saltfjellet-Svartisen National Park

Combining lush valleys and spectacular fjords with echoing caves and imposing glaciers, Saltfjellet–Svartisen National Park is also a land that reverberates with history.

The edge of Svartisen glacier

Saltfjellet-Svartisen

Straddling the Arctic Circle, Saltfjellet-Svartisen National Park was established in 1989 to eliminate the threat of damming and hydroelectric power development. It covers an area of 2,105 sq km, bordered by Sweden to the east and the Norwegian Sea to the west. The park's scenery ranges from fertile valleys and fjord landscapes to windswept moors, limestone caves and perpetual ice.

History at Saltfjellet

An old path across Saltfjellet, between Rana and Salten, is thought to have been used as far back as the Stone Age as an alternative to sailing the rough seas along the Nordland coast. Stone axes, found during the ploughing of a field at Bjøllånes, support this theory. From more recent times, many of the farmsteads that are seen date back to the 18th century.

For centuries, the hills and moors of Saltfjellet have been used as grasslands for reindeer by the indigenous Lapp or *Same* people, and Saltfjellet is rich in sites displaying their cultural heritage. Practically all Saltfjellet place-names in Norwegian have been translated from the Same's Samisk language.

Ancient sites used by the Same for animal sacrifices are also found in the mountains: a well-known offering site is the Hedningesteinen – the massive Heathens' Stone – between Vestergila and Stormdalen.

Another sacred location was Jaureøre, where a stone shaped like a man's head used to lie. Earlier this century, the stone was stolen by two men from a nearby village. However, fearful of the taboos still connected with the sacrificial stone, they buried it at Eiterå further down the valley, and it has not been seen since.

More than ice

Stormdalen valley enjoys Saltfjellet's richest and most varied vegetation, with Norway's northernmost spruce forest found here. The glacier-fed river running through the valley floods its banks every year, fertilising the surrounding fields, where bird's-foot trefoil, bluebells, ferns and various perennials add colour to the landscape. Plants in the area get additional nourishment from avalanches, which tear mineral-rich soil from the mountainsides on their tumultuous way downhill.

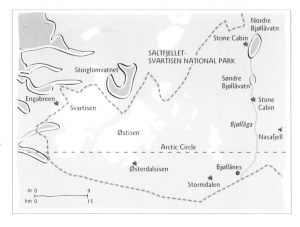

Saltfjellet's fauna is plentiful and varied, ranging from lemmings to brown bears. Birds of prey are often seen, and include golden eagles, sparrowhawks, falcons and owls. The hillsides are breeding grounds for capercaillie and ptarmigan, and the lynx is common here, as is the bloodthirsty wolverine which preys on Saltfjellet's reindeer herds.

Svartisen glacier

Svartisen – the Black Ice – is northern Scandinavia's largest glacier at 370 sq km. Svartisen is a *kåpe* glacier; a type of snowfield characteristic of Norway, it covers a large mountainous area into which ice flows steadily from all directions. Some parts of the glacier lie at around 1,200m above sea level, and at this height, massive snowfalls are not unusual. Svartisen has at times been very fast moving, and the force behind its countless tonnes of ice can be destructive. In 1723, a glacier arm advanced so far as to completely crush a farmstead at Storsteinøyra.

These days, Svartisen is a favoured destination in the summer, not just for tourists, but for local people. This applies especially to the Engabreen and Østerdalsisen ice-flows. Most visitors are content with wandering

along the edges of the ice, but there are many opportunities to traverse the glacier itself, conditions permitting. Few experiences can equal a ski-trek along the perpetual ice and snow on a summer night, with the midnight sun glowing in the north. Caves in the ice sometimes allow access into the blue depths of the glacier, but at their entrances there is always the risk of avalanches.

Despite its popularity with hikers and skiers, the vast majority of Svartisen is left untouched, with only the occasional solitary fox or flock of reindeer crossing the icy fields.

The Nasa silver mines

In the spring of 1634, Peder Olofsson was walking through the wilderness at Nasafjell. Looking around, as he rested on a snowless south-facing hillside, he suddenly noticed vast amounts of silver glinting in the sunshine. His spectacular find started the silver mines at Nasafjell.

Nasafjell is part of Saltfjellet, although some of it lies inside Sweden. The mines were operated by a Swedish company, and initially volunteers came in droves, but were soon disillusioned by the hard work and scant rewards. Towards the end of the

excavations the mining company was reduced to taking on convicted felons from the area's prisons. Same people were used to transport ore from the mines to the smelting huts, and old letters tell of the great privations and inhuman conditions they endured.

A graveyard was established here in the 1640s, but it is not known how many are buried here. Lying at around 1,000m above sea level, it is said to be Scandinavia's highest burial-place. The Nasa silver mines have been derelict since 1810, but visitors will still see many traces of the mining community. The area is a rocky wasteland devoid of vegetation, but with breathtaking mountain views.

ℹ CONTACT INFORMATION

Bodø Regional Hiking Association
Storgt. 17
Pb. 751
8001 Bodø
Norway
Tel: (00 47) 75 521413
E-mail: bot@online.no

Nordland Tourist Board
Postboks 434
8001 Bodø
Norway
Tel: (00 47) 75 545200
Fax: (00 47) 75 545210
E-mail: nordland@
nordlandreiseliv.no
Web: www.nordlandreiseliv.no

Lake Kvitbergvatnet is centrally located in Saltfjellet-Svartisen National Park

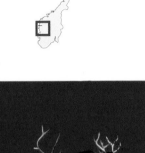

Hardangervidda National Park

This spectacular park is an opportunity to return to a less complicated time, to walk in the footsteps of hunters or to follow the tracks of reindeer across windswept moors and beneath towering mountain tops.

At 3,422 sq km, Hardangervidda is the largest national park in Norway. Established in 1981, it protects a valuable mountainous wildlife habitat. Open vistas of treeless moors and hills dominate the landscape, while the west offers deep valleys, steep mountain peaks, waterfalls and fjords. Hardangervidda, or Vidda as it is often called, is home to Europe's largest population of wild reindeer, and is the southernmost extent of arctic species such as the snowy owl and arctic fox. Rare plants are also found here, and the park is known for the fine brown trout in its lakes and watercourses. Along the famous Hardangerfjorden, lush orchards blossom in spring.

Vidda's history

10,000 years have passed since the ice disappeared from Hardangervidda, leaving only the two glaciers called Folgefonna and Hardangerjøkulen. Because of the flatness of Vidda's inland areas, the effects of thirty or forty ice ages have been relatively gentle. Slow movements of ice created more than a thousand shallow lakes in Vidda's wide valleys.

Certain sites, like Sumtangen at the Finnsberg lake, show signs of continuous human habitation for more than 8,500 years. During the first 5,000 years, hunting and fishing were the only human activities here. Hillside paths following the tracks of early hunter-gatherers are still in use. The first permanent settlements appeared during the Stone Age when the development of farming reduced the need to travel for food. Corn pollen has been found at Røldal, indicating that crops were grown there around 1,000 BC. At Hereid, a Viking burial site containing 350 graves is the biggest collection of ancient graves in western Norway.

With the rise of tourism, however, people's uses of Hardangervidda have changed more in the last century than during the preceding 9,900 years.

Walking in Hardangervidda

Whether seeking the peace of the open moors or the drama of craggy peaks and torrential rivers, hikers in the park will be kept happy. There are 700km of marked summer routes and numerous cabins in Vidda. The central and eastern parts of the Hardangervidda plateau offer gentle walks and short distances between the tourist cabins.

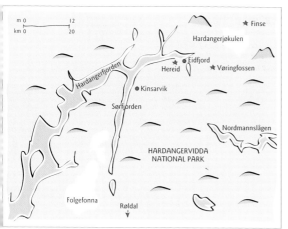

Although many visitors approach Vidda on the spectacular railways, one beautiful way to enter the park is on foot up the steep path from Kinsarvik to the Stavali cabin, with the string of dramatic waterfalls along the trail. Norway's best-known waterfall is at Eidfjord: the thundering Vøringfossen has a total fall of 182m. Those wishing to explore the perpetual ice at Hardangerjøkulen should start at Finse, where a marked route follows the edges of the entire glacier. During winter, the highland moors provide perfect conditions for cross-country skiers. There is even a ski-sailing club, where participants speed across the snowy moors while strapped to colourful sails.

Wild reindeer

Around 18,000 wild reindeer live in the park. Watching a herd of these graceful animals glide like a wave across the moors is an unforgettable experience. The hardy reindeer survive around seven months of harsh winter conditions, when they have to search for moss underneath a thick covering of snow. During the short summer season, they feast on lush mountain pasture. People have been hunting wild reindeer on Hardangervidda since prehistoric times – walled animal traps have been found on the moors dating back 6,000 years. These days, an annual cull keeps the population healthy. Reindeer have also been tamed and farmed on Hardangervidda through the ages – the first record of tame reindeer goes back to 1779. At one time, herds of up to 10,000 were kept and watched by herdsmen.

During the Occupation

Hardangervidda played an important role as a 'free area' for the resistance movement during the German occupation of Norway between 1940 and 1945. The resistance organisation, Milorg, established bases and hideouts in the remote hills. The occupying forces prohibited all use of Vidda from 1943 onwards, and the Gestapo and the SS carried out thorough, yet fruitless, searches of the area. During the war's final winter, British bombers made frequent flights across the region, dropping weapons and supplies for the home guard.

ℹ CONTACT INFORMATION

Hardangervidda Nature Centre
5784 Eidfjord
Norway
Tel: (00 47) 5366 5900
Fax: (00 47) 5366 5984
E-mail: post@hardangervidda.org
Web: www.hardangervidda.org

Destination Hardangerfjord
Postboks 66
5601 Nordheimsund
Norway
Tel: (00 47) 5655 3870
Fax: (00 47) 5655 3871
E-mail: info@hardangerfjord.com
Web: www.hardangerfjord.com

Jotunheimen National Park

Jotunheimen's wild and craggy landscape makes it a challenging destination, but the numerous walkers and mountaineers who return year after year will testify to its rich rewards.

Jotunheimen National Park was established in 1980 to protect the highest mountainous region in Scandinavia. The many majestic summits give the area its character, and among them is Galdhøpiggen, Norway's highest peak at 2,469m. Although dominated by high land, Jotunheimen's climate is surprisingly favourable, as the park lies inland and towards the south of the country. The eastern part of the park in particular, often enjoys sunny, warm summers and cold, dry winters.

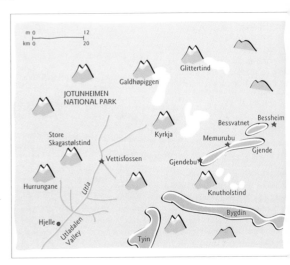

Besseggen and other walks

Although Jotunheimen was used as a hunting-ground for reindeer for several thousand years, it was not discovered as a location for tourism and recreation until the 1820s. Since then, scores of walking and climbing routes have been charted. There are more than 800km of trails marked with cairns. One of the most popular walks follows Besseggen, the narrow, sharp ridge between the Gjende and the Bessvatnet lakes. With the green

waters of Gjende and the blue of Bessvatnet hundreds of feet below, the lakes are so close together that it is possible to drop a stone into each of them from the ridge. This is where Peer Gynt, the eponymous anti-hero of Ibsen's play, had his wild flight on the reindeer's back, so dramatically described in the First Act.

Bukkelægret is another spectacular route, though not as well-known as that along Besseggen. Not for the faint-hearted walker, the path follows the steep mountainside down towards Gjende. The trip from Memurubu over to Gjendebu is said to be one of the most beautiful walks in Jotunheimen, offering panoramic views across brooding glaciers and rugged peaks.

Peaks and waterfalls

There are hundreds of mountain-tops in the park which can be conquered without climbing equipment. Reaching the summits of Galdhøpiggen and Glittertinden, the two highest points in the country, is a must for energetic ramblers, but the lower peaks are also well worth the effort. Kyrkja – the Church – is one example. The 2,032m

summit can be reached in a two hour hike. An isolated fell at the meeting point of four valleys, Kyrkja is unmistakable – a dark, distinctive triangular shape, just like a church spire, at the heart of Jotunheimen.

Vettisfossen

Olavsbu

The sharp, broken pinnacles of Hurrungane are a climber's paradise. The highest and most popular peak in Hurrungane is Store Skagastølstind, first completed by the Englishman William Cecil Slingsby in 1876. There are walking routes in the area too, but these are unmarked and only suitable for experienced walkers.

The Utladalen valley is an example of Jotunheimen's gentler aspect, with its old pine forests and sheltered hill farms. This is where Norway's highest waterfall, Vettisfossen, is situated, easily accessible along a good path from Hjelle. The perpendicular cascade of water dropping in free-fall for 275m is an unforgettable sight.

Traversing the glaciers

None of the glaciers in Jotunheimen are typical plateau glaciers. Because of the park's alpine landscape, the snowfields lie surrounded by peaks or nestle in the valleys. For hundreds of years, the glaciers were regularly traversed by local farmers and hunters, who used them as rather risky shortcuts between villages. Glacier walking is now a popular sport in Jotunheimen. The Norwegian Mountain Touring Association organises courses and provides guides to take walkers along safe routes.

Bridging the River Utla

Jostedalsbreen

Jostedalsbreen is the largest glacier on the European mainland. Over 60km in length, its icy wastes lie slightly to the west of Jotunheimen, in a national park of its own. People have lived close to the edge of this glacier for centuries, and such proximity to nature at its grandest has been the inspiration behind many legends. One of them dates back to the 1350s, when the Black Death ravaged the country. As the plague started to spread, inhabitants of some villages by the Sognefjord moved up into the isolated valley of Jostedal to escape contagion. They forbade visits from their friends and relatives, but asked them to leave any messages under a big rock at the entrance to the valley – there is still a rock there called the 'Letter Stone'. Despite these precautions, the plague caught up with them and laid the valley waste. Years later, only one survivor was found; a little girl who had fled into the mountains. When finally caught, she was as shy and wild as a bird, and was given the name of *Jostedalsrypa* – the Jostedal Grouse.

ⓘ CONTACT INFORMATION

Oslo and Akershus Mountain Touring Association
Postboks 7 Sentrum
0101 Oslo
Norway
Tel: (00 47) 22 822800
Fax: (00 47) 22 822823

The Utladalen valley

Rebild Bakker

Rebild Bakker is a place of legend and tradition, its strong links with social history evident almost everywhere. Nature and man seem to co-exist, as they have done for centuries, in a state of tranquillity.

Ironically, the only real national park in flat, open Denmark is dominated by hills and woodland. Located in Himmerland county, Rebild Bakker is set in the country's largest public forest, the Rold Skov. Its valleys carved by the meltwater of a glacier, the south of the park is dominated by deciduous trees, while to the north, cattle graze on heather-covered moors.

Purchased by a group of Danish-Americans in 1911, it was presented to the state the following year. Three conditions were attached to this unusual gift: that the park should remain in its natural state; that it should be open to everybody; and that Danish-Americans be permitted to celebrate their national holidays there. The third condition in particular is generously fulfilled – Rebild now plays host to the largest 4th of July celebration outside the USA, with thousands of Danes and Americans arriving each year to reinforce the friendly links between the two nations. In Gryden, the natural amphitheatre to the west of the park, American Independence Day is

commemorated through drama, music and speeches. The Lincoln Log Cabin, built from American timber in the 19th century style, stands nearby as a constant reminder of these links. One tenth of the Danish population emigrated to the USA between 1870 and 1920, and exhibitions in the cabin tell their story.

Cimbri and Vikings

The people of this region are no strangers to foreign travel. It was from here that the Cimbri tribe set off in 100 BC to conquer most of Europe. Although they were defeated before twenty years had passed, they are remembered for their bravery in facing down the Romans. A commemorative stone, carved in the likeness of a charging bull, stands amongst the Rebild hills, proudly claiming that 'The Cimbri set out from this place.'

Evidence of those later wandering soldiers, the Vikings, can be seen in the form of burial mounds throughout northern Jutland. At Lindholm Høje are 682 Iron Age and Viking graves, some marked with stones arranged in the shape of a ship.

Enchanted hills

A peculiarly spiritual place, Himmerland county abounds in myths and legends. One beech wood in Rebild Bakker is known as Troldeskoven – Forest of the Trolls.

Danes and Americans celebrate American Independence Day together on the Rebild hills

The Rebild hills in their autumn colours

Some of the trees here date back to the 17th century, and are gnarled and twisted from decades of coppicing and stump sprouting. They are known as *purker*, or little fellows, lurking in the woods to pounce mischievously on unsuspecting walkers. Some trunks and branches are so deformed that they bend back on themselves to form 'eye trees'. Locals believed that illnesses could be slipped off the body like a cloak if the afflicted person could pass through an 'eye'.

Indeed, the entire park is associated with health and cleanliness. Here are the most copious springs in northern Europe. In particular, the Ravnkilde (Raven's Spring) gushes 60 litres of water every second, while the Kovrsbæken (Kovr's Brook) carries even more. Their waters maintain a constant temperature of 7°C.

A number of endangered plants and flowers grow along their banks, which may once have been collected by wise women for use in their healing potions. Although this area is now restricted, visitors are free to gather their own selection of more common fruits – mountain cranberries, bilberries, blueberries, blackberries, raspberries and juniper berries.

Craft and sculpture

Of the many small folk museums in the region, one of the most charming is the Spillemands Museet. This is devoted to the traditions of clog making, charcoal burning, pottery, basket weaving and woodsmanship.

Another unusual attraction is the Thingbæk Kalkminer. This cavernous chalk mine is now a dramatic gallery exhibiting the work of sculptors Anders Bundgård and C.J. Bonnesen. These are the original gypsum figures for bronze sculptures that can be seen throughout Denmark. On special occasions, such as Christmas and Easter, the mine-workings are lit by 3,000 candles and host processions and classical concerts.

Aalborg

Even away from the hills, Himmerland remains in touch with its past. The nearest large town to Rebild Bakker is Aalborg, whose proud history is suggested in its refusal to 'modernise' its name to 'Ålborg. The Old Town contains many buildings that date back to the 15th century. The ostentatious five storey Jens Bangs Stenhus is the largest Renaissance mansion in northern Europe. Jens Bang was the richest man in Aalborg but seems also to have been the bitterest. The ugly gargoyles are said to represent his enemies, while the stone figure sticking out his tongue at the town hall opposite is Jens Bang himself, who was never elected onto the town council.

Aalborg's pedestrian area, lined with shops, cafés and over 300 restaurants, generates a festive atmosphere which is perhaps responsible for Aalborg's nickname, 'Little Paris of the North'.

ⓘ CONTACT INFORMATION

Rebild-Skørping Tourist Bureau
KulturStationen
DK-9520 Skørping
Denmark
Tel: (00 45) 96 820220
Fax: (00 45) 96 820223
E-mail: info@roldskovturist.dk
Web: www.roldskovturist.dk

Aalborg Tourist and Convention Bureau
Østerågade 8
P.O. Box 1862
DK-9100 Aalborg
Denmark
Tel: (00 45) 98 126022
Fax: (00 45) 98 166922
E-mail: info@tourist-aal.dk

North Zealand

Walk in the footsteps of royalty in the solemn grandeur of palace gardens; savour the tranquillity of a nature reserve; wander in a dappled woodland; or explore the historical towns of Hillerød and Roskilde.

Copenhagen has much to offer, but sometimes only nature can satisfy the soul. Although there are no national parks in North Zealand, there are plenty of other green areas, all within an hour's drive of Denmark's capital.

Hillerød, for example, nestles in some of the most extensive woodland in Denmark, the last vestiges of a wilderness that has never been completely tamed by humans. To the south lies Store Dyrehave woodland, while one of Denmark's largest forests, Gribskov, stretches to the north. Spoked with paths, the woods were popular hunting grounds for the monarchs of the 17th and 18th centuries. Indeed, the royal influence on the region has contributed to many of its beauties and successes. Hillerød was an insignificant market town until 1602, when King Christian IV began work on his castle, Frederiksborg Slot.

Ledreborg Slot near Roskilde

Frederiksborg

Frederiksborg Slot – *slot* means castle – is a fine example of Renaissance architecture, spread majestically over three linked islets in Castle lake. Often regarded as the Danish Versailles, the red brick palace is a treasure house, its apartments crammed with silver, tapestries, paintings and priceless furniture.

The spectacular chapel features the famous Compendius organ, which attracts musicians from all over the world. Frederiksborg's Baroque garden was restored in 1996 as part of Copenhagen's Cultural Capital of Europe celebrations. Perfectly symmetrical, paths and intricately planted squares are set off by magnificent cascades and a circular lake flanked by trees.

Fredensborg

Further to the north-east of Hillerød, on the eastern shores of the lake Esrum Sø, are the parklands of the queen's palace, Fredensborg Slot. Built slightly later than Frederiksborg, it has been favoured as the summer residence of Danish royals since the early 18th century.

Visitors, however, are welcome to absorb the atmosphere of relaxed opulence. The queen's private grounds, her orangery and herb garden are open to the public each summer. Less regimented than Frederiksborg's parklands, the grounds are built along Romantic lines, rich in hidden pleasures and with 16km of winding paths which ultimately lead to the lakeside.

Ledreborg

The landscapes surrounding Frederiksborg and Fredensborg were designed by the most important figure in Danish architecture in the 1720s,

Horse-drawn carriages in Jægersborg Deer Park

Johan Cornelius Krieger. His revolutionary vision involved the cohesion of house and gardens into a single experience, the grounds arranged around a central axis to suggest the imposition of beauty and order over a chaotic world.

The third palace to be associated with Krieger is further south, near the beautiful city of Roskilde. Ledreborg Slot is an impressive example of rococo architecture and landscaping. A yellow jewel set in eighty hectares of undulating terraced gardens, its avenues stretch languidly deep into the countryside.

Lejre

The region of Lejre, where Ledreborg is located, will please those who prefer history to be rougher and nature to be wilder. With its rich meadows and clear streams, it has been inhabited and cultivated since the last Ice Age, and was once a powerful political centre.

An old legend tells of a ship that came sailing down the river, bearing gifts from the gods and a small child. The boy grew up to become King Skjold, a King Arthur-like figure who ruled Lejre from the court of Hjort-Hallen. However, Lejre's glory days came to an end when the court was attacked and the hall burnt down.

Recent excavations have revealed that the stories have an historical basis: an enormous hall, nearly 50m long, with the curved walls typical of the Viking period has been recently discovered. Other local finds include the elaborate costume jewellery of great nobles. Pottery and glassware of Baltic origin has also been found nearby, suggesting a once thriving trade.

Jægersborg Deer Park

Just to the north of Copenhagen sprawls a convenient outlet for urban stresses. Jægersborg Dyrehave is now a state-owned forest but it was originally established in 1669 as Frederik III's royal hunting ground. The park was subsequently doubled in size by the next king, Christian V, who razed a village to the ground in order to make way for it.

Perhaps, therefore, it is poetic justice that the park has been open to the public for 250 years, and that it is something of a tradition for the residents of Copenhagen to come to Jægersborg. This enchanting forest can be explored on foot or, more romantically, in one of the horse-drawn carriages that takes passengers to the stately mansion which forms the centrepiece of the park.

Jægersborg is home to about 2,100 red, fallow and sika deer. Numbers are carefully managed, a by-product of which is venison, which has become a local delicacy.

Urban recreation

Vestskoven, the West forest, was established in 1967 to offer outdoor recreational facilities to those living in the expanding urban areas around Copenhagen. Now covering about 10 sq km, it has developed into a varied landscape, comprising lakes, hills, forest and heathland, the marshes overgrown with willow and alder.

Humans are not the only species to benefit from its creation – as well as woodland creatures, nightingales, moorhens, greylags, grasshopper warblers, water rails and grebes have all found a home here.

The park is dominated by Hersted Heights, constructed from 3 million cubic metres of earth and rubble rescued from urban building projects to form the highest man-made hill in the whole of Denmark.

ℹ CONTACT INFORMATION

Roskilde-Egnens Tourist Bureau
Gullanddstræde 15
PO Box 637
DK-4000 Roskilde
Denmark
Tel: (00 45) 46 352700
Fax: (00 45) 46 351474
E-mail: info@destination-roskilde.dk
Web: www.destination-roskilde.dk

The Lejre countryside

Skaftafell National Park

The continuous fusion of fire and ice is dramatically performed against a backdrop of primitive beauty in this corner of south-east Iceland.

Skaftafell National Park is often regarded as the most magnificent area in a country whose endless landscapes define magnificence. Nestling on sandy plains, beneath encroaching glaciers and forbidding mountains, it is an accessible green paradise in the midst of a region dominated by ice.

Endless variety

Skaftafell is a perfect example of an active glacial landscape and is filled with textbook examples of associated landforms such as hanging valleys, rolling hills, ridges of sandy moraine, tranquil lakes, tumbling rivers and jagged rocks. The glaciers themselves resemble strange ice sculptures, with shimmering arches and shadowy tunnels that are all the more beautiful for their impermanency.

Sheltered by mountains and glaciers, the national park can boast more sunshine hours, less rainfall and a milder climate than any other part of southern Iceland. However, there is no shortage of water which gushes from rocks, bubbles from crevasses, trickles in brooks and surges through rivers. On a calm summer evening, there is a special quality to the light that further heightens the effect of the scenery.

A glacial kingdom

Established in 1967 and expanded in 1984, Skaftafell National Park now covers about 1,600 sq km. Skaftafell is situated at the southern extent of the massive Vatnajökull glacier which is, excluding Greenland, the largest expanse of inland ice in Europe. The park also includes three valley glaciers that have squeezed their way southwards from the main ice sheet.

These include Skaftafellsjökull (part of the larger Öræfajökull glacier); Morsárjökull, which descends by successive waterfalls into the Morsá valley; and Skeiðarárjökull, which measures 25km across with a *sandur*, or outwash plain, that extends 20km to the coast. The glaciers are still active, groaning and creaking as they advance or retreat – Skaftafellsjökull, for example, can recede up to a metre every day, dropping debris as it goes.

Svartifoss

Jökulhlaup

When farms built on the sandur were destroyed by lava flows in the 14th century, the area became known as Öræfi (meaning 'wasteland'). As recently as 1996, volcanic activity beneath a glacier resulted in the dramatic and devastating release of water and ice that is known as a *jökulhlaup*. The sheer power of such an eruption is breathtaking. The flow cut a canyon into the ice margin 1km long, 250m wide and 40m deep.

The topography of the national park was transformed as sand and gravel flattened the Skeiðarársandur to create a coastal desert. More practically, bridges were destroyed and roads made impassable, virtually isolating south-east Iceland for several days. It is not surprising that the area is of great interest to geologists and glacial scientists, for whom Skaftafell is more than mere beautiful scenery.

Svartifoss

About 45 minutes' walk from the main campsite, Svartifoss, 'the black waterfall', is the park's major attraction. There are mightier waterfalls in Iceland, such as Gullfoss or Godofoss, but few are as instantly recognisable.

Svartifoss obtains its name not from the colour of its waters, which foam white over the cliff edge, but from the black basalt columns that flank the waterfall. Arranged in a regular hexagonal pattern, the rocks hang off the cliff face like the pipes of an organ and were the inspiration for the architectural design of the National Theatre in Reykjavik.

Hiking in Skaftafell

The national park contains enough hiking trails to keep walkers of all abilities occupied for several days. Most paths are well marked with signs that indicate distances as well as approximate times.

Tracks to landmarks such as Svartifoss and Skaftafellsheiði heath are popular to the point of overuse but elsewhere, hikers can lose the crowds and strike out for a different perspective. It is

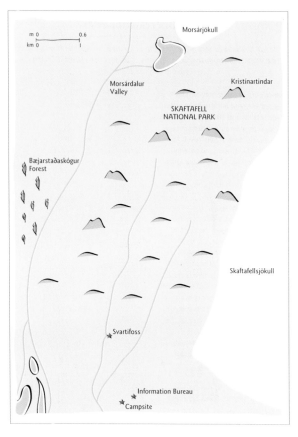

possible to climb almost any of the nearby mountains for dramatic views and endless photo opportunities.

The Kristínartindar trail, for example, is a strenuous six hour climb from sea level to 1,100m above the plains. The path passes a number of waterfalls, including the strangely named Hundafoss, or 'Dog Falls'. Its name is believed to derive from stories of travellers who often lost their dogs over the cliffs when fording the flood-swollen river.

The Kristínartindar trail gradually rises through an increasingly sparse landscape to eventually reach the peak of Nyrdrihnaukur and its views of the Morsárdalur valley below. This valley is itself a rewarding destination for a hike, brimming with a fine birch forest and clear springs which help the trees grow to over 12m in height.

Plants and wildlife

The park's sheltered position and rich volcanic soil encourages a profusion of lush vegetation. More than 200 species of plants have been found here, including wildflowers that carpet the plains and valleys in the summer. Insects also thrive, providing an ideal habitat for heath and upland birds such as snipe, brambling, skua, meadow pipit and redwing. A sub-species of wren, unique to Iceland, is also known to nest in the park.

ⓘ CONTACT INFORMATION

Iceland Travel Group Ltd
Lágmúli 4
PO Box 8650
128 Reykjavik
Iceland
Tel: (00 354) 569 9300
Web: www.iceland-travel.is

Þingvellir National Park

Most tourists experience Þingvellir as a half hour stop-off on a tour of the whole island. Just thirty minutes, however, can hardly do justice to such a fascinating area.

The word *Þingvellir* means 'plains of parliament' and although the national park spreads out over a broad forested plain, Þingvellir's main attraction is Iceland's historical parliament, dramatically surrounded by gently sloping mountains and sheer cliffs.

Established in AD 930, the *AlÞing* (parliamentary assembly) is the oldest surviving democracy in the world. The Icelandic parliament has met ever since, first at Þingvellir and more recently at Reykjavík. The only rupture in the unbroken line of the AlÞing was caused by political squabbles in the early 19th century, but today the AlÞing symbolises the independence and success of the modern Icelandic state. As a result, the significance of Þingvellir to the Icelandic people cannot be overestimated, inspiring not only political dreams but also romantic and nationalist literature.

Although the AlÞing has not met there since the late 18th century, Þingvellir remains the focal point of the country. Here, Iceland's independence from Denmark was declared in June 1944, while thirty years later, 60,000 people gathered in the park to celebrate the 1,100th anniversary of the arrival of the first settlers. Meetings and conventions continue to be held here, either outside beside Þingvellir itself, or at the nearby Valhöll Hotel.

The AlÞing

The AlÞing would meet annually at Þingvellir not only to review and enforce the country's laws but also to arrange contracts, settle disputes and carry out executions. Anyone who wanted to propose a new law could do so, while all participants in the sessions were permitted to build shelters, pitch tents, graze their animals and gather wood. It is still possible to see the remains of the *búðir* (turf booths) that were used as shelters and market stalls. The most

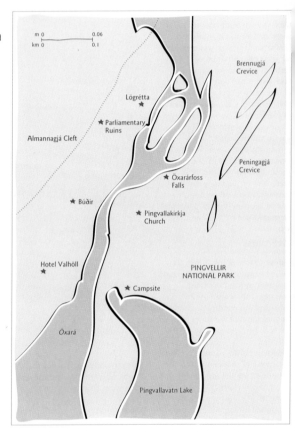

recent examples were built in the 18th century. Also still evident is the *logberg*, possibly Iceland's most revered site. This is the rock on which the speaker of law would stand to address the people. He would amplify his words by directing them at the opposite wall so that all those who attended the AlÞing could hear. Although the stone has sunk into the plain over the years, the spot is still proudly marked by an Icelandic flag. Concentrated on the northern shore of Lake Þingvallavatn, the ruined stone wall and earthwork known as the *lögrétta*, once the main parliament buildings, can still be seen.

A dramatic location

Like much of Iceland, the present scenery is relatively new. Chasms bisect the park as the North American plate continues to pull away from the Eurasian plate, creating a huge fissure that has widened by 20m since the AlÞing was first established. Lava has gushed out of the Earth, filling the hole and brimming over onto the plains on either side. The resulting landscape has been developed further by glacial erosion. The largest canyon, known as Almannagjá, or Everyman's Cleft, is about 8km long, 30m deep and up to 50m wide.

Öxara

Þingvellir's main river is named Öxara after an axe that was once lost to the current. Its waters are said to turn into wine for an hour at the start of every new year. The river tumbles into the Almannagjá ravine to form the Öxarárfoss waterfall, yet evidence suggests that the river was diverted here when the Alþing was founded, for practical or aesthetic reasons. Early Icelanders are known to have been preoccupied with the loveliness of their country, and a parliament is likely to be inspired by the backdrop of a majestic waterfall.

Mysterious pools

One pond formed by the river is known as Drekkingarhylur (Drowning Pool). It was here that, under laws passed in 1564, women convicted of murder, adultery or giving birth to an illegitimate child were drowned. Men were usually executed by hanging or decapitation, although nine men convicted of witchcraft were once burnt at the stake in the fissure now called Brennugjá, the Burning Chasm.

Less morbidly, visitors can stand on the bridge over Peningagjá (Money Chasm), dropping coins into the water and making a wish. If the coin's fall can be followed to the bottom, the wish will come true. There is an eerie beauty as the coins reflect the light through the calm turquoise pool.

Looking down into Almannagjá

Þingvallavatn

Covering 84 sq km, Þingvallavatn is the largest lake in Iceland. In some places, it is over 100m deep but only 5% of its water is supplied by the inflowing River Öxara. The rest is derived from groundwater springs making the water a clean habitat for a variety of water plants, birds and fish. Four species of trout thrive here, including the murta which is regarded as a great delicacy. Low trees and shrubs create a tranquil atmosphere along the shores of the lake, but the bed of Þingvallavatn has a tendency to subside, flooding nearby farmland and reminding the local people that this is a land of constant change.

Þingvellir church

Þingvallakirkja, a simple white church, is located near the remains of the parliament. There has been a church near the site since the days of Olaf the Fat of Norway, an 11th century king who donated timber for its construction. The church's tiny cemetery was established in 1939, and is known as the Skaldareitur (Poets' Graveyard) after the two poets who are buried there. Conveniently, the pastor of the church is also the warden of the national park.

Þingvellir National Park

It is worth taking the time to leave the Alþing and follow the network of hiking paths to the springs, streams, canyons and caves that intersperse the plain. Rocks are strewn about in bizarre formations. Vegetation here is hardly spectacular, but is surprisingly rich for a country as barren as Iceland. In addition to the colourful tundra plants, groves of birch trees and thick grasslands lend Þingvellir a refreshing lushness, and wildflowers flourish in the damp, secluded fissures.

[i] CONTACT INFORMATION

Iceland Travel Group Ltd
Lágmúli 4
PO Box 8650
128 Reykjavik
Iceland
Tel: (00 354) 569 9300
Web: www.iceland-travel.is

Imposing walls of rock at Þingvellir

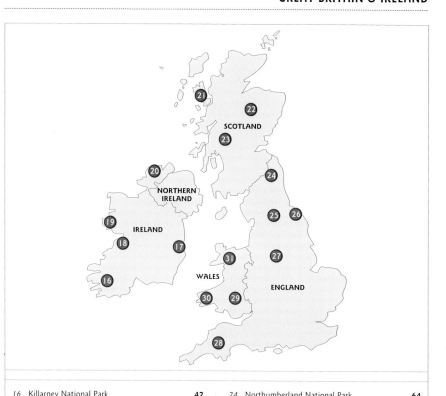

ℹ CONTACT INFORMATION

Britain Visitor Centre
1 Regent Street
London SW1Y 4XT
Tel: 020 8846 9000
E-mail: enquirydesk@bta.org.uk
Web: www.visitbritain.com

Irish Tourist Board
150 New Bond Street
London W1Y 0AQ
Tel: 020 7493 3201
Fax: 020 7493 9065
Web: www.ireland.ie

Northern Ireland Tourist Board
59 North Street
Belfast BT1 1NB
Tel: 028 9024 6609
Fax: 028 9031 2424
E-mail: general.enquiries.
nitb@nics.gov.uk
Web: www.ni-tourism.com

Scottish Tourist Board
23 Ravelston Terrace
Edinburgh EH4 3TP
Tel: 0131 332 2433
Fax: 0131 315 4545
Web: www.visitscotland.com

Wales Tourist Board
Brunel House
2 Fitzalan Road
Cardiff CF24 0UY
Tel: 029 2049 9909
Fax: 029 2048 5031
E-mail: info@tourism.wales.gov.uk
Web: www.visitwales.com

Killarney National Park

*Killarney, with its lakes and woods, has a stateliness and history
that befits its status as the oldest national park in Ireland.*

Established in 1932, Killarney
National Park consists of the lands of
the old Muckross and Kenmare
estates, although the three lakes of
the park – Lough Leane, Upper Lake
and Muckross Lake – make up almost
a quarter of its surface area.

Named after the town of Killarney,
which encroaches onto its north-
eastern border, the park is shadowed
by MacGillycuddy's Reeks in the west,
the highest mountain range in Ireland.
Within the park itself are the slightly
lower peaks of Mangerton, Torc and
Shehy, which contrast with the
lowlands near the shores of the lakes.
The park is designated a biosphere
reserve by UNESCO, and the variety
of protected wildlife – from the
Killarney fern to native red deer – is
rich and rewarding for visitors.

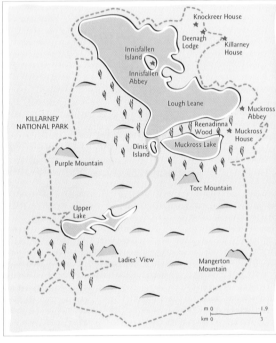

Ancient woods

Since the last Ice Age, Ireland has
seen a succession of vegetation types,
from tundra-like conditions to a
progression of woodland stages.
Birch, hazel, pine, oak and elm have
all covered the land. Since the arrival
of human settlers in Neolithic times,
woodland has been felled so that now
there is relatively little forest cover
left. From the 16th to 18th centuries,
the wood was cut for charcoal, whilst
until the 19th century, oak was used
to tan leather. Today the woods in
Killarney National Park are the largest
remaining examples of these ancient
forests. Oak trees are the most
common species, and provide a
habitat for mosses and lichens.

Reenadinna wood on the Muckross
peninsula is one of only two or three
yew woods in Europe; it is rare to see
so many yews growing together. Few
flowers or plants grow on the floor
because of the dense shade cast by
the trees, but a soft covering of
yellowy-green moss, combined with
the darkened atmosphere, gives the
wood an eerie underwater feel.

Although woodlands is widespread,
more of the park is actually covered
by peat and bog. Blanket bog is
common on low lying flat and sloping
land, while heathland commands the
higher peaty soils. Plant species
native to the Atlantic coasts of
Europe and North America, and to the
Arctic and Alps, all occur naturally in
Killarney, together with the Killarney
fern, which was nearly made extinct
by the Victorians' obsession for
collecting precious plants.

Muckross House

42

Kerry cows

As well as badgers, foxes and field mice, and swallows, swifts and redwings – birds and mammals familiar to much of Britain and Ireland – the park's secluded habitats offer protection to rarer species. Red squirrels prosper, as grey squirrels have not yet populated the south-west of Ireland, whilst the number of pine martens has been augmented by the release of animals from breeding populations in County Clare.

The park also safeguards the only remaining herd of native red deer in Ireland. All the other herds of deer derive from animals introduced from elsewhere. Killarney also has Japanese sika deer, brought from County Wicklow in the 19th century. A herd of pedigree Kerry cattle, descended from the dairy breed which was used extensively in the past to crop the grassy uplands of the county, are conserved as an important part of farming heritage.

The lakes, with their expanses of water and shelter along the shores and between the islands, offer a safe habitat for waterfowl and fish.

Muckross Gardens

The three lakes are connected, and all drain into the River Laune, which enters the sea at Killorglin. Fishing for brown trout and salmon is possible. A flock of Greenland white-fronted geese comes to winter each year on the lakes and bogs. The geese used to feed entirely on blanket bog, but in recent years have tended to browse more on agricultural grasslands as their traditional habitat has become increasingly less common in Ireland.

Early history

From evidence of copper mining on Ross Island, the earliest inhabitants of south-western Ireland arrived in the Bronze Age. After this period come the Iron Age ring forts, some dating from early Christian times. These defensive settlements dot the surrounding countryside, and there is one in the depths of Reenadinna wood. Two monasteries from the

Gap of Dunloe

7th century, on Innisfallen Island and at Aghadoe in the north, show how and where early Christian settlers lived. At Innisfallen the remains of the monastery are well preserved and there is a famous written history, the *Annals of Innisfallen* from the 11th to 13th centuries, which tells of early Irish life. Other ruins include Muckross abbey – a Franciscan friary – and Ross castle on the shore of Lough Leane, both dating from between the 15th and 17th centuries.

Estates

The grand houses of the estates within the park tell the more recent history of the area, and of the people who have lived here. Muckross House, though built in Elizabethan style, dates from 1843. Open to the public, it paints a picture of those fortunate enough to have lived in the mansion in the late 19th century. The basement contains displays of crafts and folk life of County Kerry, and also includes the main visitor centre for the park. The informal gardens surrounding the house are extensive, with brilliant displays of rhododendrons.

Knockreer House, dating from the 1950s, is now the park's research and education centre. It stands on the site

of a Victorian mansion, belonging to the Kenmare estate, which was destroyed by fire in 1913. The stables of a previous house were converted after the fire into Killarney House, which is situated on the very edge of the town of Killarney.

Two tea rooms are provided for visitors in old houses of the estates, one at Dinis Cottage on Dinis Island, near the Meeting of the Waters by Muckross Lake, and the other at Deenagh Lodge, a thatched cottage at the park entrance.

Walking in the park

The climate of Killarney is oceanic, with the prevailing winds off the Atlantic Ocean producing mild winters and cool summers. As a consequence, humidity is high, but with average temperatures of only around 15°C it is not uncomfortable. Woodland and heath dominate the park, so autumn can be a beautiful time to visit, with mists melting into the glowing colours of the changing leaves, gorse and heather. Spring and summer are also popular, owing to the warmer weather, but as Kerry experiences such a stable climate, winter is only quieter because of the bareness of the landscape.

Four guided nature trails are laid out in Killarney National Park, and one of them, the Cloghereen Trail, has been designed specifically for the visually impaired. The path has a guide rope, and stopping points at which walkers are encouraged to touch, feel and listen to the textures and noises of the immediate environment.

The hills, forests and heaths of the park are ideal for walking, and the tops give magnificent views across the lakes. The area in the east and north of the park has off-road tracks leading through woodlands to the lakesides. Ladies' View, in the south-west, has glorious sweeping panoramas, and for a challenge, there are always MacGillycuddy's Reeks just outside the park. Although the landscape of Killarney does not seem wild, walkers should take the usual hillwalking precautions and are advised not to hike alone.

ⓘ CONTACT INFORMATION

Killarney National Park
Muckross House
Killarney
Co. Kerry
Ireland
Tel: (00 353) 64 31440
Fax: (00 353) 64 33926

Ross castle

Wicklow Mountains National Park

Near enough to Dublin for a day's outing from the city, the woods and heath of the Wicklow mountains and Glendalough valley offer a timeless image of the Irish landscape.

The Wicklow Mountains National Park covers 200 sq km to the south of Dublin. The mountains form a ridge of granite, with the Glendalough valley as the central section of the park. The area has been managed by Dúchas, the official body responsible for preserving Ireland's heritage, since 1991, and much of it is soon to be designated as a Special Area of Conservation under the European Habitats directive.

Glendalough valley

Dublin's park

The national park is the local natural playground for Dubliners, so the weekends and holidays can be very busy. Summer is the best time for visiting if fine weather is important, though it is likely to be as wet underfoot or overhead as in the colder months. However, the mildness of the climate means that the park is enjoyable at any time of the year. Spring offers carpets of bluebells, while autumn displays the changing colours of the woodlands.

Land of bogs and woods

The land is typical of Ireland, with peaty soils on the steeper and drier slopes, and blanket bogs lower down. Upland heather vegetation, such as ling and bell heather, fraughan and bilberry grow in the peat, whilst sedges and bog mosses prefer the moist areas. The bogland is protected by artificial walkways; visitors can marvel at the fragile habitat beneath their feet, without damaging it.

The woodland which dominates Glendalough valley is semi-natural oak, and throughout the park there is a mixture of deciduous and evergreen

trees, including Scots pine planted by mining companies in the 19th century. In spring, bluebells, wood sorrel and wood anemones turn the ground beneath the newly budding trees into a fairytale world, whilst woodrush, bracken, ferns and mosses form a rich undergrowth.

Among the oak trees are other native species, such as holly, hazel and mountain ash. Young trees are protected by fencing, as the tender shoots tempt the red deer. This protection, together with a project for recovering private forested land originally used for timber, means the woodland areas are growing in size.

Wicklow's deer

The deer, originally native Irish red deer, are now mostly a hybrid of imported red deer and sika deer. The former prefer moorland and the latter the conifers; the hybrids seem to have inherited one or other preference, and are found in both wooded and open areas.

Over eighty species of bird inhabit the park, a diversity recognised by the European Birds Directive. Species range from peregrines, merlins and kestrels, hunting over the open moorland, to grouse, pipits and skylarks on the uplands.

Glendalough

Glendalough means 'the valley of two lakes', and an upper and a lower lough meet in its centre. The medieval monastic settlement of St Kevin forms the most obvious focal point, and the churches, stone slabs and crosses are worth visiting. These monuments probably marked the way for pilgrims coming to St Kevin's shrine, but do just as well nowadays as markers for walking in the Wicklow mountains.

A section of the long distance Wicklow Way, running from the north-east to the south-west of County Wicklow, passes through Glendalough. The information office, near the Upper Lough, marks the beginning of a variety of self-guided walks throughout the valley, as well as the meeting point for summer nature walks and children's art groups. There are also weekly evening lectures in June, July and August on the history and geology of the park.

St Kevin's monastery

The religious site at Glendalough was founded by St Kevin in the 6th century. Although the Dublin and Glendalough dioceses were united in the 12th century – resulting in a decline in the ecclesiastical importance of the monastery – Glendalough remained a significant centre for another 400 years.

The geology of the area is evident in the ruined structures, with mica-schist and slate dominating the remaining walls. Some of the buildings were rebuilt in the 18th and 19th centuries, but as the renovators chose their materials carefully, none appears out of place. There are seven churches, as well as a gateway, round tower and priest's house – a small sample of the community which thrived in medieval times.

WICKLOW MOUNTAINS NATIONAL PARK

Glencree

Kippure

Tonduff

Gravale

Mullaghcleevan

Tonelagee

Roundwood

Lough Nahanagen

Glendalough

Laragh

Visitor Centre

Information Office

m 0   2.5
km 0   4

[i] CONTACT INFORMATION

Wicklow Mountains National Park
Glendalough
Co. Wicklow
Ireland
Tel: (00 353) 404 45338
Fax: (00 353) 404 45306

Burren National Park

The limestone landscape of the Burren is renowned among botanists for the diversity of wildflowers in late spring and early summer. For others, the flowers contribute to the beauty of an unusual landscape.

The area known as the Burren covers over 750 sq km in the west of Ireland, in northern County Clare and south-western County Galway. 'Burren' comes from the Gaelic word *boireann*, which means rocky, and refers to the limestone pavements and karst formations which dominate the landscape.

Burren National Park is in the south-eastern corner of this great area. Established in 1991 as Ireland's fifth national park, it only covers 13 sq km, but the park authorities, through Dúchas, The Heritage Service, share ownership of the surrounding land; the overall size of the park is expected to increase gradually. Although small, all types of landscape and vegetation which are present in the wider Burren are represented in the park. The area is particularly famous among botanists for arctic plants growing alongside mediterranean flowers.

A limestone world

The national park's corner of the Burren is found around limestone hills fading into drift-covered lowlands, with the hill of Mullagh More as the focal point. The huge beds of Carboniferous limestone were formed 320 million years ago from the compacted remains of marine plants and animals. Fossils and coral can be spotted among the layers of rock.

Mountain avens

The effects of water and ice have given the Burren a typical karst landscape, the ground covered with cracks and fissures through which water drains. Many turloughs, or disappearing lakes, are formed seasonally on the surface when underground water levels rise. The water seeping through the grikes also helps form caves.

The effects of previous ice ages are also evident in the landscape. Glaciers deposited a covering of ground-up rock on much of the higher land. These mineral-rich fines permitted the development of a more fertile soil than elsewhere, and the greenness of the hills in certain areas is testament to this. The movement of the glaciers also smoothed away the most jagged outcrops to produce a soothing horizon of clean and gentle lines.

Human history

As with many parts of Ireland which have been populated for thousands of years, the Burren has more open vegetation than native woodland. Human settlers have lived in the Burren for over 5,000 years, and megalithic tombs, stone forts, cairns and dolmens reveal the history of ancient peoples.

The little woodlands and scrubs of hazel trees that now dot some of the park are due partly to to the Great Famine of the 1840s, when so much of Ireland was left empty and desolate through emigration and death. The lack of constant attention by farmers allowed the trees to grow, where in more fortunate times the land was cultivated and grazed.

A wealth of wildflowers

The flora in the park is most significant for its unique variety. Whilst there the are usual limestone-loving plants among the rocky crevices, there are also acid-loving heathers. Sub-arctic plants, such as

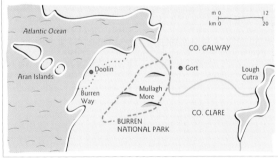

Walking in the park

The Burren is ideal for walking as it is neither too mountainous nor too flat, and is usually dry underfoot – a distinct advantage over other parts of Ireland. The rolling hills give good views, particularly rewarding when flowers carpet the rocky crevices in late spring.

The Burren area as a whole has old green tracks and byroads which are good for easy walking. To the west of the park is the Burren Way, which trundles past the village of Doolin. The route once led to the Cliffs of Moher, which fall 200m into the Atlantic, but this has now become too dangerous, and the walk has been redirected away from the coast. However, there are still marvellous views of the Aran islands.

mountain avens, grow alongside bloody crane's-bill, most often found in southern Europe. A proliferation of orchids, including the small dense-flowered species, decorates the park in a Mediterranean manner. Other spring and summer flowers include delicate gentians, shrubby cinquefoils and hoary rock-roses.

The Burren is home to the pine marten, though it is seldom seen. Hares, foxes, pygmy shrews and stoats are spied more often, while the remainder of the park's mammals are nocturnal. Seven types of bat include the lesser horseshoe bat, which is an endangered species.

Forty six species of bird breed in the Burren, whilst eighty four have been recorded as visiting. Meadow pipits, skylarks and wheatears frequent the limestone pavement and grassland, whilst sturdy yellowhammers tweet insistently among the fields and hedgerows. Common woodland birds, such as the cuckoo, nest and feed in the hazel scrub and deciduous woodland, whilst above all these landscapes kestrels, peregrines and hen harriers hover. Many species of butterfly add colour to the sometimes bare landscape in the warmer months. The large yellow brimstone feeds on purging buckthorn, which grows by the turloughs.

CONTACT INFORMATION

Burren National Park
2 Riverview
Corofin
County Clare
Ireland
Tel: (00 353) 65 37166
Fax: (00 353) 65 37165

IRELAND

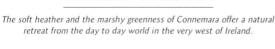

Connemara National Park

The soft heather and the marshy greenness of Connemara offer a natural retreat from the day to day world in the very west of Ireland.

Connemara National Park in County Galway is made up from the Kylemore Abbey estate, the old grounds of Letterfrack Industrial School, and some previously private land. Despite only being 20 sq km, the park contains both valleys and hills within its boundaries, including part of the Twelve Bens range, whilst the Maamturk mountains cast their shadow from the east.

The Twelve Bens

The very tops of Connemara's mountains are hard quartzite, but on the lower slopes crystalline schists are found, formed from upheavals in the Earth's crust millions of years ago. The last Ice Age has left its mark through the sand, gravel and clay deposits, as well as a scattering of boulders, all of which help determine the various plant communities.

Benbaun, Bencullagh, Benbrack and Muckanaght – four of the Twelve Bens – together with Diamond Hill, are the main peaks. Muckanaght is the highest at 656m, while Diamond Hill

St Dabeoc's heath

just reaches 440m, but they are all worth climbing for views across the county and towards Killary harbour in the north-east.

Bogs and rain

Western Ireland is damp. A stream at the centre of the park, in the Valley of Glenmore, flows into Polladirk river and on into a gorge further north. This tributary is one of many and

contributes to the wetness of the land. Although it usually rains on at least 250 days of the year, Connemara can still be enjoyed, as long as suitable clothing is worn. The weather contributes to the well-being of the vegetation; there is always colour in the landscape, whether it is green hills or purple heather.

Heather and heath

The flora in the park is dominated by heather, purple moorgrass and bogland plants, all of which flourish in the blanket bog and heathland. Three different types of heather – ling, cross-leaved heath and bell heather – grow in clumps across the hills, ensuring the scenery is never dull.

Insectivorous plants, such as sundew and butterwort, grow in the bogs, obtaining nutrients by trapping insects. Other flowers, such as pink lousewort, white bog cotton, milkwort and yellow bog asphodel, brighten the flat expanses, whilst bog myrtle, lichens and mosses lie flat to the ground.

Diamond Hill

Rare plants, usually found in either colder northern climates or the heat of the Mediterranean, also grow in Connemara, but have to be searched out more diligently than the common flowers. Purple and starry saxifrages, roseroot and mountain sorrel live high up in the hills, whilst pale butterwort, St Dabeoc's heath and St Patrick's cabbage are all found in warmer areas.

Deer and ponies

Native red deer used to roam western County Galway, but were hunted to extinction 150 years ago. The park is trying to reintroduce the animals, and the numbers are steadily growing. Connemara ponies are another native. In the past they were domesticated, but the park is now establishing a pure strain herd, to ensure all the native wildlife is conserved. Less visible inhabitants are badgers, hares, stoats, foxes, field mice and shrews, all of which keep themselves well hidden in the wilds, whilst bats are sometimes seen at dusk.

Past times

The land still bears the marks of inhabitants of previous centuries, through the remains of cultivation ridges and old turf banks. The lower lying localities were once used for grazing sheep and cattle, as well as growing vegetables, whilst peat was dug from the bogs for fuel. The old Galway road is also evident, recording past journeys to the hub of the county, although it is now overgrown.

Kylemore Abbey

History of the estate

Whilst the landscape reveals how the park was once cultivated, there are other signs of both ancient and modern generations. Megalithic court tombs, dating from 4,000 years ago, are found in the north, while an early 19th century graveyard reflects burial practices of more recent times. The most famous land owner in the region, Richard Martin (or 'Humanity Dick'), also dates from the 19th century. He left his legacy to animals by establishing the Society for Prevention of Cruelty to Animals in Ireland.

Although ruined houses, disused drainage systems and sheep pens, and an abandoned limekiln dot the park, other old parts of the Kylemore estate are still operational. The well of Tobar Mweelin, originally bored in 1870 to supply water to Kylemore castle, is still used today, while the administrative office and visitor centre are housed in the old farm buildings and infirmary of Letterfrack Industrial School, dating from the late 19th century. The Kylemore estate itself is still in private use; a girls' school and Benedictine nunnery are based at the castle and lake. However, visitors may wander in the grounds, and the nuns run a restaurant and craft shop.

Park facilities

The visitor centre is open from April to mid October. Specific summer activities include nature days for children, guided walks, and talks on Connemara ponies. Information is provided on two self-guided nature trails, and a variety of short and long-distance walks. A tea room and picnic area ensure that all visitors are well catered for whatever the weather.

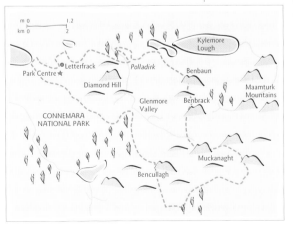

CONTACT INFORMATION

Connemara National Park
Letterfrack
Co. Galway
Ireland
Tel: (00 353) 95 41054
Fax: (00 353) 95 41005

Ireland West Tourism
Aras Failte
Victoria Place
Eyre Square
Galway
Ireland
Tel: (00 353) 91 563081
Fax: (00 353) 91 565201

Glenveagh National Park

A peaceful corner of north-west Ireland, Glenveagh's mixture of hilltops, bogs, woods, rivers and loughs has been preserved in its natural state for visitors.

Glenveagh National Park covers over 140 sq km in the remote north-west of Ireland, in County Donegal. Most of the park was originally a private estate and was only given to the state in the 1970s and 1980s, opening to the public in 1986. The park is composed of three areas: the original Glenveagh estate contains the Derryveagh mountains, whilst to the west are the quartzite hills around Crocknafarragh and to the south the peat and boglands near Lough Barra.

Walking in Glenveagh

Most of the area is in a semi-natural state, hardly even brushing with civilisation, let alone industry. The unspoiled landscapes are preserved for their wildness and desolation, offering peace and solitude for nature lovers. So, although there are few outdoor activities, the park is popular among walkers and visitors. The grand designs of the 19th century country house, its landscaped gardens and the surrounding countryside can fill a summer day.

Walks around the park range from strenuous hillwalking to following the gentle 2km nature trail near the visitor centre in the far north-east. Hikers are advised to be careful in the mountains which dominate the park, and of the low lying boggy areas, as both can be harder to navigate than at first appear. For shorter strolls, there is a path along the shore of Lough Veagh from the castle to the calm of the Poisoned Glen.

The park authority offers guided walks, including weekly nature walks in July and August, tours of the gardens, and a hillwalk every month between May and October.

Mountain building

Most of the hills are granite, except for the high peaks of Errigal and Muckish which were formed when continental collision forced layers of sedimentary rock upwards. Under considerable pressure, the rock metamorphosed into hard white quartzite, as a result of which Errigal and Muckish still stand tall.

Amongst the granite, basalt has formed ancient rocky dykes. During the great continental shifts, volcanic basalt poured into huge granite fractures and cooled into sheets stretching across the valleys. The basalt contains the magnetic mineral ilmenite, which can affect magnetic north on compasses.

Wet landscapes

The harsh granite and undisturbed state of much of the land sometimes makes Glenveagh National Park seem an empty place. Settlers in the Bronze Age, over 3,000 years ago, felled most of the forest to make the area inhabitable for themselves, but left behind a legacy of featureless blanket bog. Livestock grazing, together with

Lough Veagh

native and imported deer herds, has contributed to this clearance of the land, so that an area which was once dominated by natural oak woods is now characterised by its peatland and waterlogged soil.

Due to frontal depressions, and westerly winds, from the Atlantic, it rains in the area on most days of the year. This, unfortunately, means that the striking beauty of the hills contrasting with the glacial valleys and lakes is not always seen clearly. The wet weather and the moist ground can make a visit to Glenveagh quite a damp experience.

Plants and animals

All the hills are covered with purple moor grass and heathers, but the flowers which peep among the grasslands change from arctic–alpine species, such as bearberry and silvery moss, on the hilly crags, to white bog-cotton and flaxen-coloured asphodel on the wetness of the lower slopes. The hills in the north and west offer shelter to the rare golden plover, as well as peregrines and ravens, plus snow buntings in winter. Red grouse and deer feed on the young shoots of heather, but the purple moor grass tastes too bitter, so it flourishes,

providing ground cover for the prey of kestrels, merlins and buzzards. In the bog pools are minute aquatic plants and shimmering dragonflies, bringing beauty out of the dank ground.

The park contains over 100 hectares of woodland, some of it oak stands thousands of years old. Birch, rowan, holly, hazel, yew, aspen and bird cherry also appear among the native growth. Birds range from chaffinches,

woodpigeons and great tits to pine wood birds such as crossbills, goldcrests and wood warblers, all of which inhabit the woods year round. Rhododendrons, imported in the 19th century, are beginning to take over the natural woodland, but the park authorities work continually to ensure this exotic intruder does not choke the native species. Deer also are a threat to the woodland, feeding on the tender shoots beneath the trees.

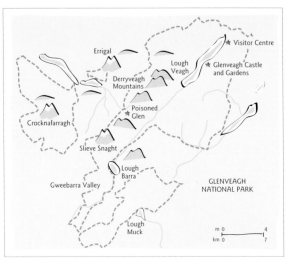

The herd, one of the largest in Ireland, was imported in 1891, after the native deer were hunted to extinction in the mid 19th century. The deer are controlled by a fence stretching for miles all around the park, as well as with a programme of seasonal culling. The deer mate between September and November, but for the rest of the year they are seen in separate groups of stags and hinds.

Water bodies range from compact Lough Nambraddan, to great Lough Veagh, which cuts the north-east of the park in two. Salmon and sea trout are found in the latter, while brown trout and eels prosper elsewhere. Graceful herons and otters are attracted by the fish, and can be spotted occasionally. The high plateau of the Derryveagh mountains is the birthplace of four rivers – the Owencarrow, the Leannan, the Gweebarra and the Clady – which flow through the park. Over 200 species of lichen testify to the lack of pollution in the area.

Glenveagh castle

John George Adair bought up the tenancies of the Glenveagh area to make the land into one estate in the 1860s. Infamously, he evicted all the tenants in 1861, leaving them to go to the poorhouse or emigrate to Australia. Once he had established the estate as his own he commissioned his cousin to build Glenveagh castle in 1867. Country houses in the style of castles were popular at the time, and Glenveagh was designed to resemble Balmoral, which had been recently renovated by Prince Albert. The battlemented ramparts are reminiscent of ancient Irish tower houses. As the castle is built out of Glenveagh's native granite it melds into its surroundings.

Its different inhabitants have influenced the style and furnishing of the house, from the modernisations and extensions of Adair's American widow, Cornelia, to the acquisitions of Victorian landscape paintings by

the last owner of the estate, the American curator Henry McIlhenny. The castle is open to visitors from mid-spring to early autumn, timed to coincide with the deerstalking and house parties of bygone days.

The gardens are also open to the public and form a focal point from which to view the park. Cornelia Adair imported many exotic plants and Henry McIlhenny cultivated them, perfecting the design and flowering cycles. Attractions include the walled garden, which is at its most colourful in August, and the Belgian Walk, built by wounded Belgian soldiers during the First World War.

ⓘ CONTACT INFORMATION

Glenveagh National Park
Church Hill
Letterkenny
Co. Donegal
Ireland
Tel: (00 353) 74 37090
Fax: (00 353) 74 37072

Errigal

Glenveagh castle

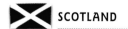

The Isle of Skye

*Once the subject of persecution on the island, Skye's Gaelic
culture is now its springboard for a renewed vibrancy.*

Situated off the frayed western
coastline of the Scottish Highlands,
Skye is a paradise for walkers,
mountaineers and afficionados of
Gaelic culture. Home to a large Gaelic-
speaking community and the
challenging Cuillin peaks, Skye's
magical mountain settings have
bolstered its appeal to visitors in
recent years.

This, in turn, has consolidated Skye's
economy, curbed the decline in its
population and encouraged cultural
activities. Although not a national
park, Skye is respected as an important
cradle of 'Scottishness' and as an area
with many landscape treasures.

The Cuillin mountains from Portree

Consisting of six peninsulas, with
many little islands speckled around its
shore, Skye is partnered by the 22km
long Raasay Island to the north-east.
The island is connected by bridge to
the mainland, but visitors can still
arrive by ferry from Mallaig in the
south. Through Uig harbour in the
north, Skye is also a gateway to the
Western Isles.

What's in a name?

The earliest Gaelic name for the island
was An t-Eilean Sgitheanach, the
winged isle, which is perhaps a
reference to the jagged peninsulas
which stick out. For the Vikings,
however, who arrived at the end of
the 8th century, this did not quite

capture the essence of the place.
They called the island Skuyo, the
cloud island, a reference to the ever-
present mist. As was their style, the
Norsemen initially arrived as raiders
and pillagers, their sole intention
being to rifle the area for goods and
control the land. The result of their
efforts was that between the 9th and

Churchton Bay, Raasay

Dunvegan and Duirinish

At the same time as the rise of the Clan Donald in the south, the Clan MacLeod were establishing themselves at Dunvegan in the north. Their castle has been home to the chief of the Clan for over 700 years, a lineage which continues today. The site overlooks Loch Dunvegan which has a colony of common and Atlantic seals, whose antics can be observed by boat.

The castle holds many intriguing artefacts from the Clan's past, including a flag with supposed magic powers which warriors once brought into battle. More recently, members of the Clan recruited the flag for good fortune when they were flying missions in the Second World War. To the west of the Clan's castle is the Duirinish peninsula dominated by Macleod's Tables, two flat-topped hills named Healabhal Bheag and Healabhal Mhór. Walking up the former is a popular trip which begins at the Forest of Varkasaig.

13th centuries Skye was considered to be more a part of Norway than Scotland. Gradually, however, the Norse people began to integrate themselves into the life and culture of the natives and the place names on the island are a testament to that fusion. Names ending in -bost (meaning a farm) and -shader (a homestead) suggest Norse origins.

Armadale and Sleat

In the 12th century, the Norse were overthrown as rulers of Skye, and Gaelic culture began to consolidate itself under the clan chieftains. One of these, the Clan Donald, whose progenitor was the Norse king Somerleder, set up their power base in the south of Skye at Armadale, and when arriving by ferry, a visitor will soon come across this stronghold.

Armadale castle is situated on Sleat peninsula, an area formed from some of the oldest gneiss rock in Europe (2,800 million years old). Surrounded by sixteen hectares of woodland and gardens, it was home to the Clan Donald for hundreds of years.

Woodlands are at their best in the south of Skye and, besides the castle gardens, there is also an oak and ash forest near Ord, north of Armadale. In late spring, the peninsula is speckled with bluebells, red campion and the aroma of wild garlic.

A popular walk to the Point of Sleat culminates in a trip across the moor to a lighthouse. Skye's moorland is shrouded in deer-grass and cotton-grass, the latter once used for stuffing pillows.

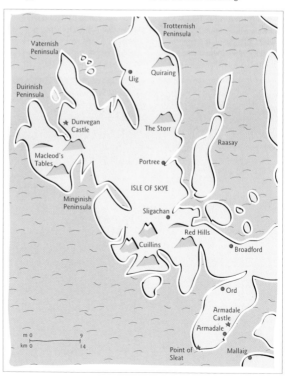

The Cuillins

Macleod's Tables were created by the Cuillins, mountains which dominate the Minginish peninsula to the south. An Cuilthion, as the range is named in Gaelic, is formed from the eroded roots of large volcanoes, whose lava flows form the northern half of Skye; the flat tops at Duirinish were shaped when the lava solidified.

The Cuillins are notorious for the challenge they pose to serious walkers and climbers. Consisting of thirty peaks, including twelve Munros – summits over 3,000 feet – the main Cuillin ridge is eight miles long, with the mountains in the west coloured an austere black. On the east side of the range, from Glamaig to Beinn na Caillich, the spiky Red hills glow a stunning shade of pink. Sgùrr Alasdair, the highest point at 993m, is named after Alexander Nicholson, who reached the top in 1873.

Trotternish

In the north-east of Skye, above the town of Portree, is the Trotternish peninsula whose mountains, stretch down its east flank. At 32km, the main ridge is the longest landslip in the British Isles, reaching its highest

Quiraing, Isle of Skye

point at The Storr (719m) on the southern end. The assent to the summit is a popular walk that begins just north of Portree. The Old Man of Storr and Quiraing are two peculiar rock formations formed by landslips. The latter's name comes from the Gaelic *Cuith-raing*, meaning 'pillared stronghold', and on its high crags walkers may hear the loud, wild song of the ring ouzel.

At the tip of the peninsula is Kilmuir, an area popular for windsurfing, kayaking and sailing, but also where the elusive corncrake can be heard. A grassy plateau at the centre of the Trotternish massif is known as the Table. In violent times, this was a safe spot where cattle could be hidden from raiders, but it has also been used as a venue for playing the Scottish sport of shinty.

View towards Blaven

Flora MacDonald

A memorial at the top of Trotternish marks the final resting place of Flora MacDonald, a heroine of Skye. After Bonnie Prince Charlie and the Jacobite army were defeated at the Battle of Culloden in 1746, the Prince, on the run from English soldiers, hid out in the Western Isles. MacDonald came to the rescue by disguising him as her maid and rowing the Prince to Skye, from where he made his escape to France.

The Highland clearances

After the defeat of the Jacobite movement – which had the support of many Scottish Highlanders – Gaelic life and culture came under intense persecution. In order to support the new landlord system, as opposed to the old Scottish clan system, the people of the Highlands were evicted from their land to make way for large-scale sheep farming.

First of all they were moved to the coast, but, not able to eke out a living from the poor fishing and unsuitable soil, they emigrated. Between 1770 and 1815, 15,000 Scots left for America. *Feannagan*, or lazy-beds, which were strips built up with seaweed and used to grow potatoes and oats on particularly poor land, can still be seen around Skye.

The mass exodus left many areas deserted and in Sligachan on Skye, and Boreraig and Hallaig on Raasay Island, there are still examples of 'cleared villages'. Hallaig is famous, having been immortalised by one of the area's most treasured sons,

Raasay-born poet Sorley Maclean (1911-1996). The poet often dealt with the torn history of his native islands and, although he wrote in Gaelic, his poetry attained international acclaim and he was a winner of the Queen's Medal for Poetry. On Raasay, a cairn has been erected in memory of Maclean, who brought together in his work the many disparate strands of Skye's and Raasay's history.

ⓘ CONTACT INFORMATION

Isle of Skye & South West Ross Tourist Board
Tourist Information Centre
Meall House
Portree
Isle of Skye
Tel: 01478 612137
Fax: 01478 612141
Web: www.skye.co.uk

Walkers on Am Basteir

The Cairngorms

This mountainous region, famed for its skiing and distinctive wildlife, can be enjoyed throughout the year.

Located in the north-east of Scotland, the Cairngorms border Aberdeenshire, Moray and the Grampians, with the range stretching from the River Spey and the town of Aviemore in the west to the River Dee in the east. Scheduled to become a national park in 2002, the Cairngorms have been the cause of much environmental wrangling of late.

The area has been a popular ski resort since the 1960s, but the demands of that acclaim have intensified concerns over its unique ecosystem. Its designation as a national park is an attempt to maintain a balance between recreation and conservation. The proposed national park will take in the central massif, but exclude the Monadhliath mountains to the west, and the land north of Nethy Bridge and Tomintoul.

The Cairngorms are an all year round attraction for visitors, with hillwalking in summer and skiing in winter. In the coldest months, the peaks offer precarious ice climbs for the adventurous. The range contains the largest single mass of high ground in Britain, is rich in pine forest and alpine grasslands, and encompasses four of the country's highest peaks.

Skiing

The Cairngorms developed as a ski resort when a road was built from Aviemore to the foot of the slopes. Since then, Aviemore has grown from a small railway town to a busy tourist resort, popularising the Cairngorms as

Loch Morlich

a haven for people seeking the rugged outdoors. Shaped by glacial corries cutting into the plateau, and deep defiles and gullies, Coire Cas and Coire na Ciste host the main concentration of pistes. At the head of the ski slopes, and overlooking them, is the mountain of Cairn Gorm.

From humble beginnings, the ski area now includes thirty ski runs. Although the Cairngorms are suitable for families and beginners, the difficult West Wall piste attracts those looking for a greater challenge. Over to the north-east, the Lecht is a more compact arena, but offers good conditions for Nordic skiing.

Cycling

The region's combination of rugged mountains, deep forests and less frantic river valleys creates plenty of cycling opportunities for visitors. The hilly ground and woodlands have many off-road trails and dirt tracks which allow mountain bikers to penetrate both the Cairngorm plateau and the surrounding countryside.

Glenmore Forest Park has signposted cycle routes which lead through the conifer woodland surrounding Loch Morlich. Cyclists can also head north to Loch Garten, where observant watchers could spot an osprey. There were no ospreys in Scotland at the beginning of the 20th century, but in the 1950s a pair began nesting on Loch Garten. The RSPB organises a diligent security operation and the bird numbers continue to increase.

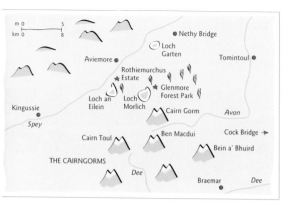

Ben Macdui

Walking in the higher reaches of the Cairngorms can be extremely taxing and poor preparation is dangerous. When sure of a clear day and a suitable route, however, the rewards can be great. Walking up Cairn Gorm is a popular outing and offers fine views over Loch Morlich.

For experienced hikers, Ben Macdui is probably the most difficult trek. It is the highest mountain in the range with a rounded top and a stony summit bereft of vegetation. Folklore has also pronounced it a special place, with tales of a Fear Liath More – a big grey man – on the peak. On clear days, the summit provides views across to Ben Nevis, Britains's highest mountain. It was once thought that Ben Macdui was the taller of the two; the issue was finally resolved by the Ordnance Survey in 1847.

Wildlife trails

The choice of walking routes in the Cairngorms caters for both the serious hiking enthusiast and the casual wayfarer. Furthermore, each trek benefits from a stunning backdrop, with snow-capped mountains, acres of forest and rare bird species for keen-eyed walkers to watch for.

Some of the birds are found in few other places in Europe. The dotterel, of which a third of the UK population breeds in the Cairngorm grasslands, is only seen elsewhere in Scandinavia. Golden eagles patrol the skies, whilst snow buntings build their nests amongst boulders. Walkers should also look out for ptarmigans which inhabit the corries and the high peaks.

Hiking

Although accomplished walkers may be primarily interested in the tops, the area to the west – a wooded glen stretching to Aviemore – offers more moderate challenges. Much of the forestry is commercial but there are remnants of the Scots pine and juniper which once covered much of the Highlands. The area encompasses Glenmore Forest Park, with its nature trails, and the Cairngorm Reindeer Park. Further west, on the banks of the River Spey, is Rothimurchus estate whose forest is criss-crossed with footpaths. This land, owned by the Grant family for over 400 years, is particularly appealing to walkers, providing views of the Cairngorms, and the Lairig Ghru mountain pass.

ⓘ CONTACT INFORMATION

Aberdeen Tourist Information
St Nicholas House
Broad Street
Aberdeen AB10 1DE
Tel: 01224 632727
Fax: 01224 620415
Web: www.agtb.org

Aviemore Tourist Information
Grampian Road
Aviemore PH22 1PP
Tel: 01479 810363
Fax: 01479 811063

 **SCOTLAND**

Loch Lomond and the Trossachs

Lochs tussle with mountains for space, and high roads and low roads meet on the stomping ground of a Scottish hero.

Situated in central Scotland, Loch Lomond and the wooded and mountainous area known as the Trossachs will constitute the first of the nation's new national parks. Stretching from the banks of Loch Lomond in the west to the town of Callander in the east, the park will encompass several other smaller lochs, the Queen Elizabeth Forest Park and a string of hills and mountains.

Perhaps most famous for the immortal song inspired by Lomond's 'bonnie banks', the area also profoundly influenced the novelist Walter Scott. The antics of the Trossachs' favourite son, 18th century outlaw Rob Roy, had a particular fascination for the Lowland writer. A cherished stretch of the West Highland Way, the long-distance walk from Milngavie north to Fort William, passes through the area.

Scotland's national parks

It is ironic that Scotland has been so late in embracing the national park movement – it was only in 1997 that the government decided to designate areas – for it was a Scotsman, John Muir, who through his oratory and article writing in America at the end of the 19th century, laid the foundations for the first such environmental movements.

Loch Lomond

The countryside of Scotland is, of course, an obvious candidate for protected status and many areas are already under the eye of organisations such as the National Trust for Scotland, or are designated national forests. National parks, however, are to give specific areas even more control over their conservation.

Loch and forest

It is the blend of lochs, forests, hills and mountains, all at the meeting point of the Highlands and Lowlands, that gives the region its individual quality. The banks of Loch Lomond are shrouded in oak trees which in spring are lit up by sheets of wild hyacinths. The Queen Elizabeth Forest Park, home to Loch Ard forest, Achray forest and Strathyre forest, is also notable for its old oak woodlands which contrast with the modern conifer plantations. Flitting between the lochs and the woods are great crested grebes, great spotted woodpeckers, oystercatchers, osprey and peregrines. On the ground, chief inhabitants of the hills are the roaming roe deer and red deer.

Cycling

Winding through woods and along the banks of lochs, with Munros – peaks over 3,000 feet – forming an impressive backdrop, there are hundreds of kilometres of cycle track in the Trossachs. For families, there are plenty of gentle byroads and side tracks in the south, while mountain bikers can take on the challenges of the hilly north.

South from Luss across Loch Lomond

Roy and Trossachs Visitor Centre in Callander. It provides an introduction to the history and folklore of the area as well as a chance to learn more about Scott's hero.

Callander is also the ideal starting point from which to explore the rest of Rob Roy's domain. He was raised to the west of the town, while to the north, in the village of Balquhidder on the banks of Loch Voil, is his simple grave. A network of paths, which span the triangular area between Callander, Balquhidder and Aberfoyle, makes the countryside accessible to visitors.

och Katrine, where Walter Scott set s 1810 novel *Lady of the Lake*, is an ngaging setting. After cycling north ong the banks of the loch to ronachlachar, cyclists can return on ie *S.S. Sir Walter Scott*, Scotland's ily passenger steamer still in service. nother option is the Queen izabeth Forest Park, which covers 0,000 hectares and offers 250km of acks. At the centre of the park is its sitor centre which has audiovisual resentations, displays, exhibitions nd resident craftsmen.

ngling and water sports

hrough the combination of the River ndrick feeding in at the southern nd, and the colder inlets further orth, Loch Lomond has cultivated a ealthy variety of fish species. It is otable for its pike and coarse fishing, hilst its tributary, the Endrick, offers ach, dace and bream. For game shing, Lochs Ard, Lubnaig and Katrine e marked spots for brown trout, hile the Teith, which flows through allander, is good for river angling.

/ith so many surrounding lochs, ater sports are naturally another otion in the Trossachs, with boating, ater skiing and sailing all available. ie partnership of lochs with rivers so means that canoeing at various vels of difficulty is possible. or relaxed outings the lochs are ideal, is the Teith. More adventurous noeists can find a challenge west Crianlarich in the slightly faster ower Orchy, or in the whitewaters the Middle Orchy.

Exploring Trossachs history

The Trossachs are forever associated with Rob Roy MacGregor (1671–1734), the notorious Scottish daredevil and cattle outlaw. Sir Walter Scott's novel, *Rob Roy*, written in 1817, gave weight to the national admiration for the adventurer, which is carried on today through the Rob

ℹ️ CONTACT INFORMATION

Argyll, the Isles, Loch Lomond, Stirling & Trossachs Tourist Board
41 Dumbarton Road
Stirling FK8 2QQ
Tel: 01786 475019
E-mail: info@scottish.heartlands.org
Web: www.scottish.heartlands.org

Loch Lomond Park Ranger Service
Balloch Castle
Balloch G53 8LX
Tel: 01389 758216

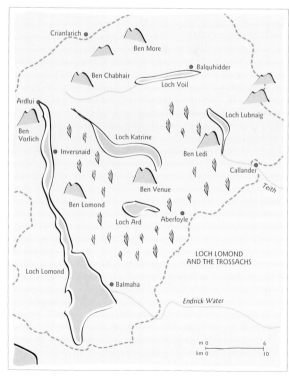

Northumberland National Park

Situated on the Scots–English border, Northumberland's history was always going to be tempestuous, but what were once battlefields are now the serene moorlands of the national park.

Created in 1956, the Northumberland National Park sits landlocked on the west side of the county, reaching from the Roman remains of Hadrian's Wall right up to the Cheviot hills and the Scots–English border. It is a sparsely inhabited moorland, interrupted by little else but rivers and valleys, and speckled with ruins from its turbulent past.

The wall, built on the orders of the Roman Emperor Hadrian in AD 122, was an attempt to separate the land of the Britons from the land of the Picts. Since then Northumberland has seen plenty more battles and gory feuds, not only in Scots–English wars, but also between the medieval warring families known as the border reivers ('reive' means to rob or plunder). However, conservation is

Coquetdale at Shilmoor

the only battle being fought today, and over 500km of public footpaths and bridleways permit visitors to explore the fruits of the park's work.

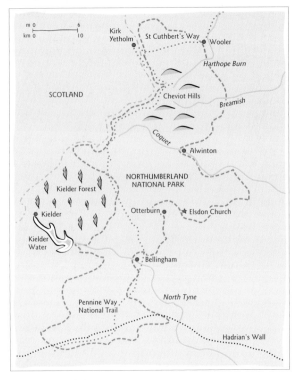

Walking the ways

There are two long distance walks that traverse the national park. From the south comes the Pennine Way, a 434km trek which begins near Manchester. The walk makes its way up through the park, initially shadowing a section of Hadrian's Wall, before heading north through Bellingham and then along the park's west edge. It ends just inside Scotland St Cuthbert's Way, which follows the life of the 7th century saint, goes from Melrose in Scotland south-east to the island of Lindisfarne. It cuts across the Cheviot hills in the north via Kirk Yetholm and Wooler.

Kielder forest and water

Although the park has only a small amount of native woodland, Kielder forest sits on its doorstep. Combined with Kielder water, a man-made lake, the area just west of Bellingham is a haven for walks and watersports. Consisting of 500 sq km of woodland the forest has thirteen waymarked walking routes. It is also home to 6,000 roe deer and is one of the few places in Britain where the red squirrel can be found. The reservoir was opened in 1982 to supply water to the North East, and since then has become popular with windsurfers, waterskiers, canoeists and anglers.

The Cheviot hills

The north of the park is dominated by the Cheviot hills, a breathtaking stretch of high ground. Cheviot Hill (815m), from which the area takes its name, is the highest point in the park. It sits in the middle of the valleys of Harthope, Breamish and Coquetdale, whose rivers and surrounding land provide excellent habitats for birds.

The curlew can be seen here in spring when it returns to the moors to breed. Sparrowhawks, dotterels and snow buntings also make their presence felt, as do roaming feral goats. In Upper Coquetdale dippers, grey wagtails and the noisy common sandpiper are attracted by the flowing water, while on the heather moorland ring ouzels and wheaters are common.

Ad Gefrin

With 130 ancient hut remains, Yeavering Bell (360m) is the site of the largest Iron Age fort in the north of England. It is also the setting of a royal Anglo-Saxon palace – Ad Gefrin – which once stood at the foot of the hill. The palace is closely associated with Edwin, the 6th century King of Northumbria, after whom the city of Edinburgh is named. Breamish valley, also in the Cheviots, is home to Brough Law, an Iron Age fort dating back 2,500 years, the remains of which consist of stone ramparts encircling the crest of a rounded hill.

Harthope valley

Reiver country

Northumberland has seen many battles between the Scottish and the English, but between the 14th and 16th centuries, battles had less to do with allegiance to the two crowns as they did with loyalty to family names. A hostile environment arose in which families such as the Charltons, Elliots, Robsons and Grahams fought, killed and stole from each other, in a society where only the most brutal survived.

It wasn't until the joining of the Scottish and English crowns in the 17th century that the area began to settle. Bellingham was, at the time, at the heart of reiver country and around the area are the remains of bastels – fortified houses – which were occupied by reiver families.

The Battle of Otterburn

The reivers were generally not rich families and were in conflict as a matter of survival. At Otterburn in 1388, however, a famous meeting took place between two wealthy land-owning families, the Percys of Northumberland led by Harry Hotspur, and the Douglases of Scotland. Many of the dead from that battle are buried at Elsdon church near Otterburn, which dates from the 14th century.

Hadrian's Wall

This great Roman wall was originally 117km long and 5m in height. Some of the best remaining stretches are in the national park where there are also forts and guardhouses. To the south is the fort of Vindolonda, a great source of historical finds and home to a reconstructed Roman temple. Housesteads, the most complete Roman fort in Britain, is located north of the wall and has granaries, barracks, latrines and even a hospital.

[i] CONTACT INFORMATION

Northumberland National Park
South Park
Hexham
Northumberland NE46 1BS
Tel: 01434 605555
Web: www.nnpa.org.uk

Bellingham Tourist Information
Fountain Cotttage
Main Street
Bellingham
Hexham NE48 2BQ
Tel: 01434 220616
Web: www.northumberland.gov.
uk/VG/natpark.html

River Breamish

Yorkshire Dales National Park

Undulating golden hills and valleys contrast with stark limestone landforms in this corner of northern England, where the atmosphere is always warmly welcoming.

The Yorkshire Dales was established as England's seventh national park in 1954. The park covers 1,769 sq km in the heart of the north of England, across the counties of North Yorkshire and Cumbria. As with many other national parks in Britain, the area is very much 'alive', with the local population living and working in the farms, villages and small towns.

Over twenty main dales shape the rolling landscape, with smaller valleys, moors and hills contributing to the region's distinctive contours. The size of the park means there is great variety of walks and sights for visitors. Any description or visit can only give a taste of what is on offer.

The limestone pavement at Ingleborough

Shaping the land

The familiar scenes of high fells, hay meadows in the valleys and dry-stone walls have become famous through regular appearances in novels and on television. This landscape is, in truth, a collaboration between the forces of nature and the steady influence of the district's inhabitants. This part of England has been populated for over

10,000 years, and these lives have left as much of a mark as the last Ice Age. After the passage of the glaciers, settlers cleared and cultivated the land, moulding it to their own requirements. Primitive settlements and old mineral workings record early activity, while native breeds of sheep still graze the fells thousands of years after their introduction.

The natural landscape is composed of limestone, millstone grit, shale and sandstone, the softer rocks being weathered to leave scars, caves and

waterfalls. The dissolving action of rainwater on the limestone has produced pavements of fissured rock in the south-west. Moorland on the high ground and meadows in the valleys contrast with the bare rock, particularly in summer, when purple heather and bright wildflowers flourish. Woodland is not as extensive as it once was, but there are oak woods in the far south, and 'hanging' ash woods grow along the sides of dales, a unique feature of the area.

Northern dales

The northern dales, particularly around Arkengarthdale, can feel the most untouched part of the park. The area, which retains something of an old world charm, is known as 'Herriot country', from the books by James Herriot and the subsequent television series, *All Creatures Great and Small*. There are many walks, whether across bleak moors, through the gentle valleys of Wensleydale, or in Swaledale's flowery meadows. At Richmond, at the very edge of the park, the climb up to the castle gives refreshing views of the Vale of York to the east and Swaledale to the west.

Other ancient monuments include the ruins of Middleham castle where Richard III stayed; Bolton castle in Bishopdale where Mary Queen of Scots was imprisoned; and the ruined abbey of Jervaulx in Lower Wensleydale. A visit to the northern dales is not complete without tasting Wensleydale cheese, the particular penchant of Wallace, the placid hero of Nick Park's animated adventures, *Wallace and Gromit*.

Western dales

The three peaks of the Pennines – Whernside, Ingleborough and Pen-y-Ghent – are the main attraction of the westerly reaches of the Yorkshire Dales. The hills, each about 700m high, can be climbed via different routes, with the town of

The view over Kettlewell with snow on the high ground

Horton-in-Ribblesdale a central starting point. The Ribblehead viaduct, part of the Settle–Carlisle railway, is a noticeable landmark, and the Pennine Way passes through this part of the park.

The Reginald Farrer Nature Trail explores the Ingleborough area, beginning at Clapham village. The Farrer family established themselves at Ingleborough Hall, and landscaped the estate with lakeside woodland, as well as exotic plants brought back from overseas by Reginald Farrer in the early 20th century. The trail commemorates his explorations, and leads to the Ingleborough show cave, which was discovered by the Farrers in the 1830s. The cave is part of Yorkshire's extensive subterranean network which includes Gaping Gill, Britain's largest cavern. This impressive pothole contains the country's highest unbroken waterfall, Fell Beck, which falls from the moor above.

Looking down into a gentle dale from Gordale Scar, Malham

Southern dales

In the south of the park, the most popular attraction is Bolton Abbey estate in Wharfedale. The estate includes Strid wood, a Site of Special Scientific Interest; a 12th century ruined Augustinian priory; and 120km of footpaths. Owned by the Duke and Duchess of Devonshire, Bolton Abbey has been in their family since the mid 18th century. The nave of the priory was saved after the dissolution of the monasteries in the 16th century and is now the parish church of Bolton Abbey village. The estate stretches for over 11km along the River Wharfe, and both Landseer and Turner were inspired to paint the particular beauty of these dales.

To the north-west of Bolton Abbey is the town of Malham, surrounded by the craggy limestone scenery that characterises the south-west of the Dales. Malham is best known for its limestone pavement, formed by the regular patterns of clints (the blocks) and grikes (the crevices). As well as admiring nature's intricacies, a trip to the pavement gives excellent views over the valleys towards Malham tarn. The Pennine Way passes nearby, leading towards Horton-in-Ribblesdale and the three peaks in the west.

CUMBRIA
Arkengarthdale
Richmond
YORKSHIRE DALES NATIONAL PARK
Whernside
Pen-y-Ghent
Nidderdale
Ingleborough
Ingleton
Horton-in-Ribblesdale
Clapham
Wharfe
Malham
LANCASHIRE
Bolton Abbey Estate
Wharfedale
Ilkley
m 0 — 10
km 0 — 16

[i] CONTACT INFORMATION

**Yorkshire Dales
National Park Authority**
Colvend, Hebden Road
Grassington
Skipton
North Yorkshire BD23 5LB
Tel: 01756 752748
Fax: 01756 752745

Yorkshire Tourist Board
312 Tadcaster Road
York YO24 1GS
Tel: 01904 707961
E-mail: ytb@ytb.org.uk
Web: www.ytb.org.uk

North York Moors National Park

Dry-stone walls appear amid the rolling purple moors of this national park, somehow taming the exhilarating wild bleakness of the landscape.

The North York Moors National Park covers over 1,436 sq km in Yorkshire. The park's land is a combination of moorland, woodland and farmland, with the latter taking up the most surface area, a reminder that over 25,000 people live and work in the park. The North York Moors, however, still contains the largest expanse of open heather moorland in England, an area which was designated a Site of Special Scientific Interest in 1998.

Contrasting landscapes

Despite being named after bleak moorlands, the park is actually full of contrasts – from the Cleveland hills and the Heritage Coast along the North Sea to the 4,000km of streams and rivers and the coniferous forests in the south-west. The coast is still characterised by villages clinging to cliffs, fishing boats moored in harbours, and stone quarries, which through disuse are now a haven for wildlife. Down in the bays, fossils can be found, a record of prehistoric life.

Walking by the River Esk

The land has been settled and worked for over 8,000 years, and this is reflected in its shape. Dales divide the moors, with dry-stone walls marking out the farmland, whilst once boggy areas have been drained to produce rich soils. The creamy-buff colours of Yorkstone are ubiquitous, whether in houses and dales' walls, or in the hills and cliffs from which it is taken. European Union funded schemes are currently helping farmers to repair and conserve Yorkstone buildings, ensuring that local construction materials continue to be in evidence.

The animal world

Nature's contribution ranges from a scattering of wildflowers on the limestone escarpment of the Tabular hills, to breeding golden plovers on the moorland, and crayfish in the Rye and Derwent rivers. Kittiwakes nest on the high cliffs along the coast, and merlins on the high moors. The rivers offer a safe and clean habitat for otters and water voles, whilst the Esk is the only salmon and sea trout river in Yorkshire, with the trout spawning in the tributaries each year, making stretches of it excellent for fishing.

The view of Rosedale from Blakeley

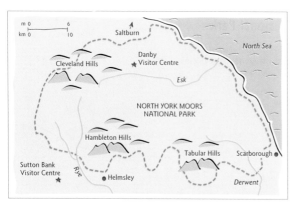

which are open to the public. In the Hambleton hills are three medieval abbeys, the 14th century Carthusian Mount Grace priory, the Cistercian Byland abbey and the early medieval Rievaulx abbey. Also worth visiting are Spout House, a 16th century cruck-framed cottage with curved timbers, and Helmsley castle, witness to sieges from both King John in 1216 and the Parliamentarians in 1644.

i CONTACT INFORMATION

North York Moors National Park
The Old Vicarage
Bondgate
Helmsley
York YO62 5BP
Tel: 01439 770657
Fax: 01439 770691
E-mail: info@northyorkmoors-npa.gov.uk
Web: www.northyorkmoors-npa.gov.uk

Yorkshire Tourist Board
312 Tadcaster Road
York YO24 1GS
Tel: 01904 707961
E-mail: ytb@ytb.org.uk
Web: www.ytb.org.uk

Walking and cycling

The Cleveland Way National Trail cuts across the park from Helmsley up to Saltburn before turning south towards Scarborough. The Tabular Hills Walk links the two southerly ends of the trail, enabling walkers to trek around the entire perimeter. This route is obviously long, but there are many shorter walks, some of only a few hours, to suit all ages and abilities. The gentle hills around Bilsdale are particularly good for families.

The park authorities offer self-guided nature walks near the visitor centres at Danby and Sutton Bank, as well as ones exploring the landmarks of the area. The stone crosses and standing stones which dot the moors make useful pointers to hike between. They were originally erected by the local monasteries to reassure visitors that they were not lost.

The park is also popular with cyclists, and there are bridleways to follow, as well as off-road tracks in the Boltby and Daltby forests. Leaflets describe the routes. For the more adventurous, rock climbing, canoeing, windsurfing, gliding and sailing are all available. The watersports take place mainly on Wykeham lakes in the southern dales, and there is of course the coast for traditional, bracing seaside visits.

The Moorsbus, which runs regularly in the tourist seasons, offers a cheap and green way to get around the park. Buying a ticket for the bus also entitles visitors to free entry to attractions and events.

Monuments

As well as the dales and moors, the national park also conserves the remains and monuments of the many settlers. An archaeologist is employed to help preserve sites such as the Rosedale ironstone kilns, a record of the old industries of Yorkshire. English Heritage and the National Trust manage a variety of properties, all of

Looking down to Robin Hood's Bay from Ravenscar

Peak District National Park

The Dark Peak and the White Peak; historical villages and barren wildernesses; high fells and deep river valleys; the Peak District is a dynamic region of contrasts.

The Salt Cellar on Derwent Edge, one of many unusual rock formations found in the Peak District

The Peak District was Britain's first national park and is still its most popular. Covering 1,438 sq km, it is located at the southern tip of the Pennines near the cities of Sheffield and Manchester, where many of the Peak District's most loyal visitors live.

Peak District National Park

The word peak is derived from the old English word *peac* meaning hill or knoll, although as there is no single peak, this name may be rather misleading. In fact, the region is divided into two halves, the Dark Peak and the White Peak. Large tracts of land remain relatively untouched, with approximately a third designated as being of special scientific interest.

In addition to nature trails and short footpaths, the famous Pennine Way runs through the open moorland and spectacular cliffs of the Dark Peak. Other easily accessible activities include cycling, horse-riding, hang-gliding, sailing, canoeing, windsurfing and fishing. The Peak District's numerous interesting rock formations make caving and climbing particularly popular. Losehill Hall, the national

park centre at Castleton, offers study holidays and courses covering a range of creative and active interests.

Around 38,000 people live in the hundred or so villages encompassed by the national park. The park authorities are responsible for preserving the historical and architectural heritage of each settlement, including over 2,700 listed buildings. The Peak District as it is today has evolved from centuries of forest clearance, mining and farming. Half of the national park is enclosed farmland, but the climate is too harsh for the cultivation of crops. Sheep and dairy cattle are kept in the valleys, while beef cattle are reared on the higher, rougher slopes.

The Dark Peak

England doesn't get much more desolate than the Dark Peak area. Gritstone, a hard rock that does not produce rich soil, forms bleak moorland broken only by occasional rocky tors and steep cliffs. Much of the moorland area is over 500m above sea level. Exposed to the elements it is covered with a layer of peat too

acidic for any plants other than hardy cottongrass, crowberry, purple moor grass, bracken and heather. Red grouse and sheep are raised here, further frustrating the growth of larger plants. Oak woodland survives only in sheltered, steep-sided cloughs and is often interspersed with birch and mountain ash. Redstarts, wood warblers and pied flycatchers sing amongst the trees. Elsewhere, broad, flat shale valleys with gentle rivers tend to be milder and more fertile than the higher land.

The White Peak

Formed from a limestone plateau, the White Peak contrasts sharply with the Dark Peak. A patchwork of low hills, rolling dales, ancient woodland and green fields are separated by dry-stone walls. Over the centuries, water has dissolved the soft rock, producing dramatic cliffs and caves. The area forms the northern boundary for many species of plants and animals. The woodlands are a mixture of ash and wych elm, along with dogwood, cherry and hazel. Dale grasslands are filled with cowslips, orchids, small scabious and bloody crane's bill.

Dovedale

Despite hosting an often overwhelming number of visitors, Dovedale is undisputedly one of the most beautiful areas in the Peak District. The River Dove rises on the high moorlands and descends for much of its course with one bank in Derbyshire and one in Staffordshire. North of Hartington, the natural boundary between the counties is even more pronounced, with the Derbyshire bank formed from limestone and the Staffordshire bank from shale. As a result, the scenery and wildlife on each side of the river are very different. Footpaths along the banks enable visitors to compare the two types of landscape at close hand.

Losehill Hall, Peak District National Park Centre

Castleton

At the boundary between the Dark Peak and White Peak areas lies the village of Castleton. Situated beside an extensive cave network, this is the only place in Britain where the decorative mineral called blue john can be found. A type of fluorospar, its jaunty name is derived from the French words for the mineral's colours, *bleu* and *jaune* (yellow). Many of the caves are open to the public. Blue John cavern and Treak Cliff cavern display some fine stalactites and stalagmites as well as several of the only known veins of blue john itself. Peak cavern – the largest natural cavern in Derbyshire – has a gaping entrance so huge that a village of rope-makers thrived there for three centuries. Boat trips can be made through the flooded workings of Speedwell cavern, which was mined in the 18th century.

Eyam

Eyam is a picturesque little village with a tragic history. A travelling tailor from London brought the plague to the village in 1665, but rather then spread the epidemic to the surrounding countryside the villagers heroically chose to isolate themselves in Eyam. Four fifths of the community died, and their sacrifice is remembered today at Eyam museum. Less morbid attractions include the ancient church with its lovely sundial and the intricate carvings of a magnificent Saxon cross. Most of Eyam's cottages date back to the 17th and 18th centuries, while Eyam Hall itself can be found on the main street.

Derwent and Chatsworth

The Derwent is the longest river in the national park, and its idyllic valley is a major attraction. Its southern reaches pass Chatsworth House. Sitting comfortably in carefully landscaped parkland with wooded hills rising behind, Chatsworth suggests on a small scale the success with which humans have interacted with nature throughout the park.

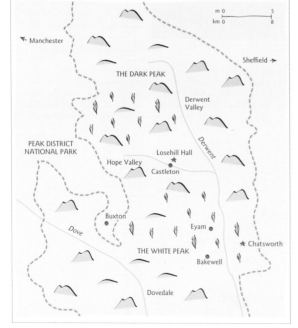

[i] **CONTACT INFORMATION**

The Peak District National Park
Aldern House
Baslow Road
Bakewell
Derbyshire DE45 1AE
Tel: 01629 816200
Fax: 01629 816310
E-mail: aldern@peakdistrict-npa.gov.uk
Web: www.peakdistrict.org

Exmoor and Dartmoor National Parks

These two national parks capture some of England's finest moorland, tors and coastline. Unperturbed by the splendid countryside, rambling Dartmoor and Exmoor ponies let it all go by.

Situated in Devon and Somerset, Exmoor and Dartmoor National Parks are characterised by vast moorlands and sylvan valleys. In close proximity to one another, with Exmoor on the north coast and Dartmoor to the south, these conservation areas offer different sides of the peninsular landscape whilst still sharing much of its beauty. Although Dartmoor, landlocked with over 160 tors, is regarded as much more of a wilderness, Exmoor's sheer coastal cliffs, the highest in England, give it its own edge.

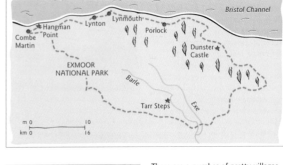

Walking the moors

The south-west is lined with many walks, both short and long distance, which criss-cross, surround, and even link the two parks. In fact, a sizeable part of the park authorities' work is repairing or containing the erosion created by walking visitors.

The South West Coastal Path, at 965km Britain's longest marked trail, begins in Exmoor and travels around Cornwall to Poole harbour on the southern coast. The Two Moors Way (166km) combines the best of both parks, meandering from Ivybridge at the base of Dartmoor up to Lynmouth on the Exmoor coast. Alternatively, the Dartmoor Way is a circular route that journeys 145km around the park.

Porlock Bay

Despite its beauty, Dartmoor is hardly an isolated wilderness. Scattered archaeological remains range from prehistoric stone monuments to 20th century tin mines and old farms.

There are a number of pretty villages, such as Widecombe-in-the-Moor. Situated on the route of the Two Moors Way, it is famous for its magnificent church and for its fair, which is held annually on the second Tuesday of September. Princetown, in the west, claims to be the highest village in England, and is the site not only of Dartmoor prison but also of a visitor centre run by the national park authority. Exhibitions and interactive displays help to provide a snapshot of Dartmoor's nature and history.

Exmoor National Park

Stretching from the Brendon hills in the east to the village of Combe Martin, Exmoor's moorland escapes the ruggedness of Dartmoor. Around Simonsbath, what was once a royal

Dartmoor National Park

Covering 953 sq km and dominated by wild moorland, granite tors and wooded river valleys, Dartmoor is the largest open space in southern England. Nearly half of the national park is open to the public, with about 900km of footpaths and bridleways enabling visitors to reach secluded corners as well as expansive vistas. The heather-clad hills, surrounded by forest and speckled with hundreds of historical sites, provide endless scope for exploration, although some areas are intermittently off-bounds for Ministry of Defence training.

Walkers on Bossington Hill, near Porlock

hunting forest has wilted away, and been replaced by purple moor grass, with cotton grass and bog asphodel in the wet mires.

Exmoor does, however, have its steep coastal cliffs. Reaching a height of 433m at Hangman point in the west, the cliffs are accompanied by the longest stretch of naturally wooded coastline in Britain, most of which is sessile oak. For its protection, the area has been designated Heritage Coast and is home to guillemots, razorbills, kittiwakes and gannets.

Coastal features

Exmoor's coast has room for just a few fishing and holiday resorts. Porlock is a prized village – with thatched cottages, and a medieval manor-house and church, it is home to the Ship Inn where Samuel Coleridge is said to have written part of *The Rime of the Ancient Mariner*. The sea reached the edge of Porlock in medieval times but as a pebble ridge developed and streams silted up behind it, Porlock marsh was formed. The tree stumps of a submerged forest can still be seen just beyond the ridge at low tide.

Further east along the coast is Dunster castle, the fortified home of the Luttrell family for 600 years. The gardens are famous for their lemon trees, camellias and sequoias. Between Porlock and Dunster, and forming a large part of Exmoor National Park, is Holnicote estate. An area rich in

Ponies on Haddow Hill

woodland, the estate includes the coastal path to Selworthy Beacon and a circular nature walk from Webbers Post carpark to Dunkery Beacon, the highest point of the park at 519m.

Tarr Steps

A popular feature of Exmoor, the Tarr Steps on the River Barle is an ancient clapper bridge, one of the oldest types of crossing structures. Constructed by laying granite slabs across supports in the river bed, their weight is the only thing that holds them in place. In 1952, however, when torrential rain swept the area, large logs floated down the river and knocked the bridge out of place. A cable hung across the water now protects the steps.

Ponies

Throughout both parks an indigenous breed of pony can be seen grazing on the moors. The Exmoor and Dartmoor ponies, sturdy animals with short legs, are an important feature of the area. Although their origins are not entirely clear, the animals were once used as pack ponies when the south-west had a busy tin-mining industry and were turned loose when the mines closed. The ponies were also used by Dartmoor prison guards right up to the 1960s for escorting people to and from the prison.

i CONTACT INFORMATION

Dartmoor National Park
The High Moor Visitor Centre
Princetown
Yelverton
Plymouth PL20 6QF
Tel: 01822 890414
Fax: 01822 890566
E-mail: info@dartmoor-npa.gov.uk
Web: www.dartmoor-npa.gov.uk

Exmoor National Park Authority
Exmoor House
Dulverton
Somerset TA21 9HL
Tel: 01398 323665
Fax: 01398 323150
E-mail: exmoor.natpark@
somerset.gov.uk
Web: www.exmoor-
nationalpark.gov.uk

Dunster castle

Chagford

Postbridge

Krap's Ring

Widecombe-in-the-moor

Princetown

Ashburton

DARTMOOR NATIONAL PARK

m 0   6
km 0   9

Ivybridge

Brecon Beacons National Park

A mountainous region in the part of Wales traditionally characterised by coal mining, the Brecon Beacons offers much for both energetic visitors and those interested in more leisurely pursuits.

The Brecon Beacons National Park covers 1,347 sq km of South Wales. Stretching from the mass of the Black Mountains in the east to the lonesome Black Mountain in the west, the park embraces ice age valleys, royal forests, man-made reservoirs, Iron Age hill forts and Roman roads. The area is excellent for walking and cycling, but the many reservoirs, lakes and rivers also make it ideal for canoeing, sailing and windsurfing.

None of the towns have grown much in size since the 18th century when they held important agricultural markets. However, all are worth visiting, mostly for their Georgian architecture and medieval castles. The Beacons Bus offers excellent transport to all attractions and activities, and visitors are encouraged to use public transport by the park authorities.

Ice and coal

The landscape of the park is formed by a combination of red sandstone and porous limestone. To the north, among the highest hills, the soil and rocks are red with iron oxide and date from the Devonian period over 300 million years ago. To the south, these

Walking on Pen-y-Fan

red layers were weighted down with limestone and millstone grits from the Carboniferous period, forming the rich coal seam that characterises the area.

The porous limestone in the south and east allows rivers and waterfalls to hide underground, forming spectacular dripping caverns and producing sudden gushes of water from the rocks. Glaciers have left their shape in the *cwms*, or mountain basins, which now contain icy lakes, whilst the effects of snowbanks are clear in the long, straight ridge on the Black Mountain.

Nature reserves

The forests, moorland and lakes give the scenery in the Brecon Beacons the familiar tones and shapes of many of the higher parts of Britain. However, arctic and alpine flowers in the boggy areas of the Craig Cerrig Gleisiad Nature Reserve, together with rare aquatic plants by Llangorse lake, distinguish the flora from other areas.

Beech woods in the south-east offer a home to rare flowers, whilst polecats and pine martens thrive in the mountains. Buzzards and ravens populate the northern cliffs of the park, where visitors are less likely to disturb them.

On foot and by pony

Walking in the hills and mountains is very popular, particularly on Pen-y-Fan, which is the highest point in the Beacons. There are over 2,000km of public paths, and a good variety of marked trails, catering for lengthy hikes as well as shorter strolls.

The central section of Lon Las Cymru (the Welsh National Cycle Network) passes through the park, tracing scenic cycle rides without going up too many hills. The Taff Trail is suitable for both cyclists and walkers, whilst the mountain bike festival in August, at Llanwyrtd Wells, just north-west of the park, has become an annual event.

Brecon Beacons National Park is one of the oldest centres for pony trekking, and specially designed bridleways take ponies and their riders across the Beacons, Black Mountains, Upper Swansea valley and Epynt Mountain. For those who like to take their feet off the ground, Talgarth is a centre for hang-gliding, paragliding and gliding, Llangorse has a rope centre for abseiling and climbing lessons, whilst there are enough quarries and crags for climbing throughout the park.

Llangorse lake

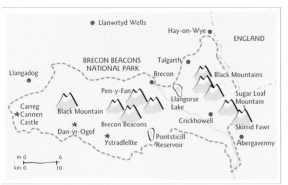

and is now famous for its annual jazz festival. The cathedral used to be a medieval priory, but was given cathedral status in 1923.

Hay-on-Wye is particularly renowned for its Georgian character, which lends a welcoming atmosphere to the annual literary festival. Abergavenny to the south-east of the park is shielded by the peaks of the Sugar Loaf Mountain and Skirrid Fawr, whilst Crickhowell, to the west, rests on the slopes of Table Mountain.

The geology of the area makes it ideal for cavers, with many underground crannies to be explored, particularly to the south of the Black Mountains by the Tawe Taf Fawr and Fechan rivers. The Dan-yr-Ogof show caves offer a dry and lit alternative for those who are not attracted by caving. The show caves are the largest and longest in Britain.

Monuments to the past

From the original Mesolithic hunter-gatherers to the Victorian industrialists, there are remains and monuments to record all the inhabitants of the region.

Iron Age forts and stone henges dot the hills, with the largest hill-fort in Wales, Carn Goch, at Llangadog in the west. Tombs, cairns and barrows from the Bronze Age indicate ancient burial sites. Straight Roman roads have left their mark in the Brecon Beacons, just as elsewhere in Britain, and a Roman fort was excavated in the 1920s near Brecon. Norman castles protect what are now the boundaries of the park, at Hay-on-Wye, Brecon, Trecastle, Tretower, Crickhowell and Careg Cannen, recording the warfare of the early Middle Ages.

In more modern times, the coal mines in the south, and limestone furnaces at Clydach gorge, are a testament to the heavy industry of the 19th and 20th centuries. The Brecon and Monmouthshire canal was originally built as a transport link for local industry, but now offers a peaceful haven for birds, as well as holidaymakers on canal boats.

Market towns

The local towns flourished in the 18th century, street names announcing individual markets, and prosperity reflected in the architecture. Brecon, as befits the main town of the area, has a castle and county museum,

[i] CONTACT INFORMATION

Brecon Beacons
National Park Authority
7 Glamorgan Street
Brecon
Powys LD3 7DP
Tel: 01874 624437
E-mail: enquiries@brecon
beacons.org
Web: www.breconbeacons.org

Ystradfellte waterfall

Pembrokeshire Coast National Park

The salt spray of the sea and the screeching of the seagulls typify this coastal area, where any holiday will almost certainly involve a soaking.

Whitesands Bay

Pembrokeshire Coast National Park covers 622 sq km in south-west Wales. Both the landscape and attractions are dominated by the coastal location, but the Preseli hills to the north and the Daugleddau estuary in the south are also worth visiting. The islands around the coast are peaceful havens for birds and seals, while the many forts and castles on the cliffs reveal much about Britain's past as an island guarding against invasion.

From sea to hills

The combination of hard limestone rocks with soft shales and sandstones has produced a landscape of alternating headlands and bays; the pattern of St Bride's Bay squeezed between the protruding pincers of St David's Head and Marloes peninsula is repeated in microcosm around the coast.

Sea cliffs, sand-dunes and inter-tidal areas are all features of the seashore, whilst further inland, woodlands and

lowland moor and heath offer greater variety. The tidal estuary of Daugleddau and Milford Haven, where the east and west tributaries of the Cleddau river meet, is a drowned river valley, with coppices of oak, ash and sycamore lining the river banks.

The Preseli hills to the north are characterised by heather, grasses and bracken in the dry inland areas, and mosses and rushes in damper hollows nearer the sea. The vegetation creates a subdued collection of royal colours in late summer and autumn, with the golden gorse intermingling with the purples of the heather and reddish-brown bracken.

Hedgerows and mudflats

The varied habitats of the national park form supportive environments for many plants and animals. Beneath the traditional high hedgebanks flower lesser celandines and primroses, while cow parsley, hawthorn, blackthorn, gorse and honeysuckle blossom among the greenery of the hedgerows.

In spring and early summer the sea cliffs and islands are spread with blankets of white, yellow, blue and pink flowers, including scurvy grass, gorse, sea campion, pink thrift, kidney vetch and vernal squill.

Unusual flowers, such as rock sea lavender, wild chives, Newport centaury and spiked speedwell, can occasionally be found near the cliffs. Samphire, sea lavender and rice grass prosper on the tidal mudflats of the Daugleddau estuary.

Many birds, as well as breeding populations of grey seals, dolphins and porpoise, congregate around the coast and islands. The native seabirds, buzzards, peregrines, skylarks and ravens are joined from April to August by razorbills, puffins, petrels and guillemots. On the mudflats, waders such as oystercatchers and curlews feed alongside ducks.

Rare fritillary butterflies, horseshoe bats and otters are among the protected species found in the park.

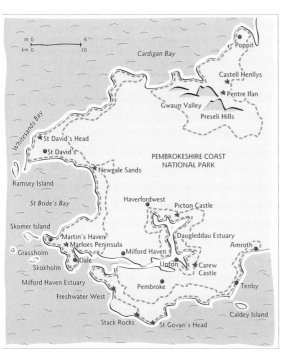

Early summer is the best time to visit Skokholm when it is carpeted with pink thrift and white scurvy grass. Grassholm, 17km out to sea, is the only gannetry in England and Wales. The white 'blob' visible from the mainland is the mass of gannets nesting. The island is managed by the RSPB; boat trips are available, but visitors are unable to land.

Ramsey Island, off St David's peninsula, is a RSPB reserve, but the snowy-furred grey seal pups born in late summer and autumn attract more visitors than the birds. The rugged Bitches to the east form part of Welsh maritime history, many ships having floundered on the treacherous rocks.

Caldey Island, near Tenby, offers different attractions to the westerly islands. There is a Cistercian monastery where the monks make perfumes and chocolates, whilst the medieval priory and lighthouse are also interesting. Clean sandy beaches are ideal for a day at the seaside.

Outdoor activities

The coastal and tidal areas make Pembrokeshire synonymous with water-based activities, whether whitewater kayaking or more sedate angling. The Pembrokeshire Coastal National Trail, from St Dogmaels in the north to Amroth in the south-east, attracts many walkers, from day-trippers to serious hikers. Pony trekking, cycling and climbing are also popular, taking advantage of the varied terrain. The park authority provide information on the local codes of practice for outdoor activities.

Offshore

Skomer, the biggest of the islands off Marloes peninsula, is a National Nature Reserve and the sea around it forms one of only three Marine Nature Reserves in the UK. Boat trips from Martin's Haven enable visitors to visit the island during the day or watch the returning seabirds in the early evening. Skomer has a summer population of over 100,000 pairs of Manx shearwaters. These ground nesting birds only come ashore at night, but can be seen congregating out at sea on summer evenings. Puffins, razorbills, guillemots, kittiwakes and fulmars also nest on the island, and there are several pairs of short-eared owls.

Bluebells and red campion blossom in May, offering an idyllic spectacle on the approach to Skomer. From the paths that criss-cross the island, there are tranquil views across St Bride's Bay towards Ramsey Island and St David's peninsula.

Tenby in the south-east of the park

Beaches and watersports

Pembrokeshire has over fifty clean beaches and bays, with six Blue Flag beaches and twenty three Seaside Award beaches. If the cold Atlantic Ocean is not too off-putting, the sheltered bays are good for swimming in summer, whilst surfing is popular throughout the seasons. Whitesands Bay, Freshwater West and Newgale beach are the best places for catching the breakers, with Broad Haven and Dale beaches better for windsurfing.

Good visibility, warm currents, plentiful marine life and many wrecks make Pembrokeshire's waters ideal for divers, whether new or experienced. Martin's Haven, Little Haven and Whitesands Bay are popular launch sites. Along the more rugged parts of the coast it is possible to try the new sport of coasteering. This involves traversing the cliffs near the water line, occasionally jumping or falling in, whilst wearing a wetsuit, buoyancy aid and protective helmet.

Canoeing and sea kayaking are possible in all the waters around the national park, but some areas are only suitable for experienced paddlers. The whitewater around the Bitches in Ramsey Sound makes for exhilarating trips for accomplished kayakers.

From game fishing in reservoirs to float fishing on the rocks along the seashore, the park caters for anglers of all persuasions. Druidston to Freshwater West – from St Bride's Bay, around Marloes peninsula to the Milford Haven estuary – is famous for having some of the best sea fishing in Wales. There are some restrictions on salmon fishing and usual licence rules apply for coarse and rod fishing.

Walking and cycling

Park staff lead guided walks and give talks on local history and wildlife. Paths along the banks and woodlands of the Cleddau river, offer different scenery – views of ancient trees and the occasional fox, rather than cliffs and seabirds. The coastal path is reserved for walkers, but there are bridleways and byways inland for cyclists and horse-riders.

Pony trekking trips are organised in the Gwaun valley and in the rural lanes of Pembrokeshire. Visitors pass through the countryside at a leisurely pace, more akin to the speed of life of the herders who drove their flocks to market along the bridleways in previous centuries. The high hedgerows are thick with colour and activity, all of which comes alive to the rider out in the open air.

The Castlemartin sea cliffs are home to many nesting seabirds, but also to climbers in the appropriate seasons. Climbing usually takes place on Stack Rocks and St Govan's Head. There are courses available for beginners.

Historic castles and forts

The burial chambers and standing stones in the Preseli hills record the history of the earliest peoples. Over sixty dolerite bluestones are believed to have been taken from Preseli and transported to Stonehenge 4,000 years ago, to make the sacred inner circle of the henge. The Bluestone Trail leads walkers to sites, such as the burial chamber at Pentre Ifan.

The Mabon and Twrch Trwyth sculpture trails commemorate themes from the Mabinogion – the Celtic myths of Wales – including King Arthur fighting a giant boar.

The site at Castell Henllys, between Cardigan and Newport, reconstructs life in an Iron Age fort, with authentic thatched roundhouses and animal pens. Excavation of the site continues every summer, and the archaeological findings contribute to the authentic atmosphere. Tours, storytelling, craft demonstrations and celebrations of Celtic festivals all take place during

Walking the Pembrokeshire Coastal National Trail

The boats at Solva

the summer at the fort. Activities for children include being `woaded up' and learning about bread making and spinning wool.

The Normans established many castles in Pembrokeshire from the 11th century, including a chain of fortifications known as the Landsker Line, which even today marks the division between the Welsh-speaking north and the more anglicised south. Many other Norman castles were built on the coast. Carew castle, alongside a quiet tributary of the Daugleddau, is a Norman stronghold which was converted in Elizabethan times to a country manor house, and

has recently undergone major restoration work. Summer events include battle re-enactments, country fairs, plays and an annual herb festival. The restored tidal mill is also open to the public, and there are short walks within the grounds.

St David's

St David's is the smallest city in Britain, a status derived from its late 12th century cathedral. The bones of St David, the patron saint of Wales, are said to be buried at the cathedral, on the site of what is believed to be the original monastery he established. The city is a thriving community, with

the annual Cathedral Festival of classical music in early summer, and many art galleries, potteries and workshops exhibiting local artists' work and techniques.

ⓘ CONTACT INFORMATION

Pembrokeshire Coast National Park
Winch Lane
Haverfordwest
Pembrokeshire
SA61 1PY
Tel: 01437 764636
E-mail: pcnp@pembrokeshire coast.org.uk
Web: www.pembrokeshire coast.org.uk

Snowdonia National Park

'Snowdonia' conjures up images of cloud laden mountains, biting winds and greying slate landscapes, but the area is not only for hardy walkers.

Snowdonia National Park is named after the mountain peak of Snowdon, which dominates the north-west of Wales. Covering 2,176 sq km of rugged terrain, Snowdonia is the second largest national park in Britain. Although the region is renowned for its mountains, there are also contrasting surprises, such as steep-sided valleys, dark moorlands and forests, calm lakes and streams, and coastal estuaries and beaches. Local people live and work throughout this farming and mining region, and Welsh is the language used daily by the majority of the population.

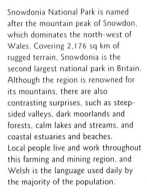

Pony trekking on Cader Idris

Powerful forces

The varied landscape of Snowdonia was formed by a combination of ancient volcanic activity and the glacial power of the last Ice Age. The highest mountains, of which there are fifteen over 914m (3,000ft), are made from volcanic lava and ash, combined with sedimentary rock. Fossils of primitive sea creatures indicate that the peaks were once below sea level. Glaciers then carved out U-shaped valleys, narrow lakes forming behind the banks of debris.

Snowdon lilies

In Cwm Idwal, a rocky basin at the foot of the Glyders which is now a National Nature Reserve, alpine and arctic flowers grow, such as mountain avens and purple mountain saxifrage. Hiding in lofty ledges is the yellow Welsh poppy, as well as the rarer Snowdon lily. This mountain spiderwort is unique to Snowdon, but is not often seen. Also unique to the area is the rainbow coloured Snowdon beetle.

Ravens, buzzards, kestrels, merlins and peregrines hunt among the mountains and valleys, whilst cormorants nest a few kilometres inland on Craig-yr-Aderyn, or Bird Rock, to the south-west. Pine martens and polecats thrive in the

more remote parts of the region. The park is committed to protecting all these species.

Climbing Snowdon

Llanberis, in the foothills of the Snowdon massif, offers a good base to explore the park. The Snowdon Mountain Railway, the only rack and pinion railway in Britain, begins near the town, and takes visitors up to the summit of Snowdon.

Alternatively, the summit can always be reached by walking, with at least six designated routes. The two most popular routes are the Miner's Track from Pen-y-Pass, which is steep at Bwlch Glas, and the longer Llanberis route. The latter follows the railway, but is much the safest and easiest, suiting those who want the

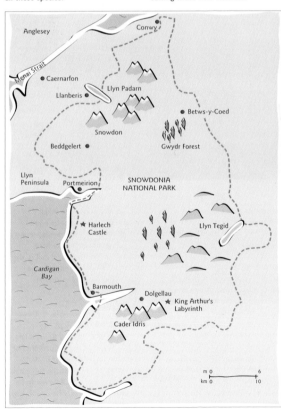

achievement of reaching the top by themselves, but not necessarily the effort of trekking. The Snowdon massif is a star shaped cluster of five peaks, offering walking routes that are not all focused on reaching the summit of the mountain. The park authorities publish guides to walking on and around Snowdon itself, as well as elsewhere in the national park.

Open air

The varied landscape of mountains, lakes and coast offers visitors a chance to try many outdoor activities. The National Whitewater Centre is near Llyn Tegid (Lake Bala) in the east of the park, and water sports such as canoeing, windsurfing and water skiing, as well as the obvious whitewater rafting, are all available on the lake.

The Cambrian coast is popular for sailing and yachting, while the Menai strait is well-known for its good surfing conditions. Fishing – for brown trout, grayling, salmon and sea trout – is excellent both at Llyn Tegid and along the coast.

The beaches offer a variety of sandy swimming areas and more rocky and deserted coves. Barmouth, a busy family resort, is a Blue Flag beach, as are Marian-y-De and Dinas Dinlle on the Llyn peninsula. The whistling sands of Porthoer are worth a visit, but preferably on a dry day when the 'whistle' is more pronounced.

The Snowdon massif is the main attraction for many walkers and climbers, but Cader Idris to the south of the park, and Betws-y-Coed near Gwydr forest in the north-east, are just as enjoyable. Walks in Betws-y-Coed explore gorges, woods and rivers, whilst Cader Idris is for the more strenuous minded.

Pony trekking and mountain biking are also possible on this mountain range. For those keen on cycling and trekking, there are marked trails throughout the park. The Lon Las Cymru (the Welsh National Cycle Network) wends its way through the region, while the Lonydd Glas follows disused rural railway lines, most of which were closed in the 1960s.

Whitewater canoeing on Capel Curig

Historical attractions

If the weather is typically British – wet and changeable – there are plenty of attractions which keep visitors dry. The park and the surrounding area have many monuments charting the history of Wales, from Roman ruins to slate mines.

King Arthur's Labyrinth, between Corris and Dolgellau in the south, records Arthur's fight against the Saxons in the Dark Ages, told through tales from ancient Welsh myths. The labyrinth is underground, and a boat glides along a subterranean river, taking visitors back in time. Out in the open, the Corris Craft Centre demonstrates the traditional crafts and artistry of the region.

The castles of Conwy, Caernarfon and Harlech are all world heritage sites, and are only three of the many castles built by Edward I to show his dominance over the Welsh in the 13th century. Caernarfon also has excavated Roman ruins dating from AD 78. Conwy is the last remaining medieval walled town in Britain and has Plas Mawr, a well-preserved Elizabethan town house. Other 16th and 17th century manor houses are found throughout the region. At Bodnant in the Conwy valley, the gardens cover 40 hectares and reflect the changing seasons.

The copper mine near Beddgelert and the Welsh Slate Museum record the livelihoods of many of the people in North Wales from the 18th to the 20th centuries. The Museum of the Quakers in Dolgellau tells the story of the growth of religious dissent in Wales and the subsequent emigration of local Quakers to America.

[i] CONTACT INFORMATION

Snowdonia National Park
Penrhyndeudraeth
Gwynedd LL48 6LF
Tel: 01766 770274
Web: www.gwynedd.gov.uk

Llynnau Mymbr, Snowdonia

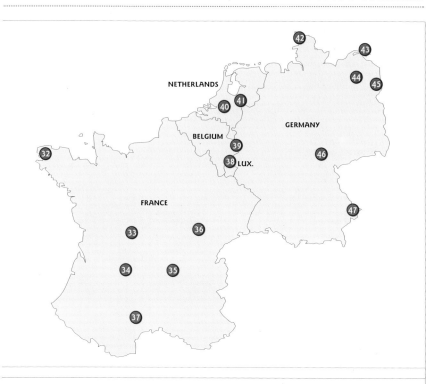

ℹ CONTACT INFORMATION

Belgian Tourist Office – Flanders
31 Pepperstreet
London E14 9RW
Tel: 020 7458 0044
Fax: 020 7458 0045
E-mail: office@flanders-tourism.org
Web: www.visitflanders.com

Belgian Tourist Office – Brussels and Ardennes
255 Marsh Wall
London E14 9FW
Tel: 0800 9545 245
Fax: 020 7531 0393
E-mail: info@belgium-tourism.org
Web: www.belgium-tourism.net

Maison de la France
178 Piccadilly
London W1V 0AL
Tel: 0891 244123
Fax: 020 7493 6594
E-mail: info@mdlf.co.uk
Web: www.franceguide.com

German National Tourist Office
PO Box 2695
London W1A 3TN
Tel: 020 7317 0908
Fax: 020 7995 6129
E-mail: German_National_Tourist_Office@ compuserve.com
Web: www.germany-tourism.de

Luxembourg Tourist Office
122 Regent Street
London W1R 5FE
Tel: 020 7434 2800
Fax: 020 7734 1205
E-mail: tourism@luxembourg.co.uk
Web: www.luxembourg.co.uk

Netherlands Board of Tourism
PO Box 523
London SW1E 6NT
Tel: 0906 871 7777
Fax: 020 7828 7941
E-mail: hollandinfo-uk@nbt.nl
Web: www.holland.com

Armorica Regional Nature Park

*A rural retreat, Armorica has the best of both worlds:
the marine beauty of cliffs and beaches blends quietly
into a hilly inland countryside.*

There is a story in Brittany that when Christ was born, God asked the trees of the Monts d'Arrée to go to Bethlehem to greet him. All except the humble pine, gorse and heather refused point blank to cross the sea, and were shrivelled to the ground by heaven's wrath. This little tale is a handy introduction to the Armorica Regional Nature Park, where the Monts d'Arrée lie: it explains the general barrenness of the inland countryside; it reminds people of the sea's dominant influence; and it shows the curious mix of Christianity and folk tradition that is everywhere present in Breton culture.

Créac'h lighthouse

Landscape and climate

Established in 1969, the Armorica Regional Nature Park comprises thirty nine communes in the département of Finistère, the most westerly region of Brittany. The park extends over 1,720 sq km from the Monts d'Arrée to the Crozon peninsula, and seawards to the islands of Sein, Molène and Ouessant. Incorporating both inland and marine environments, the countryside is immensely varied, from the river estuaries and splendid cliffs of the shoreline to the mysterious moors, bogs and heathland of the mountains. While the omnipresence of the Atlantic gives the land a temperate climate, the sea breezes keep the atmosphere fresh.

Arrée mountains

Created 600 million years ago, the Arrée mountains are some of the oldest geological features in Europe. A high ridge of land stretching into Finistère, the hills peak at Roc'h Trédudon (387m), and are characterised by a craggy profile. The moorland heather and gorse, interspersed by rivers, ponds and lakes, softens the rock somewhat, but apparently has its own perils. In the Yeun-Elez valley, the peatland used to include a shifting mire, said to be the Gate of Hell, and in the Huelgoat forest, moss-covered boulders seem to be the entrance to a fairytale land.

Despite the proximity to the underworld, people still settled here, and various museums run by the park authorities display the region's heritage. La Maison Cornec, made from local slate, is the 18th century home of a well-to-do peasant, and with restored period furniture gives an authentic insight into everyday life of the time. The Country Priest's House helps explain the role of the clergy in society, while the Moulins de Kerouat (Kerouat mills) are a complex of some fifteen buildings. Built between the 17th and 20th centuries, the group includes houses, mills, bread ovens, springs, washing pools and common land.

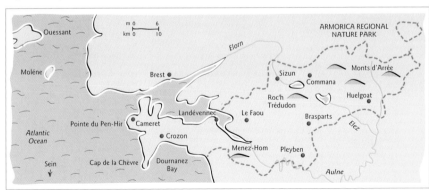

Aulne estuary

From the top of the Menez-Hom, a hill situated at the beginning of the Crozon peninsula, there is a magnificent panoramic view over Dournanez Bay to the south. To the north, the outlook is over the River Aulne, and the almost fjord-like estuary where it flows into the Brest Channel. For about 20km inland from the sea, the river is lined with creeks, marshes, mudflats and reedbeds; the rich wetlands are home to herons and cormorants.

At the mouth of the Aulne lie the remains of the ancient Landévennec abbey, within easy reach of the gentle town of the same name. Founded in 485 by St Gwennolé, the abbey was built in a clearing open to the rising sun. Destroyed by the Normans in 913, a later abbey was built, but the ruins of the original have been excavated by archaeologists.

Crozon peninsula

On this headland, expanses of gorse-covered open moorland end at sheer cliffs falling away to the sea below, or gently slope down to sandy beaches. The capes of Roscanvel, Toulinguet, Pen-Hir and La Chèvre (the Goat) all offer splendid ocean views,

Ouessant sheep

particularly in the evening when the sunset turns the water into a mass of rippling oranges and reds. The villages that crouch on the promontory have low rows of houses, built with their gables aimed into the prevailing wind.

The Vauban tower at Camaret, built between 1680 and 1695, played a vital role in defending Brittany in the Battle of Camaret in 1694. Open to the public, the building is known as 'the gilded tower', its slated roof having a pinkish coating. For history of a different kind, the aligned standing stones at Lagatjar just west of Camaret are a mysterious reminder of ancient tribes. Over 143 menhirs dating from about 2,500 BC are representative of the vast wealth of megaliths found in Brittany.

The islands of the park

The islands of Sein, Ouessant and Molène all come under the park's jurisdiction. Home to lesser and great black-backed gulls, puffins and storm petrels, the Molène archipelago also offers shelter to dolphins, European otters and grey seals. In 1988 the chain of islands was declared a UNESCO biosphere reserve.

Accessible by boat from Brest or Le Conquet, Ouessant rests 20km offshore at the meeting between the Atlantic and the English Channel. The museum in the Créac'h lighthouse tells the history of maritime signalling, with special attention given to the beaconing of the French coast, begun by Augustin Fresnel. A final site is the Maison du Niou, a 19th century cottage. Its simplicity calls to mind the hard life of the islanders, when the women tilled the land whilst the fishermen braved the cruel sea.

[i] CONTACT INFORMATION

Armorica Regional Nature Park
15 Place aux Foires
BP 27
29590 Le Faou
France
Tel: (00 33) 2 9881 9008
Fax: (00 33) 2 9881 9009

Elez river near Loqueffret

FRANCE

Brenne Regional Nature Park

*Pools, ponds and lakes surrounded by lush green vegetation
create a soft watery landscape with a calming atmosphere.*

The Brenne Regional Nature Park is found in the département of Indre, to the south of the low-lying Loire valley region in central France. Established in 1989, the park extends over 1,660 sq km, within which are forty six townships with a total population of only 30,000 people. The defining characteristic of the landscape is without doubt water. While the Creuse, Anglin and Claise rivers flow through the area, over a thousand ponds and lakes provide a still wetland environment that nourishes many threatened plant and bird species.

Chèrine reserve

On either side of the Creuse

Running through Brenne, the River Creuse is a natural boundary between the two distinct landscape types found within the park. Undulating countryside covered with woodlands, hedgerows and meadows leads south of the river, with the hills becoming more pronounced towards the foothills of the Massif Central. Through this region flows the Anglin,

an erratic river into which many tributaries run; if the river floods, the results can be terrible. While the Creuse and Anglin have expanses of wooded valleys, further downstream they pass by scenic limestone cliffs; the waters and rocks offer excellent canoeing, fishing and climbing.

To the north of the Creuse is the Brenne's famous lakeland. Otters and kingfishers can be glimpsed in the gentle, moist landscape of ponds and heaths. Curious sandstone mounds known as *buttons* break up the level plains. In local myth they were created by the giant Gargantua. Large as he was, on his way from Tours to Limoges, Gargantua could not help occasionally putting his feet down, which sank into the muddy ground. Each time he had to scrape his boots, he left behind a hillock.

The lakes of the Brenne

The French word for the myriad expanses of water in the Brenne, *étang*, is not easy to translate. Literally, it means 'pond', and with some 1,400 ponds within its boundaries, the area is known as the 'land of a thousand ponds'. However, the waters are frequently too large to suit such a humble title, and really merit the status of lakes.

Although their appearance is now natural, the lakes are in fact artificial, having been created for fish-farming. The impermeable clay and sandy soil makes for poor agricultural land, but is ideal for ponds, and according to the locals it was the monks of the

7th century St-Cyran and Méobecq abbeys who first began building them. In reality it was probably the religious communities of the Middle Ages who started the tradition, but many of the ponds were drained during the Revolution, as they were supposedly insanitary. With the 20th century, however, fish-farming has regained its importance and 2,000 tonnes of carp, tench, roach and pike are harvested here each year.

Flora and fauna

Little touched by intensive agriculture or industry, the lakes are a quiet home to 150 nesting bird species, while 267 species have been recorded using the countryside as a resting or feeding ground. Black-necked grebes, warblers, bitterns, marsh harriers and many varieties of duck benefit from the vast reedbeds, while even rare purple herons hide amongst the sedges, bullrushes and willows. The mudflats that appear during the summer dry periods swarm with worms and molluscs, providing a banquet for plovers, sandpipers, snipes and godwits.

Waterlilies spread themselves across many of the lakes, where the water violet is also found, while on land, varieties of orchids, martagon lilies and wild sweet peas are amongst the wealth of summer wildflowers. The park authorities work with Indre Nature (a regional nature protection society) to arrange guided nature walks, whilst the local branch of the French equivalent of the RSPB arranges outings in English.

Exploring the lakes

Many of the lakes are private owned, but there are nevertheless plenty of ways of accessing their beauty. The Chérine nature reserve near St-Michel-en-Brenne includes one of the largest remaining reedbeds of the Brenne, and was created to protect rare plant and animal species. It is a good place to see the European pond tortoise as it bumbles its way through the watery landscape.

The Massé, Neuf and Foucaults étangs are owned by the park and have bird observation hides open to the public.

European pond tortoise

The Blizon Nature Trail at Rosnay mixes pleasant walking with dragonflies – sixty one of the ninety one species recorded in France are found in the Brenne.

Private lakes that can be reached by marked footpaths include the Etang de la Mer Rouge and the Etang du Sault, and, for these and longer hiking circuits, the park suggests 107 marked trails between 6 and 32km long. Routes for cyclists and motorists are also available.

Heritage and history

The park's visitor centre in Hameau du Bouchet is situated in the farm buildings of an old castle, and has exhibitions on the local countryside and history, with eight slide shows in English. Local delicacies such as the renowned Pouligny-Saint-Pierre goat's cheese are on sale. The red sandstone houses around the centre are

representative of the region's architecture. The traditional buildings have a large ground floor room with a loft above, only accessible by a permanent ladder.

Of castles and churches worth visiting, Château Naillac in Le Blanc dominates the town from its situation above the Creuse, and despite several reconstructions has kept its grand seigneurial hall. A museum of the Brenne's history is housed within its walls. The Notre-Dame abbey at Fontgombault is an imposing edifice with a troubled history of pillage and destruction. Since being bought and restored by Trappist monks in the 19th century, it has become home to a community of Solesmes monks. By contrast, the Saint-Sulpice chapel, hidden in a clearing of the Lancosme forest, is a simple sandstone building, perfectly suited to the unpretentious charm of the entire park.

ⓘ CONTACT INFORMATION

Brenne Regional Nature Park
Hameau du Bouchet
36300 Rosnay
France
Tel: (00 33) 2 5428 1213
Fax: (00 33) 2 5437 5696
E-mail: info@parc-naturel-brenne.fr
Web: www.parc-naturel-brenne.fr

Le Blanc Tourist Office
Place de la Libération
36300 Le Blanc
France
Tel: (00 33) 2 5437 0513
Fax: (00 33) 2 5437 3193

One of the Brenne's many lakes

FRANCE

Périgord-Limousin Regional Nature Park

The natural treasures of the Limousin are equally matched by its history and tradition, creating an area that both stimulates the imagination and satisfies the senses.

The Limousin region in mid-France is a beautiful landscape of low mountain ranges, plateaux, castles, prehistoric monuments, lakes and river valleys. The central belt of the region offers the porcelain town of Limoges, and the lakes and hills of the Millevache plateau, while to the west, the Périgord-Limousin Regional Nature Park is a pleasant introduction to some of the richest natural and cultural heritage sites of the area.

The park lies on the margins of the Aquitaine basin and the foothills of the Massif Central, half in the Limousin and half in the Dordogne area of Aquitaine. Founded in 1998, its purpose is to help protect 1,800 sq km of wooded valleys, ponds, moors, marshland, peat bogs and meadows.

Landscapes of the park

The park covers four main geographical areas: the northern *bocage limousin*, consisting of gently undulating hills covered with hedges and copses; the central Feuillard massif, land of the chestnut tree; the Jumilhac plateau to the east, with hill ranges cut through by narrow valleys; and open farmland in the Périgord valleys to the south.

Above all, the scenery offers woods and pastures, a 'green and pleasant land' interspersed with rivers, villages and farms, towers and castles, the fields dotted with the distinctive red of the famous Limousin cows.

Woods and wetlands

In the Périgord area, the marshes, reed beds and chalky meadows of the Nizonne valley are of special interest, and offer a representative sample of wildlife in the region. Over 1,000 plant species, including rare orchids, are found in the park, and purple herons benefit from the water lands. Red deer, otters and minks roam the woods, while bats haunt at night.

The Limousin countryside

The Rochechouart meteorite

In the bocage limousin, a gigantic meteorite hit the earth over 200 million years ago leaving a crater 20km in diameter. The history of the impact and its consequences can be explored through an exhibition in Rochechouart, while many of the rocks blasted by the impact can now be seen in a different setting; throughout the centuries, the local people have used them to construct their châteaux, farms and wells.

Chestnut trees and gold

St Peter, so the legend goes, was told to travel through France and report back to God on what each area had to offer. In the Limousin, his answer was 'chestnuts'. Indeed, the trees are everywhere, and were once a source

of food, firewood and building materials. The park's Feuillard massif, a plateau of rounded wooded hills, was once home to numerous *feuillardiers*, craftsmen who used the chestnut trees to produce fine strips of wood for binding wine barrels or weaving into baskets.

Around Jumilhac, mills and forges used to bear witness to the iron industry of the area. Although most of these are now abandoned, the land still produces two tonnes of gold a year from a mine to the north-east of Jumilhac. So rich in minerals, even the rivers of the area, such as the Valouze and Périgord, carry gold.

Richard the Lionheart

In 1199, Richard the Lionheart was killed whilst laying siege to the château of Châlus-Chabrol. One way of getting to know the castles, fortresses and medieval towns of Limousin is to follow a specially-designed route named after the king. Sights include Ségur-le-Château, a castle and also officially one of the 'most beautiful villages in France'; Lastours, showing the remains of a Norman keep; the Château des Cars, seat of the Limousin governors; and the restored 13th and 15th century Rochechouart castle with its splendid Renaissance courtyard.

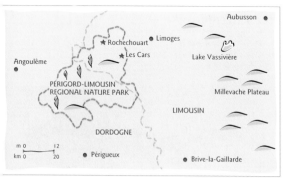

Lake Vassivière

A butterfly-shaped artificial lake developed by the French Electricity Board as part of its hydroelectric work, Lake Vassivière is a Limousin heritage site and one of the foremost attractions of the region.

Part of the lake has been cordoned off to create a haven for water sports such as water-skiing, canoeing, sailing and surfboarding, as well as angling. On the island in the centre of the lake, the Centre for Contemporary Art and a sculpture park in the nearby woodland provide an opportunity to reflect on the synergy of art and nature.

The surrounding granite plateau of Millevache, known as the 'land of a thousand springs', offers magnificent sweeping views and is ideal for walking, cycling and pony-trekking.

[i] CONTACT INFORMATION

Limousin Tourist Board
27 boulevard de la Corderie
87031 Limoges cedex
France
Tel: (00 33) 5 5545 1880
Fax: (00 33) 5 5545 1818
Web: www.cr-limousin.fr

Porcelain past

Only in 1709 did Europeans finally discover the secret formula for making china, or porcelain; fifty years later a deposit of the secret ingredient, kaolin – a fine clay – was found at Saint-Yrieix-la-Perche. Since then, Limoges porcelain has become world-famous, and the town's National Porcelain Museum displays a deserved pride in its heritage. Limoges is also worth visiting for its cathedral and abbey, and picturesque Quartier de la Boucherie, an area of 13th century buildings which at one time housed butchers selling the meat of the prized red Limousin cattle.

Tapestry

In the Creuse valley, Aubusson is home to another Limousin speciality – tapestry. Amongst the old pepper pot turreted houses is the 'Vieux Tapissier' family house. The tapestry workshop of the Corneille dynasty of weavers since the 16th century, it is now a tapestry museum that gives an insight into the ancient arts of dyeing, pattern-making and weaving.

The trade is still flourishing today; the largest tapestry in the world, the 264 sq metre modern image of Christ that hangs in the new Coventry Cathedral, was made in nearby Felletin.

Châlus-Chabrol

FRANCE

Nature Parks of the Auvergne

*Extending across the Massif Central, the Volcanoes of the
Auvergne and the Livradois-Forez parks have a grandiose
beauty mixed with old-fashioned rural charm.*

Vast open mountains and green
plateaux are the hallmark of the
Auvergne region in the Massif Central
highlands of France. Around the
central city of Clermont-Ferrand,
volcanoes and hills sprinkled with
lakes, forests, rivers and peat bogs are
home to two regional nature parks.
Separated by the River Allier, the
Volcanoes of the Auvergne and the
Livradois-Forez Regional Nature Parks
run parallel to each other, and
between them offer protection to
some of the Auvergne's most
beautiful countryside and richest
natural sites.

Massif du Sancy

Volcans d'Auvergne

The Volcanoes of the Auvergne was
established in 1977 and is the largest
French regional nature park. Visually,
it is impossible to escape from the
geological origins of the landscape;
volcanic eruptions beginning about
20 million years ago formed the four
massifs and granite plateaus that
dominate the countryside today.

To discover the area, plenty of well-
marked routes are ideal for hiking or
horse-riding. The peaks and waters
also set bigger challenges: hang-
gliding is possible from many of the
summits; downhill and cross-country
skiing is a winter delight; over fifty
equipped climbing sites range from
level 2 to 8b in difficulty; sailing and
windsurfing is possible on most lakes;
the rivers offer canoeing; and hot-air
balloon trips simply let the vast
panoramas unfold below.

Puy de Dôme

The Puys chain of volcanoes in the
north are the youngest volcanoes in
France, and have just cooled down
after their fiery activity 6,000 years
ago. A line of over eighty volcanoes
stretches for 35km, creating a
mysterious silhouette visible from
afar. Just west of Clermont-Ferrand,
the Puy de Dôme rises to 1,464m, and
being the highest in the chain is

the symbol of the region. A Roman
temple to Mercury was built here in
the 1st century AD, while now the
strategic position is home to army,
meteorological, television and
telecommunication stations.

The vantage point also offers an
amazing view over other peaks, each
one formed by a different volcanic
quirk: the Puy de Dôme itself is a
rounded dome with no crater, having
been formed by lava cooling in
contact with the open air; the Suchet
was scarred by a violent explosion;
and Côme Puy has a double crater
caused by successive eruptions.

South of the Puys, the Dore
mountains are the grandparents of
the Auvergne volcanoes, and have the
highest summits of the Massif
Central, with the dark lava rocks of
the Puy du Sancy reaching 1,886m.

The Cantal mountains

Lying at the southern edge of the
Volcanoes Park, this range was
created between 11 and 4 million
years ago and is the largest volcanic
massif in Europe. From the central
peaks around the Puy Mary and the
Plomb du Cantal, about a dozen
glacial valleys spread out in the
distance, covered with beautiful
beech forests and rich pastureland.

L'Artense and Cézallier

Between the Dore and the Cantal
mountains, the Artense plateau and
Cézallier massif offer a diversion from
volcanic craters. A granite plateau
with glacial gorges, the Artense
displays green meadows with
scattered rocks and small lakes.
Interspersed are beech and coniferous
forests, broom-covered slopes and
peat bogs in the valleys.

In the Cézallier region, a high bare
plateau to the east is covered in
mountain pastures, creating a
summer kingdom where insects
abound. Wild wooded gorges pierce
the eastern slopes, and the Pinatelle
forest is home to the park's largest
deer population. The two glacial lakes
either side of La Godivelle village have
been designated a nature reserve to
protect their natural peat bogs.

Spa towns

After a few days' wandering in the volcanic wilderness, another of the Auvergne's specialities might be needed for relaxation. The region is home to ten spa towns. The curative properties of the natural hot mineral springs have been used for centuries, and today's thermal resorts are centres for recuperation and calm.

At Le Mont-Dore, part of the spa centre is a classified historical monument, having wonderful neo-Byzantine architecture. The most famous spa, Vichy, lies to the north-east of Clermont-Ferrand and is worth visiting for its elegant architecture from the Second Empire and the Belle Epoque.

Clermont-Ferrand

A convenient central point between the two parks, Clermont-Ferrand's bustle of commerce and nightlife offers a striking contrast to the surrounding Auvergne. However its dark buildings, built from the black volcanic rock of the area and earning it the name of *ville noire* (black town), help it to blend in. A statue of the Gallic chieftain Vercingétorix in the Place de Jaude and the dark, soaring Gothic cathedral of Notre-Dame de l'Assomption, are two of the city's main attractions.

Livradois-Forez

The Livradois and Forez mountains were formed by movements in the Earth's crust during the Tertiary geological period. Two ridges were thrown up, which over time slowly moved away from each other, causing the ground between to collapse. This is seen today in the Dore valley that separates the ranges. West of the Livradois peaks, the fertile Limagne plains near Billom have a mild climate. The black earth produces maize and sunflowers, the tall houses have red roofs, and the area is known as the Auvergne Tuscany. This gentle land soon gives way to the Livradois'

Côme Puy's double crater

wooded slopes and bare open tops. To the south, the Bar Mount near Allègre is a volcanic cone sheltering a peat bog in its crater, a unique site in Europe, and at nearby Sembadel, a picturesque rail route begins.

A 'discovery train' runs through most of the park, first across La Chaise-Dieu plateau and then up alongside the river, allowing spectacular views to the surrounding mountains.

Highland life

Trees don't grow on the windswept highlands, and the high stubble fields, or *hautes chaumes* as they are called locally, stretch their thrilling bleakness for miles across the sub-alpine Forez peaks.

Dotted about are *jasseries*, granite mountain cottages with thatched roofs, where once women, children, dogs and livestock would have lived whilst the cows were out on the mountains' summer pasturage. Although this custom has practically

Capercaillie

vanished and there are now more sheep than cows, the Fourme cheese that used to ripen in jasserie cellars is still made in the region.

At Col des Supeyres, a jasserie has been restored with care and is open as a museum to offer visitors a taste of the past – local ham, sausage and cheese can all be sampled along with the old-fashioned atmosphere.

Water power

Hardly benefiting at all from the rich volcanic soil of its western neighbours, the Livradois-Forez is generally poor agricultural land, and the local farmers have always needed to diversify to survive. From the Forez and Livradois ranges, numerous mountain streams rush down the slopes, chiselling out enclosed valleys, and since the Middle Ages the locals have used this natural force to power mills of all kinds.

To the north of the park, Thiers was a medieval industrial city, and is still the cutlery capital of France. The waters of the River Durolle were used for the cutlery works, and the old factory buildings are now home to a contemporary art museum.

A wander along the Durolle reveals the tenacity it must have taken to capture the river's energy. Here, in the Vallée des Rouets, knife-grinders would lie on their stomachs across planks above the mill wheels. Their body weight would hold the knives against the grinding wheels, the continuous motion whetting the blades to their final sharpness.

Ingenuity and local trades

The knife trade was only one of many that have become part of the Livradois tradition. Near Ambert, another water-based industry can be witnessed at the Moulin Richard de Bas, a working mill that houses a museum of the history of paper. Paper is still made by hand in the style of the 14th century, and visitors can help. In Arlanc, a lace-making factory shows off the intricacies of the point and bobbin tradition, while in Lavaudieu a museum workshop displays the less well-known craft of stained glass-making.

Besides these durable products, the edible specialities of the Auvergne are also honoured. Local producers delight in offering guided tours round their apiaries, goose, goat, fruit or herb farms, and a working museum demonstrates how Fourme d'Ambert cheese is made. An 'Artisan's Route' introduces visitors to all the trades, as well as the many castles and churches.

Vallée du Fossat, Livradois-Forez

Schnapps

The upland moors of both parks let the carnivorous drosera, or sundew, flourish to the peril of unwary insects, and grass of Parnassus grows in the moist fields. The volcanic soil provides nourishment for andromeda, spotted cat's ear and autumn crocuses. Martagon lilies and anemones are amongst the rarer species, and yellow gentians spread over the plateaux. These plants are prized for their roots, which grow thick and deep. Dug up, sorted, cleaned and crushed, they are soaked in alcoholic spirits to produce the golden gentian schnapps.

CONTACT INFORMATION

Auvergne Regional Tourist Board
43, avenue Julien - BP 395
63011 Clermont-Ferrand
France
Tel: (00 33) 4 7329 4949
Fax: (00 33) 4 7334 1111
Web: www.cr-auvergne.fr

The Volcanoes of the Auvergne Regional Nature Park
Centre d'information
Montlosier 63970
France
Tel: (00 33) 4 7365 6400
Fax: (00 33) 4 7365 6678
E-mail: parc.volcans@wanadoo.fr

The Livradois-Forez Regional Nature Park
63880 Saint-Gervais-sous-Meymont
France
Tel: (00 33) 4 7395 5757
Fax: (00 33) 4 7395 5784
E-mail: info@parc-livradois-forez.org

Auvergne architecture

From the 9th century, Romanesque art began to make its presence felt in the Auvergne, and today over 500 churches in the region display the rounded arches and vaults typical of the period.

The only intact Romanesque cloister at Lavaudieu abbey, and the recently restored mini-church at Glaine-Montaigut are of special note, particularly for their religious wall-paintings. Thiers, Arlanc and Billom are all home to magnificent churches, while even village churches are worth a visit. The imposing abbey at La Chaise-Dieu offers a contrast with its Gothic style.

Auvergne birds

For ornithologists, the Auvergne has many valuable sites. Birds of prey such as royal and black kites, kestrels, peregrines and eagles swoop over the steep slopes of the volcanoes; hawks and harriers scan the pastures for prey; and riverbanks shelter herons and stone curlews.

Rock thrushes find their diet of insects and berries on the sub-alpine meadows, and woodpeckers and finches hide in the woods, as does the shy black grouse, symbol of the Livradois-Forez Park. The Bird Protection League does a lot of work in the area, setting up platforms for white storks to nest on.

A jasserie in the Livradois-Forez

Morvan Regional Nature Park

*From Celts to Crusades and mountains to music,
the Morvan Regional Nature Park in Burgundy
presents a fascinating history and culture.*

Think of Burgundy, and immediately the deep rich red colour of good wine springs to mind. But what else is known of the region's riches? Perhaps Dijon mustard, or the Benedictine monastery at Cluny, but most people have probably not heard of its delightful heartland, the Morvan.

Designated a regional nature park in 1970, the Morvan is a thinly-populated area between the towns of Avallon, Saulieu and Autun. Pasturage and copses in the north give way to central forests and bogs, which in turn rise to the southern mountains. The area's name, deriving from the Celtic for 'black mountain', hints at magic, with great lakes and wild rivers adding to the enchantment.

Rafting on the River Cure

Celtic and Roman roots

Although today the Morvan is hardly touched by urbanisation, it was once home to the principal commercial centre of Ancient Gaul. Bibracte, situated on Mont Beuvray, was the largest hillfort of the Eduens, the most powerful Celtic tribe. It was here that Vercingétorix was chosen as leader of the combined Gallic forces against the Romans, and it was here

that Julius Caesar wintered after defeating the Gauls at Alésia in 52 BC. A walking route leads north-east from Bibracte through the Morvan to the battleground. Alternatively, for those more interested in the conqueror's influence, part of the GR 13 marked trail runs east from Bibracte to Autun, the Roman town of Augustodunum. Built by Augustus Caesar to replace the old Gallic hillfort, the town walls are the best preserved of the period in France, and the remains of a 1st century Roman amphitheatre are as impressive as any in southern France.

Medieval piety

The Romanesque basilica in Vézelay is dedicated to Mary Magdalene, whose relics were supposedly brought to the monastery in the 9th century. The town became a central focus for medieval pilgrimages and religious fervour. In 1146, St Bernard made an impassioned call for the Second Crusade outside the church, and it was here too that Richard the Lionheart launched the Third Crusade.

The town itself is set on what is known as 'the eternal hill', but sadly the church was to lose its prestige. Several centuries later, an Avignon Pope declared that the 'real' relics were in fact in a church in southern France, and Vézelay lost its attraction, consequently falling into physical decay. However, the basilica is still a wonderful example of Burgundian Romanesque architecture, and is now a UNESCO world heritage site.

Revolution

The château of Saint-Brisson, the main centre for the Morvan Regional Nature Park, bears witness to more recent turbulence. The original castle was burnt down after the aristocratic owners fled to England during the French Revolution, but the family were lucky enough to survive.

On returning to their home, they had another château built, this time designed by an English architect. The new estate consisted of a central manor house, surrounded by a farmhouse, storehouses, a chapel, hunting lodge and gardens.

In 1975, the estate was acquired by the Burgundy region, and it now houses the park's visitor centre and library. An arboretum has over thirty types of trees and bushes representing the woodlands of the Morvan, whilst a herbarium houses over 170 plant species. Based on monastic herb gardens, the herbary is organised into themes such as medicinal or forest plants. For nature enthusiasts, the park organises specialised walks and tours, both during the day for simple bird-watching or discovering the flowers, and at night on the trail of bats, owls, badgers and snakes.

Museums

The park's ecology museum is one of many that celebrates the culture and traditions of the Morvan. The rye museum in Ménessaire shows how the golden crop, which until the Second World War dominated the landscape, was used by the local people for everything from bread to

The wren, a Morvan inhabitant

household goods and thatched roofs. The ox drivers' museum in Anost tells the story of the men who, to supplement meagre incomes, would often leave homes and families for months to work elsewhere. In Saint-Léger-Vauban, there is a museum to Field Marshal Vauban. A famous military engineer, Vauban was also something of a social philosopher, writing two books relating to the poverty of his region, which earned him a royal disgrace.

Lakes and leisure

In central and north-western Morvan, the lakes are a link between past necessity and current pleasure. Lake Settons was created to raise the level of the River Cure to help float logs,

and Lac du Crescent was built to control river flow. Now, along with the lakes of Pannecière, Chamboux and Saint-Agnan, the waters offer peaceful fishing, sailing, and swimming, while the whitewaters of the Cure and Chalaux rivers challenge kayakers.

Plenty of marked walks use old forest tracks as a means of discovering the countryside, including the GR 13 that leads from Vézelay to Mont Beuvray and Autun, or the GRP route 'Tour du Morvan'. Whilst wandering, it can be fun to sample the local entertainments: classical concerts in Bazoches; Anost's folk music festival; the Augustodunum carnival in Autun; or the food festival in Saulieu.

i CONTACT INFORMATION

Morvan Regional Nature Park
Maison du Parc
58230 Saint-Brisson
France
Tel: (00 33) 3 8678 7900
Fax: (00 33) 3 8678 7422
Web: www.parcdumorvan.org

Burgundy Regional Torist Board
Conseil Régional
BP 1602
21035 Dijon cedex
France
Tel: (00 33) 3 8050 9000
Fax: (00 33) 3 8030 5945
E-mail: promotion@crt-bourgogne.fr

Lac du Crescent nestling in the Morvan countryside

Grands Causses Regional Nature Park

Immense gorge-gouged plateaux, strange rock formations and sheep flocks are the hallmarks of an imposing region in southern France.

The Grands Causses Regional Nature Park in the département of Aveyron covers a vast expanse of contrasting altitudes and landscapes. Established in 1995, it incorporates ninety four communes over an area of some 3,150 sq km. Its name comes from the *causses*, huge limestone plateaux that make up over half the territory.

Bordered by the Cévennes National Park to the east, and to the south by the Haut-Languedoc Regional Nature Park, the Grands Causses is part of one of the largest protected natural regions in Europe. Whether explored by car, bike, or on foot, numerous routes open up the area's natural, historic and culinary specialities.

The Causse du Larzac

East and west

The three limestone causses that run down the east side of the park were formed between 150 and 205 million years ago. The gorges, grottoes, underground rivers and peculiar boulder formations that make the region so fascinating have been gradually carved out by the action of water on the soft limestone rock.

All the causses are also adorned with human handiwork. Medieval villages blend subtly into the rocky landscape, while on the great plains traditional stone houses are covered by *lauzes*, heavy limestone slabs. The large stones help protect against the freezing winters and summer heat. The sheep trails of the dry open pastureland are bordered by *lavognes*, clay marshes lined with stone to help collect rainwater for the flocks during the long dry summers.

By contrast, the western countryside is more fruitful, dedicated to agriculture and raising sheep. Green valleys, wooded hillsides and warm red sandstone create a land rich in natural colour, whilst human history is revealed by ancient dolmens, and medieval abbeys and castles.

The Causse de Sévérac

In the north of the park, the Sévérac Causse rises to peaks of 1,000m, providing a natural barrier between the harsh mountain weather beyond and the Mediterranean climate to the south. Many trout streams ripple through the green meadowlands where the River Aveyron has its source. At the centre of the region, the medieval village of Sévérac-le-Château is dominated by a castle on the hill above. Dating from the 13th century, the castle often hosts exhibitions on the music, cuisine and costumes of the Middle Ages.

The Causse Noir

The almond, prune, cherry and apricot trees that cheer the sunny hillsides in the spring belie the wild nature of the Causse Noir. Sheer cliffs loom over the savage gorges through which the Jonte and Dourbie rivers run. Around Montpellier-le-Vieux, strange chaotic boulders are named after their peculiar shapes: an arch is called the 'gate of the Mycenae', whilst the local dialect has christened others as the 'bear' and the 'cooking pot'.

From the Causse Noir, it is worth venturing into the Causse Méjean in the Cévennes National Park. Along the Jonte, griffon vultures have been released into the wild by the park authorities. In the show caves at Aven Armand and Dargilan, intricate stalactites and stalagmites vaunt nature's secret creativity.

The Causse du Larzac

The Larzac Causse in the south is both the most rugged of the plateaux and the cradle of sheep-rearing. In spring, the heaths are decorated with orchids, dog-roses and yellow flax, whilst wild thyme and lavender attract the honey-bees. However, as the summers dry out the land, the colours disappear, and the landscape takes on the barren aspect of the steppes.

Besides its flocks, the Larzac is known for its old walled villages of the Knights Templars and Knights Hospitallers. These military religious orders, originally created in the 12th century to help protect pilgrims journeying to the Holy Land, received land in Larzac from the King of Aragon in 1159. They developed agriculture and sheep farming, and built strongholds such as Ste-Eulalie-de-Cernon and La Couvertoirade.

When the Templars were suppressed in the 14th century, their possessions were given to the Hospitallers who subsequently fortified the villages further during the turmoil of the Hundred Years' War. Within external protective ramparts, narrow medieval streets, houses and civic buildings are still remarkably well preserved.

Le Rougier and the Lévezou

In the south-west, the St-Affrican and Rougier hills are gentler, with good farmland yielding various crops and supporting the sheep that produce milk for the renowned Roquefort blue cheese. Here the historic landmarks are even older – there are more dolmens and menhirs, dating from around 2,500 BC, than in Brittany.

The Lévezou plateau rises up to the north, above the Tarn and Muse valleys. Numerous springs and streams tumble down through the Raspes du Tarn gorge, while the woods in autumn become a paradise

The statue of Jean-Henri Fabre in St-Léons

for mushroom-hunters. Amongst the villages that cling to the slopes is St-Léons, the birthplace of Jean-Henri Fabre, father of modern entomology. A museum pays tribute to the largely self-taught teacher whose dedication to the insect world did much to increase interest in the subject.

Millau and its surroundings

The focal point of the park, Millau relaxes beneath the protective shadow of the Noir and Larzac Causses. In Roman times, the town achieved importance through the export of its red clay pottery. Now it is known for its leatherwork; in the 1950s it had no fewer than 140 factories. Despite a recent decline, the *Peau de Millau* (Millau leather) is still a guarantee of quality, the luxurious leather goods prized by many Parisian fashion designers.

i CONTACT INFORMATION

The Grands Causses Regional Nature Park
71, Boulevard de l'Ayrolle
BP 126
12101 Millau Cedex
France
Tel: (00 33) 5 6561 3550
Fax: (00 33) 5 6561 3480
E-mail: parc.grands.causses@ wanadoo.fr

The Causse Noir

Nature Parks of Luxembourg

The Upper-Sûre Nature Park and the proposed Our Valley Nature Park dwell on opposite sides of Luxembourg's Ardennes region, each offering the best of the outdoors intermingled with absorbing history.

The nature parks of the Ardennes are a recent attempt to strike a balance between economic development and environmental preservation. The beech and oak forested hills, enriched with rivers and lakes, are a valuable asset to the local towns and villages. Meanwhile, farmers tackle the agricultural development of the area through crop diversification. The parks are sectioned into groups of two or three villages called communes, each endowed with a plethora of natural features and organised activity to keep all visitors occupied.

Upper-Sûre Nature Park

Situated in the south-west of Luxembourg's share of the Ardennes, the nature park of the Upper-Sûre takes up almost a third of the region. It is centred around the Upper-Sûre lake and river, and came into official existence by grand-ducal decree in 1996. The lake is man-made, having been dammed in 1961 to provide drinking water. A stretch of 5km, however, is all that is cordoned off for this purpose. The rest is dedicated to leisure facilities, ranging from windsurfing and sailing to swimming and canoeing. The surrounding sylvan countryside, interspersed with streams and ponds, is equally enticing with horse-riding, walking and cycling tracks, and cultural sites illustrating Luxembourg's past.

Cycling in the Upper-Sûre

There are two principal cycling tracks in the park, both of which carry on into other parts of the Ardennes. In the southern section of the park, a track passes Eschette's forest and the ruins of the Schorels fortress. Continuing west, at the pleasant plateau of Koetschette, a 15km trek can be undertaken to Martelagne and its slate quarry museum. The quarry was worked for over 200 years before being closed in 1986. It has since received awards for nature and environmental protection.

Canoeing on the River Sûre

At the apex of the park another cycle track winds its way by the Winseler tea factory and herb garden before continuing west along the Wiltz river. On the Upper-Sûre lake, mountain bikes can be rented for exploring the 15 hectares of surrounding countryside as well as the typical Ardennes villages of Bavigne, Liefrange and Nothum.

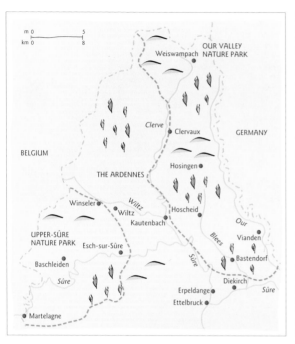

For those seeking more adventure, the rivers of the Ardennes can be canoed all year, with the race season officially beginning in Easter and heralded by an international rally. Between October and March there are wild water stretches on the River Wiltz and the River Sûre. For more tentative canoeists, the Upper-Sûre in summer offers a course that is much gentler.

The unpolluted waters of the park are also suitable for angling and are home to trout, pike, perch, eel and carp. Formal permits are required, although, for a fee, angling is possible in various fishponds throughout the Upper-Sûre without a permit.

Cultural activities

Themed walks are a good way of sampling some of the park's outdoor attractions. From Baschleiden, a religious walk trails the Catholic area, surveying churches, art treasures and hermitages. Three other separate trails introduce visitors to old watermills, Second World War monuments and local farmhouses. In Esch-sur-Sûre, the former cloth factory is now home to the Nature Park Visitors' Centre which demonstrates traditional cloth production processes. Particularly interesting for children are the restored wool machines and candle factory. Younger visitors may also be

Water activities

The Upper-Sûre lake is the focal point for watersports in the park. Its size allows plenty of room for all, and the water is of a high quality. To the west, Boulaid is host to another artificial lake which is similarly popular for aquatic activities. The nearby villages of Insenborn and Lultzhausen lie on the lakeside and are ideal for swimming, sailing and canoeing. For divers, the national Sub-Aqua Club has its base in Lultzhausen.

Esch-sur-Sûre

attracted to the pottery works at Lueresmillen and the Thillenvogtei open-air museum. For discerning tastes, the gardens of Colpach castle displays sculpture by the French neo-classicist Maillol.

Our Valley Nature Park

The Our river, on the east side of the Ardennes, lines the border between Luxembourg and Germany. The valley stretches from Bastendorf right up to the lakes of Weiswampach and encompasses the Blees and Clerve rivers. It reaches inland too, past the villages of Brandenbourg, Hoscheid and Clervaux. Owing to its length, the Our Valley Nature Park matches the Upper-Sûre in its variety. The scenic clusters of villages provide swimmers, anglers, horse-riders, canoeists, skiers, and all those of an active persuasion with the facilities for a lively holiday.

Ardennes draught horses at the rural museum in Munshausen

Equestrian activities

Exploring the Our valley by horse is made easy by the various riding schools. Assistance is also available from the Fédération Luxembourgeoise des Sport Equestres. Heinerscheid, a village in the north of the valley, has its own horse-riding centre and for exploring the 600m high plateau, the villages of Lieler and Kalborn, and the valleys of both the Upper-Our and the Clerve, horseback is an ideal approach.

Cycling in the Our valley

Two cycling tracks in particular open up some treasures of the countryside. The 13km Reisdorf–Vianden track introduces visitors to the Vianden home-in-exile of the French 19th century novelist Victor Hugo, and the town's impressive feudal manor. Once the seat of the Counts of Vianden, its medieval structure towers over the area. A 13th century church adds to the view. To sample the valley of the Clerve river properly, a 15km cycle through the centre of the Oesling is recommended. Starting at Wilwerwiltz, the trail heads south through Lellingen, host of a narcissus festival at Easter, before meeting historic Kautenbach with its castle, and then Merkholtz village.

Skiing in the Our valley

During a snowy winter, the settlements in the north of the park – namely the villages of Hosingen, Weiswampach and Asselborn – are popular for cross-country skiing. Each town has its own ski trails. At an altitude of 440m, Asselborn's trail length is 4km, while Hosingen and Weiswampach, at altitudes of 500 and 520m, have trails of 5km.

Testing the waters at the Weiswampach lakes

Culture in the Our valley

Tucked into the valleys and forests, castle remains and impressive religious buildings beckon. Clervaux's Benedictine abbey is pedestalled on the town hill, yet, save for its red roofs and steeple, it is almost entirely shrouded by the surrounding forest. Bastendorf's 10th century castle in the valley of the Blees river is another point of intrigue. Alternatively, on the banks of the Our are the remains of Stolzembourg's copper mine or, further to the north,

the Munshausen living museum is dedicated to the work of Ardennes draught horses.

A visit to Vianden in autumn brings an encounter with the town's own brand of quirky festival. The walnut street market is held on the second Sunday of October and invites a barrage of nut-based produce. Contenders for sampling include nut liqueur, nut candy, nut pizza and nut cakes. Bands of musicians hold forth on the streets while festivities are topped off by the town's nut parade.

i CONTACT INFORMATION

Upper-Sûre Natural Park
15 route de Lultzhausen
L-9650 Esch-sur-Sûre
Luxembourg
Tel: (00 352) 8993311
Web: www.restena.lu/sycopan

Luxembourg National Tourist Office
PO Box 1001
L-1010 Luxembourg
Tel: (00 352) 42 82821
Fax: (00 352) 42 828238
E-mail: tourism@ont.smtp.etat.lu
Web: www.etat.lu/tourism

The thickly forested hills of the Ardennes

BELGIUM

Hautes Fagnes–Eifel Nature Park

*The high fenlands of the Eifel plateau are protected for
their water-fed vistas and fragile ecosystems that are
a haven for wildlife.*

The Hautes Fagnes–Eifel Nature Park
covers 72 sq km along Belgium's
eastern border in the province of
Liège. The park was created in 1971
as a Belgian–German initiative to
protect the Eifel high plateau which
straddles the two countries. The
German portion is called the Nordeifel
Nature Park and is the larger of the
two sections, stretching between the
towns of Düren and Prüm.

The Belgian part runs between Eupen
in the north to the provincial border
with Belgian Luxembourg in the
south. It incorporates the picturesque
lakes of Robertville and Bütgenbach,
the Our river valley, the Hertogenwald
forest and the Losheimergraben
woods. Most importantly, it contains
the Hautes Fagnes National Nature
Reserve, from which the larger park
takes its name.

High fens

The Hautes Fagnes reserve was
created in 1957 and is both the
largest in Belgium and the only
nationally protected one. Hautes
Fagnes means 'high fens', and the
reserve's landscape is one of moors,

peat bogs, and low, grass or wood
covered hills. Belgium's highest point
falls within the park, at the modest
altitude of 694m at Botrange.
The spot is marked by the Signal de
Botrange tower, whose additional
height bumps the elevation up over
700m. The Botrange offers views over
the pale grass moors of Hautes
Fagnes, west to the provincial capital
of Liège, east to the park's German
section and south to the dark forested
hills of the Ardennes.

Seasonal change

The Hautes Fagnes is one of the
wettest and coldest areas of Belgium.
Often shrouded in mist and low
cloud, the area receives a bountiful
1.5m of rain every year. The result is
a wealth of ecologically important
raised sphagnum bogs, which cover
both the plateaux and valley basins.

The spongy sphagnum moss retains
water and forms peat as it decays,
providing habitats for rare ferns and
flowering plants. Some of the bogs are
over 10,000 years old, and much of
the park's conservation work revolves
around them. Walking within the
reserve is limited to marked paths,
and raised wooden walkways protect
both the environment and ramblers'
feet. Outside the confines of the
reserve exploration is less regulated,
and visitors are free to wander
through the forests and farmland.

In winter, all of this water translates
to snow, and the Hautes Fagnes
becomes one of Belgium's top cross-
country ski centres. This is also a
spectacular time to visit the reserve
as the walkways offer excellent views

Hautes Fagnes is carpeted in snow in winter

across the fens, blanketed in their coat of snow. No parallel ski tracks will disturb this smooth white expanse but visitors may see the prints of deer or of any of the park's 160 species of bird.

Areas of snow which look as if they have been scuffed or kicked will probably be a lek, the stomping ground of the black grouse. These birds are protected in Belgium as the destruction of their moorland habitats has endangered them both here and elsewhere in Europe.

A healthy population lives within the park and they are easily spotted perched in the bare branches of trees. Males are coal-black, with distinctive red crests raised above their eyes like startled brows. Females are less dramatically feathered, but both sexes can reach over half a metre in length.

Botrange and beyond

Most of the walks within the reserve at Hautes Fagnes begin by the visitors' centre at the foot of the Signal de Botrange. The centre hosts an exhibition on the 500 million year history of the park's landscape, imaginatively housed in an underground 'time tunnel'.

Guided walks and rides leave from the centre all year round, and both skis and bicycles can be hired here. An alternative method of viewing the park is onboard the Vennbahn, a restored steam train, which departs near Eupen for trips through Hautes Fagnes and over the border into the German Eifel forests.

For visitors wishing to explore further afield, 560km of trails lead through the rural and forested cantons

immediately adjoining the park. Environmentally friendly travel options are being extended by the RAVeL scheme, a project which aims to link more than 2,000 canal towpaths and decommissioned railway lines for cycling and walking. Routes to date include an old railway line heading towards the Ardennes, a westward trail to Liège and a crescent linking the settlements of Spa and Stavelot on the park's border.

Spa

The town of Spa sits on the boundary between the Eifel fenlands and the Ardennes and, as its name suggests, is famous for the waters which rise here. Historically frequented by European monarchy and aristocracy, the town retains an air of faded splendour in its buildings and public areas. It is still popular with visitors who wish either to take or bathe in the waters, which are rich in iron and other minerals, leached from the soil of the Hautes Fagnes.

Coo-Stavelot is the starting point for canoe trips on the River Amblève. Further north, the village of Robertville has a restored medieval castle. Using 17th century engravings, the castle was rebuilt in the 1970s and today houses displays on the Middle Ages. From Robertville it is less than an hours journey west to Liège – once an important ecclesiastical centre and now home to museums of modern, Walloon, religious and decorative arts.

CONTACT INFORMATION

Hautes Fagnes Nature Park Visitor Centre
Centre Nature à Botrange
B-4950 Robertville
Belgium
Tel: (00 32) 80 440300
Fax: (00 32) 80 444429
E-mail: botrange.centrenature
@skynet.be
Web: www.ful.ac.be/
Hotes/cnatbotrange

Liège Province Tourism
Boulevard de la Sauveniere, 77
B-4000 Liege
Belgium
Tel: (00 32) 4 232 6510
Fax: (00 32) 4 232 6511
E-mail: ftpl@euronet.be
Web: www.colvert.be/ftpliege

Walkways cross the fragile peat bogs

Biesbosch National Park

In a country perpetually struggling with the sea, Biesbosch protects the shifting zone where water and land meet.

Exploring the park's woodlands by boat

More water than land, Biesbosch National Park covers 71 sq km of the Maas and Waal river deltas. Originally the delta met the North Sea at Zeeland further to the west, but human interventions have meant that the environment which is now protected by the national park is not a naturally occurring one.

Tides of change

Until the 15th century, the Biesbosch was a polder – land below sea level which has been reclaimed using dykes and dams. Water was pumped away by windmills and the land was used for pasture and agriculture.

In 1421, St Elisabeth's flood devastated the area, covering sixteen villages and leaving behind a vast inland lake fed by the Mass and Waal. The North Sea was also free to enter and the action of the tides and rivers formed pools, as well as banks and islands where rushes, reeds, and later willows grew.

This was the natural state of the Biesbosch, but local people had not given up their claims and in the 16th century reclamations began again.

By the mid 19th century, two thirds of the Biesbosch had been reclaimed and the mighty Nieuwe Merwede canal was dug. Reclamations continued and by the end of the Second World War, the area was heavily farmed and populated, but peace was to be short lived. In February 1953, spring tides

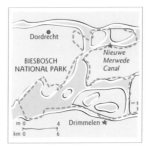

and severe storms combined forces to batter down the dykes of Zeeland. Despite an international relief effort 1,835 people died and as a result the ambitious Deltaplan was formed.

The Deltaplan

The Deltaplan aimed to prevent a similar disaster by closing the four sea-arms of the river delta.

The closure of the first two arms, the Volkerak and Haringvliet, was completed by 1970, using a complex system of locks, sluices and gates to enable ships to come in and the river waters to drain out to the North Sea. Special canals accommodated fish migration and huge slides could be lowered to completely secure the defences in the event of storms.

Before 1970, the Biesbosch had been fully tidal, experiencing differences in water levels of 2m. The Deltaplan altered the environment; some areas remained tidal (but with reduced variations in water levels), while others were cut off from the sea and formed marshes and lagoons. Certain plants and animals could not survive the transformation and disappeared, to be replaced by new species, more suited to stable environments.

The changing balance is ongoing as further outlets of the delta were blocked and the ecosystems of the Biesbosch are still evolving. Since the national park was formed in 1994 attention has been given to reopening parts of the delta to greater tidal fluctuations, enabling the Biesbosch to revert to a more natural state.

A beaver at work

Osier cutters and others

Prior to the Deltaplan, the Biesbosch wetlands were accustomed to human activity. Eel and salmon fishing, duck hunting, reed cutting and basket weaving provided employment.

The main industry, however, was osier cutting. Beds of willows were cultivated for their young branches which were used for baskets and stakes. The demand created by the construction of the Netherland's longest dyke, the Afsluitdijk, in the 1930s was such that the beds at the Biesbosch were stripped and more had to be planted.

Osier cutting was hard and dirty work and when the demand for osier declined in the 1950s the beds were neglected. They reverted to the woodlands which now cover the majority of the land in the park. In a few places the osier-beds have been maintained in the traditional manner.

On water

Today the Biesbosch is a freshwater tidal area which consists of waterways – rivers, canals, streams and pools – interspersed with small holms and islands. By far the best way to get around is by boat and it is the only way to explore certain areas.

There are several options available to visitors. Tour boats operate within the park, going as far afield as the harbours and quays of Dordrecht. Ferries operate between the islands and rowing boats, canoes and silent electric boats can be hired from the visitor centres. At present, private boats are allowed within the park, although due to efforts to reduce pollution, this is likely to cease in the future.

Using a smaller craft will enable visitors to explore narrow waterways where rushes, purple loosestrife and the yellow flowers of the spindotter, a large marsh marigold unique to the area, crowd the banks. Kingfishers flash across the water in a blue blur, while large dragonflies skim its surface. In summer the air is full of the fine song of the bluethroat. Half of the Netherland's bluethroat population breed in the park, their blue bib and red tail distinguishing them from other songbirds. The open water and mudflats are where the waterfowl and wading birds live, as well as the burrowing muskrat. Unfortunately, because of water pollution fish are unlikely to be seen.

On dry land

Most of the park's footpaths can only be accessed by water and landing stages on the islets allow boating and walking to be combined. There are a variety of tracks available, passing through rush-beds, polders and marshes. Paths which are marked as 'boot tracks' are boggy and uneven – proper footwear will be required.

Some of the more rewarding routes are through the reverted osier woods. Forty types of willow grow in the Biesbosch and, as they have aged, other plants have sprung up in their midst. Willow-herb, valerian and rich damp mosses all attract insects and birds in turn. Field voles, nordic voles, deer and beavers also live here.

For those who prefer not to take to the water, there are cycle tracks and footpaths along the Nieuwe Merwede canal. Other possibilities include guided nature walks from the visitor centres at Dordrecht and Drimmelen.

[i] CONTACT INFORMATION

**Biesbosch National Park
Visitor Centre**
Bezoekerscentrum
De Holland Biesbosch
Baanhoekweg 53
3313 LP Dordrecht
The Netherlands
Tel: (00 31) 78 630 5353
Fax: (00 31) 78 630 5350
E-mail: biesbosch@antenna.nl
Web: www.minlnv.nl/parken/
biesbosch

Traditional osier-bed with yellow spindotters

Hoge Veluwe National Park

Take advantage of Hoge Veluwe's distinctive white bikes to explore the hills and open plains of a national park in the 'Other Holland'.

The Netherlands' largest national park, the Hoge Veluwe, is found in the east of the country in the province of Gelderland. Nowhere in the Netherlands is isolated, but here, expanses of forest, heath and wetland create a surprising aura of space in this densely populated land.

The Other Holland

Gelderland, together with the abutting provinces of Flevoland and Overijssel, form a region known as the 'Other Holland'. Only an hour from Amsterdam, this area nevertheless escapes the urban sprawl. Its dominant feature is water: the Waal, Lek, Maas, Rijn and Ijssel rivers in Gelderland; the canals, lakes and rivers of Overijssel; and in Flevoland, a province reclaimed from the sea, the residual rush-filled wetlands.

The Netherlands' relationship with water is a troubled one. It was the sea which raised the country to its pinnacle of international power between the 16th and 18th centuries when the ships of the Dutch East India Company sailed the world in search of colonies and trade. Yet, with half of the country lying at or below sea level, and dykes and huge pumps working constantly to maintain the status quo, water can also claim its toll. As recently as 1995, vast areas of Gelderland were evacuated when flooding rivers threatened to burst their banks.

Hoge Veluwe

Hoge means 'high' and Hoge Veluwe National Park occupies an elevated plateau, characterised by woodlands, heaths, expanses of shifting sands and marshy fens. In summer, the vast stretch of pale heath grasses are reminiscent of prairie lands, while autumn colour is provided by the leaves of oak and beech copses, and cushions of purple heather. Red and roe deer, moufflon, wild boar and pine martens inhabit the park and observation hides increase the

chances of sightings. In forested areas both black and lesser spotted woodpeckers can be seen, as well as the more diminutive crested tit.

There are well-paved walking and cycling trails throughout the Hoge Veluwe and getting around is simplified by the 'white bike' scheme. Free bicycles can be picked up at the entrance and are ideal for exploring the park before being dropped off at the end of the day.

Art and nature

One of the park's highlights is the collection of fine art accumulated by Helene Kröller-Müller, on whose estate the park was founded. The purpose-built gallery draws as many visitors to the park as the natural landscape does. Paintings exhibited include works by Seurat, Picasso, Léger, Mondrian and Braque. A stunning room is dedicated to some of the 278 Van Gogh paintings owned by the gallery. The gallery's sculpture garden is one of the largest in Europe, where pieces by Auguste Rodin, Barbara Hepworth, Mario Merz and Henry Moore vie for attention. As the gallery is closed on Mondays, visitors can take advantage of the fact that white bikes are consequently more readily available.

In addition to St Hubertus, an art deco hunting lodge built for the Kröller-Müllers, cultural attractions

Cyclists explore the park on their white bikes

Shifting sands in Hoge Veluwe

preserved and the 34 sq km of Weerribben encompasses peatlands, reedbeds, water meadows and bogs where notable species of aquatic plants grow. Traditional human activities such as reed cutting and woodland coppicing continue in the park, and birds and butterflies abound. Wieden and Weerribben are also home to a rare sub-species of the large copper butterfly, found nowhere else in the world. The butterfly is easily recognisable in flight from the orange-white flicker of its wings.

To the south of Weerribben the villages of Blokzijl and Vollenhove were once fishing ports on the Zuider Zee, which has now been drained and access to the North Sea blocked by a dyke. The villages have been restored to reflect their maritime past, and feature well-preserved buildings, pretty streets and charming harbours.

include the Openluchtmuseum on the park's border. This open air museum displays Dutch buildings, some over 250 years old, complete with period furnishings, bicycles and toys. Houses are grouped into mock villages to represent different regions of the Netherlands through the ages.

Flevoland

Flevoland is a polder on the coast to the north-west of Gelderland. Polders are areas of low-lying reclaimed land (in the Netherlands they can be as low as 4.5m below sea level) and parts of Flevoland only emerged from the sea in the 1970s. In Oostvaardersplassen to the south, water was allowed to remain when the polder was drained and the area is now an important protected wetland. Some woodlands have developed in the reserve, but it is predominantly covered in grass, rush and scrub, a habitat which attracts vast numbers of birds. Facilities for ornithologists include walkways, a resource centre and hides, and on a bird-watching trip visitors may see cormorants, bitterns, egrets, spoonbills and herons, as well as more common wildfowl.

North of Oostvaardersplassen, two museums show opposing sides of the Netherlands' struggle with the sea. The Nieuw Land Poldermuseum at Lelystad explains the process of land reclamation, while at Ketelhaven, the National Museum of Ship Archaeology displays some of the 430 excavated shipwrecks, which have been located off the Other Holland's coast.

Overijssel

The Overijssel waterland, a province to the north-east of Gelderland, is a lacy network of rivers, canals, streams and lakes. Many of the channels were formed by extensive peat mining and now provide a habitat for wildlife and flora, as well as a playground for canoeists, walkers and nature-lovers. The most beautiful areas are within the Weerribben National Park, and in the smaller Wieden reserve. Here the fragile ecosystem of the wetlands has been

ℹ CONTACT INFORMATION

Hoge Veluwe National Park
Apeldoornseweg 250
7351 TA Hoenderloo
The Netherlands
Tel: (00 31) 318 591627
Fax: (00 31) 5318 592248
Web: www.hogeveluwe.nl

Heaths and woodlands form much of the landscape

Schleswig-Holstein Wadden Sea National Park

*A shoreline teeming with life is both a protected habitat
and an ideal place for a sunny seaside holiday.*

The Wadden Sea, or Wattenmeer, is the name given to the 500km of North Sea coastline that stretches from Den Helder in the Netherlands to Esbjerg in Denmark. *Watten* are mudflats, and the Wattenmeer refers to the seascape of tidal flats, dunes, creeks, bays, estuaries, mud and sandbanks that are characteristic of the region. The largest unbroken environment of its type in the world, it is not surprising that efforts should be taken to preserve such a treasure, and virtually the entire German section is protected by national park status. The stretch from the Dutch border to the Elbe estuary is taken care of in the Lower Saxony and Hamburg Wadden Sea National Parks, while from the Elbe northwards, the Schleswig-Holstein Wadden Sea National Park looks after this beautiful but sensitive coastline.

Avocet with young

The national park

Created in 1985, and declared a Ramsar site and a UNESCO biosphere reserve in 1990, the park aims both to preserve the natural state of the coastline, and allow visitors to experience the environment without harming it. Covering 4,410 sq km, the park includes tidal flats, salt marshes on the mainland and island coasts, outlying sandbanks, and most of the low lying salt marsh islands.

In between land and sea

Moving away from the mainland towards the sea, the terrain usually passes through the following stages: dykes; salt marshes; mudflats; mixed flats; sand flats; occasional sand banks; and finally the open sea. Through these vast expanses of tidal flats run creeks and channels that provide the main routes for the tide that for six hours floods the plain, and for six hours retreats.

Guided walking tours across the flats offer a safe way of exploring this habitat. Although the flats may seem innocuous, the tide can come in at speed; if walking alone, it is essential to be aware of the tide tables.

If the mudflats sometimes appear monotonous, the open horizons, especially when sunsets shimmer across the sea and wet sands, are often transformed into a magical combination of light and water.

The seasons are reflected too in different ways. Spring brings with it the colourful fields of yellow rapeseed on the mainland, and during summer – the most popular time for visiting – the beaches are ideal for swimming and watersports. Autumn and winter, although cold, can actually provide the more dramatic scenery. Bad weather displays the drama of the storm tides and flooding, while frozen mudflats against a pale blue wintry sky also have a desolate calm beauty.

Walking across the mudflats to one of the Halligen

Animal life

The sand and mudflats provide homes for a myriad of living organisms, which in turn become food for millions of birds and fish. The mass of living material on the floor of the Wadden Sea is ten times greater than that on the North Sea bed, and plays a prominent role in the area's ecosystem. Rag, bristle and lugworms, snails, amphipods, sand gapers, cockles and mussels provide a huge feeding ground at low tide for ducks, gulls and waders.

Both a popular bird breeding ground and resting point on migrations, the park can at times be inundated by up to 1.3 million birds, including brent geese, grey plovers, dunlins, pintails, knots, shelducks, redshanks, terns, bar-tailed godwits, avocets, curlews and sanderlings. In midsummer, a particular sight is the annual visit of shelducks; almost the entire European population arrives off the island of Trischen for their mass moult. Here the birds find ample food for their brief flightless period.

On the sandbanks, seals haul themselves out of the water to bear and suckle their young, and sunbathe to stock up on vitamin D, needed during their annual moult. The harbour seal population of the park now stands at around 6,000, with a lesser number of grey seals.

A flock of dunlins

Marsh plants

Very few plants grow in the tidal area, the main exception being the eelgrass upon which hungry brent geese feast. However, in the salt marshes that lie above the normal high-water mark, vegetation abounds with salt-tolerant plants. The lower marshes host sea-lavender, sea-aster, sea-mugwort and sea-blite, while Danish scurvygrass, sea-plantain, thrift, greater and lesser sea-spurrey and arrow grass thrive in the middle and upper reaches.

Islands

A particular feature of the area is the Halligen, low islands that are relics of a fenland expanse which was once part of the mainland. Here farmsteads are built up on embankments called *warfts*. During storms or spring tides, the Halligen, unprotected by dykes, are flooded; the farmhouses are then the only thing above land, looking a bit like Noah's Ark.

In the north of the park, the islands of Föhr, Amrum and Sylt are ideal resorts for a summer holiday, with long wave-swept beaches offering challenges for swimmers and surfers.

Towns and resorts

The cultural centre of Schleswig-Holstein's west coast, Husum, is known as 'the grey town on the sea', and was birthplace to the poet and novelist Theodor Storm. The harbour, prettily decorated with fishing boats, is a good starting point for trips to the islands, while old streets and alleys with tall gabled houses give a charm to the centre.

St Peter-Ording, on the Eiderstedt peninsula, is the biggest resort, with swimming beaches, white dunes and a farm park. The symbol of the peninsula is Westerhever's red and white striped lighthouse. At a height of 41.5m, the light can be seen for 40km in fine weather. Dagebüll is an excellent starting point for mudflat walking, while the port of Tönning is the centre for the park itself.

ⓘ CONTACT INFORMATION

Schleswig-Holstein Wadden Sea National Park
Schlossgarten 1
25832 Tönning
Germany
Tel: (00 49) 4861 6160
Fax: (00 49) 4861 61669

National Parks of Germany's Baltic Coast

Golden beaches and dazzling white cliffs characterise the peaceful mainland and islands of Germany's Baltic coast.

The chalk cliffs of Jasmund National Park

Along the coast of Mecklenburg-Vorpommern in north-east Germany, broad sandy beaches and reed and salt flats are enhanced by cliffs and elegant beech forests. The seascape is a gentle one, with a pleasant maritime climate. Between Rostock and Greifswald, the sensitive ecology of one of the few unspoiled natural landscapes in central Europe is protected by two national parks and a variety of nature reserves.

Bodden

Created in 1990, the Vorpommersche Boddenlandschaft National Park stretches east from the Fischland–Darß–Zingst peninsula over the islands of Bock, Werder and Hiddensee to the west coast of the Isle of Rügen. Within its boundaries are diverse shorelines, dunes, wind flats, salt marshes, and the *bodden* that give the park its name.

The bodden are shallow depressions carved out by glaciers during the last Ice Age. Rising sea levels have since partially flooded the land to create the islands, ridges and peninsulas that characterise the region today.

The shallow waters of the bodden hold rich stocks of worms and shellfish, and entice many migratory birds to the area. Chief amongst these are the cranes that arrive in their thousands during the autumn on their way from Scandinavia and Eastern Europe to Spain. Around the small islands of Ummanz and Kirr, inaccessible reed and salt flats offer a safe haven to shy bird species such as reed kites, redshanks, reed warblers and curlews.

Fischland–Darß–Zingst

Originally, the three sections of the peninsula were separate islands, but the action of the sea, coupled with the creation of dykes, gradually formed a peninsula. Constituting the greater part of the national park's land area, Darß is particularly scenic, with its mile-long sandy beach and wooded tracts. Darß forest is currently protected from human intervention so that it can regenerate itself, but footpaths allow access through it. In the Zingst area, footpaths also pass through the Osterwald, 800 hectares of woodland, and over the high white sand-dunes near Pramort.

Hiddensee and Rügen

East of the Zingst peninsula, Hiddensee is the largest island in the park. 18km long, it has a varied landscape of woodland, heaths, moors, sand flats and salt marshes. The western and northern coastlines also possess some of Germany's best sandy beaches. Reached by ferry from Stralsund or the Isle of Rügen, Hiddensee remains a peaceful haven thanks to the absence of private cars.

A causeway across the Strelasund, or Strela Sound, links the Isle of Rügen with the mainland town of Stralsund. The largest German island, Rügen's charm stems largely from the bodden, beech woods, rounded hills and shining white cliffs that are juxtaposed along its shores.

On the west coast, walks along the sand-bars offer views over the bodden and good bird-watching opportunities. In the north at Cape Arkona are the remains of the Jaromarsburg, a fortified Slav settlement that was once an important sanctuary of Western Slavs. The central position

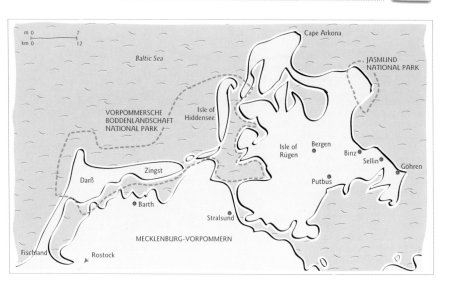

of Rügen's capital, Bergen, makes it a good base for exploring. In the town museum, the main theme is the Christianisation of the islanders that occurred after the Danish conquest in 1168. Exhibits on Slavic temples and the worship of the four-faced god Swantevit lead to displays on the 12th century Cistercian monastery.

Culture and traditions

The historic buildings in the town of Stralsund make a visit to the city a pleasant experience. It boasts three imposing brick-built Gothic churches, whilst the front of the town hall has one of the best examples of secular Gothic architecture in northern Germany. The Meeresmuseum (marine museum) has one of Europe's largest aquariums, with displays on marine

biology and the flora and fauna of the Baltic coast. The Museum of Cultural History gives an insight into folk traditions including regional craftsmanship such as medieval gold jewellery from Hiddensee.

Jasmund National Park

Covering just 30 sq km on the Jasmund peninsula of Rügen Island, and fulfilling the old adage 'small is beautiful', Jasmund is the smallest national park in Germany. Lying between Sassnitz and Lohme, the park displays the 69 million year old chalk massif that forms the bedrock of the peninsula. A subterranean upheaval during the Ice Age threw up a chalk rift, creating the Stubbenkammer chalk cliffs that rise in white sheerness from the waves.

The most spectacular are known as the Wissower Klinken, the view from which was made famous by the Romantic painter Caspar David Friedrich. These, along with the majestic Königstuhl cliff, are the main landmarks of the island itself.

Inland from the chalk coast, the colour changes of the beautiful Stubnitz beech woods mark the passing seasons, whilst ash, alder, maple, wild cherry, pear and apple offer variety, and yew and ivy provide darker shades of green. The sources of bogs, springs and brooks create wetlands for moisture-loving plants such as drosera, marsh marigolds, cotton grass and sphagnum moss. At the edge of the park, the port of Sassnitz-Mukran operates international ferry links, while local boat excursions run from Sassnitz.

ⓘ CONTACT INFORMATION

Vorpommersche Boddenlandschaft National Park
Im Forst 5
D-18375 Born/Darß
Germany
Tel: (00 49) 382 345020
Fax: (00 49) 382 3450 224

Rügen – National Park Office
Blieschow 7a
D-18586 Lancken-Granitz
Germany
Tel: (00 49) 38303 8850 (Vorpomm.)
Tel: (00 49) 38392 35011 (Jasmund)

Forest on the Darß peninsula

Müritz National Park

Sparkling or sombre lakes, golden sand-dunes and imposing beech forests are some of the many attractions to be found in the German Lake District.

From the beautiful beaches of the Baltic coast, the German state of Mecklenburg-Vorpommern spreads southward, displaying the gentle hills, sandy landscape and lakes that are characteristic features of the North German Plain. To the south-west, the lakes are so numerous that the region is known as the Mecklenburg Lake District, the largest lakeland region in Germany. Within this area are parks and plains such as the Strelitz Lakeland Plain, the Feldberg Lake District, the Nossentiner/Schwinzer Heide Park, and last but not least the Müritz National Park.

Müritz National Park

Lake Müritz, the largest lake in the Mecklenburg Lake District, and indeed in Germany, lends its name to the national park that was opened in 1990. 'Müritz' is derived from a Slavic word meaning 'sea', and with a surface area of 117 sq km the name is hardly an exaggeration. On a stormy day, the wild waters can take on the

dramatic aspect of rough sea waves. The park itself covers a total area of 300 sq km, and is divided into two parts. The bigger section to the west of Neustrelitz runs along the east side of Lake Müritz. The much smaller eastern area centres around the village of Serrahn, and is home to the park's highest point, the 143.5m Hirschberg.

Shaping the landscape

Retreating Ice Age glaciers left the hollows, moraines and sandy deposits that form the basis of the park's landscape. The hollows became lakes and ponds, of which there are more than a hundred, while the wind piled the sand into dunes, which in places are large enough to seem like hills.

Today the vast majority of woodland is pine, although the beech woods around Serrahn that have been uncultivated for over 40 years give an impression of virgin forest. Variety is also provided by indigenous alder and birch, along with the foreign Douglas

fir, European larch and American red oak that were planted from the 19th century onwards.

The park's fenland is rich and various, as the bogs have been formed in different ways. Some are the result of shallow lakes silting up; basin bogs are fed by water running down from the moraine ridges; and several moors are fed by springs. When the outlet to Lake Müritz, the Elde, was made navigable about 200 years ago, the resultant fall in water level of over 1.5m also led to the establishment of reed beds around the lake edge.

The industrialisation of agriculture, with its intensive use of fertilisers and pesticides, damaged much of the area's meadowland. However, since the 1970s Swedish Fjäll cattle and Gotland sheep have been kept on protected fields near Müritzhof; the gentle grazing has allowed the return of forest pasture, where threatened flowers such as orchids and gentians can thrive undisturbed.

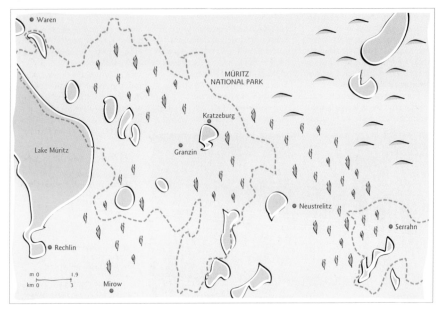

Flooded birch forest

Nearby nature parks

Mecklenburg-Vorpommern boasts a total of 261 nature reserves, some of which are to be found in two nature parks within easy reach of Müritz.

Nossentiner/Schwinzer Heide is the larger and lies to the north-west. Its lakes offer swimming, angling and boating, and the vast heathlands can be explored on foot, horseback or by bike, along the many signposted trails. A particular point of interest is the Benedictine monastery at Dobbertin that dates back to 1220.

By contrast, the Feldberg Nature Park to the east of Müritz is known for a natural phenomenon, its eagle population; every tenth sea eagle in Germany makes its home here. The forests are special too; the oldest beech trees in Germany at the Heilige Hallen reserve give an insight into the atmosphere of a primeval woodscape.

Birds

For bird-watchers, the national park is an ideal destination. Müritz is famous for white-tailed eagles, black storks and ospreys, but over 145 bird species in total breed here. Observation posts provide the opportunity to see osprey eyries, or watch the magnificent passage of cranes in the autumn.

Thousands of bean and white-fronted geese, tufted ducks, goosanders, smews and swans use the lakes as resting grounds on their migrations, some even staying until the waters ice over. Bird-watching excursions are run by the park authorities.

Waterways

Canoeing is a relaxing way of discovering some of the lakes, rivers and canals, especially as a ban on motorboats ensures tranquillity.

One route leads from Lake Müritz to the sheltered, narrow lakes near Mirow, while another runs along the River Havel from Kratzeburg, offering varied landscapes of swamps, reeds and forests. Green and yellow buoys designate the routes and closed off sections respectively. Where parts of the river are inaccessible to boats, overland paths are clearly marked, and boat-trolleys provided.

i CONTACT INFORMATION

Müritz National Park
Schloßplatz 3
D-17237 Hohenzieritz
Germany
Tel: (00 49) 39824 2520
Fax: (00 49) 39824 25250
E-mail: info@nationalpark-mueritz.de
Web: www.nationalpark-mueritz.de

There are over one hundred lakes in Müritz National Park

Lower Oder Valley National Park

*On the German–Polish border, the flood-plains of the
Lower Oder valley offer diverse habitats for many
endangered species of plants, animals and birds.*

In the region of Brandenburg in eastern Germany, an area associated mainly with agriculture, forestry and mining, lies the Lower Oder Valley National Park. Owing to its situation on the frontier with Poland, the region was left largely undeveloped, allowing the unusual flood-plains around the River Oder to survive.

The area was the first in the old East Germany to achieve national park status after reunification. Planned as part of a joint German–Polish conservation project, the park adjoins the Polish Lower Oder Valley Nature Park. The parks run for 60km along the Polish border, from Hohensaaten to Szczecin, and together protect the largest surviving natural flood-plains in central Europe.

River Oder

On the flat lands of the Lower Oder valley mingle forests, marshes, dry meadows and water meadows. During

Spring adonis

the 20th century, polder systems were constructed following Dutch models to reclaim and protect farm land. In the south of the park are dry polders, where fields are sufficiently protected by dykes to avoid flooding. However, the central area of some 5,000 hectares, between the villages of Stützkow and Friedrichsthal, consists of wet polders, flooded each year from November to April.

In the Polish area, known as the Zwischenoderland, the polder system was partially destroyed during the Second World War, and not rebuilt afterwards. For fifty years, the landscape was left to itself and has been able to revert to a natural water meadow system which is also flooded during the winter.

As a whole, the region not only acts as a retention basin, protecting towns further downstream from flood damage, but is also an ecological sewage treatment plant. Micro-organisms are able to break down many of the pollutants in the Oder's waters before the river finally recedes.

Plants

The vegetation within the park varies according to the water level. On the slopes, hardwood trees such as English oaks, elms and ash are found, whilst softwoods that appreciate water flourish in the areas that flood. White willow, common alders and black poplars constitute much of the riverside forest, especially in the polders near Lunow.

A number of steppe plants such as the blue cross-gentian, the yellow spring adonis, pheasant's eye and silver feather grass bloom in the dry meadows, along with many orchids. The woods shelter liverwort and anemones, while the water meadows offer moist habitats for lady's-smock and marsh marigolds. Reeds, bulrushes and irises grow by the riverbanks, and the still backwaters harbour waterlilies.

Ornithology

Of the 200 plus bird varieties spotted in the park, about 120 actually breed here as well, including endangered species such as white and black storks, ospreys, white-tailed eagles and lesser spotted eagles. The site is the most important breeding ground in Germany for the threatened

Red-necked grebe

A dead arm of the Oder

Szczecin

THE POLISH
LOWER ODER VALLEY
NATIONAL PARK

Gartz

West Oder

East Oder

GERMANY

Vierraden
*Friedrichstal
Canal*

Schwedt

LOWER ODER
VALLEY
NATIONAL PARK

Criewen

Oder

Stolpe

POLAND

Hohensaaten

m 0 — 3
km 0 — 5

aquatic warbler and corncrake, and
the marshy slopes are also ideal
breeding sites for cranes.

Other species include kingfishers,
grebes, woodpeckers, nuthatches,
cormorants, owls, lapwings and
herons, as well as geese, swans and
ducks. Thousands of the latter use
the water meadows as a passage and
resting point on both their winter
and spring migrations.

For keen ornithologists, the park
wardens provide information on the
best times and places to see the
various species; watch stations have
also been set up to allow observation
without disturbing the birds.

Frogs

Amongst the rarer amphibian species
found in the park are firebellied toads
and tree frogs, and visitors are asked
to report sightings to the authorities.
The creatures are often encountered
at twilight, moving from their
spawning grounds to new waters. To
prevent them being squashed by cars,
the frogs used to be escorted across
the road by a local nature group.
Now tunnels are being constructed.

Whilst beavers and otters enjoy the
waterlands, the forests are home to
pine and stone martens, badgers,
stoats, deer, boars, foxes, squirrels
and hedgehogs.

The annual flooding of the Oder

Schloss Criewen

The focal point of the park is Schloss Criewen, currently being renovated to house the park's foundation, a library and a visitor centre. The building will serve as a German–Polish meeting centre, its current status as both geographical and cultural heart of the park suiting this role admirably. Similar in style to a large manor

Common rosefinch

house, the castle was built in the 1820s as the home of Captain von Arnim. The church next to the castle used to be the focal point of Criewen village; unfortunately for the villagers, the Captain preferred privacy and they were simply relocated to what is now the present site of Criewen.

Activities in the park

The park can be discovered by foot, bicycle or horse-drawn carriage. In winter, however, the only possibility of exploring the flooded polders is by bicycle along the dyke paths. Near Stolpe, a round tower with 5m thick walls is all that remains of a 12th century stronghold. Its position gives good views over the dry meadows. Stettiner Berg, a hill to the north, overlooks part of the Polish park, and an open border at Mescherin allows walkers and cyclists to explore it.

Uniformed rangers are happy to answer questions about the ecology and nature of the region, and the park also organises themed weekend walks. Bike and boat hire is available, there are several riding centres, and boat trips run up to Szczecin.

Schwedt and Vierraden

Schwedt lies at the centre of the park on the Friedrichstal waterway, a canal that runs parallel to the River Oder. Once known simply as an industrial town, its emphasis is now being changed by the influence of the surrounding nature parks. Points of interest include the Vierradener Straße, with sculptures and fountains; and the Berlischky Pavilion, a concert hall built in 1779 as a church for the French Reformed Community.

In nearby Vierraden, a museum provides information about the tobacco plant which has been a local crop since the end of the 17th century. Drying tobacco leaves can be seen in barns all along the valley, and there is still a yearly festival to celebrate the end of the harvest.

ⓘ CONTACT INFORMATION

Lower Oder Valley National Park
Bootsweg 1
16303 Schwedt
Germany
Tel: (00 49) 3332 25470
Fax: (00 49) 3332 254733

Early morning mist in the Oder valley

GERMANY

Harz and Hochharz National Parks

Wild mountains, spruce forests, bogs and sparkling streams create an untamed land with an invigorating climate and inspiring scenery.

Torfhaus Moor •

Stretching out for sixty miles across central Germany, the Harz mountains mark the boundary between the north German lowlands and the southern uplands. Once split by the East / West partition, the mysterious hills and valleys of the region can now be explored as a unified whole.

Towards the east, the Lower Harz has fertile loamy soil, where beech wood-covered slopes gradually rise to the Upper Harz plateau. Here, huge expanses of moor and forest are fissured by gorges and torrential streams, creating a virtually uninhabited landscape where heathen rituals once took place, and legends of witches still survive.

Echoing this primordial atmosphere, the ecology of the area includes environments remarkably close to their natural states, providing valuable habitats for rare wildlife and plants. And not everything is foreboding: in the summer over a hundred lakes and reservoirs are beautiful spots for a pleasant ramble, while mountain villages and hillfoot towns offer both character and a chance to rest and benefit from the clear air.

The national parks

While the entire mountain range is designated a nature park, two national parks lie at the heart of the landscape. Founded in 1990, the Upper Harz National Park in Saxony-Anhalt covers an area of almost 65 sq km around the Brocken, which at 1,142m is the highest and best-known mountain of the Harz massif.

Adjoining this park on the west side is the Harz National Park of Lower Saxony, which offers protection to a further 158 sq km of woodland. Reaching from Bad Harzburg in the north to Herzberg and the Oder reservoir in the south, this park covers altitudes of all levels, providing at least six different vegetative regions. Between them, the parks

include evergreen and broad-leaved forests, bogs, alpine meadowland, cliff-faces and mountain streams.

Activities and awareness

8,000km of marked paths and plenty of ski trails mean that the region can be explored in winter or summer, and opportunities abound for swimming, caving, canoeing, climbing or hang-gliding. Yet, while the national parks make every effort to let the visitor appreciate the natural beauty, they also ask tourists to help by keeping to paths, making as little disturbance as possible, and generally allowing nature to be itself in peace.

Boulders in the spruce forest

The Brocken

Centrepiece of the Harz, the rounded granite peak of the Brocken is surrounded by myths to match its harsh appearance. Above Thale, a small town to the east, a rock shelf overlooking the dramatic Bode valley is known as the Hexentanzplatz – the witches' dancing place. This was a prehistoric cult site and, according to tradition, witches would meet there on Walpurgis night (April 30th / May 1st) before flying through the mountains to dance with the Devil on the Brocken.

Goethe climbed the peak in 1777, then still a relatively dangerous trek, and later recreated the wild atmosphere in nightmarish scenes in his *Faust*. Since his trip, tourist traffic has vastly increased; a popular trail to the peak named after the writer follows his route closely, while a steam railway is a pleasant way to travel to the summit.

Up to 50,000 people a day now visit the Brocken, inevitably causing damage, and unfortunately the most sensitive sites have to be cordoned off. Information on all aspects of the park can be found in the Brocken museum, housed in what is left of the old East German military buildings on the plateau.

Forests

The vast majority of the park area is forested, mostly by spruce trees. The reason for this monotony lies largely with man's interference. Since the 12th century, the Harz has been mined for its lead, zinc, copper, silver and even gold. Wood was needed for building the mines and firing the metal processing furnaces; as a result, indigenous beech, birch, maple and rowan trees were replaced with quick-growing spruce.

Now, many of the spruce have been killed by a particular bark beetle, and gradually the forests are developing into self-sustaining ecosystems. Only indigenous spruces are being retained, to allow the broad-leaved trees that belong to the area a chance to re-establish themselves, particularly the rowan.

The rocky slopes of the Harz mountains

Peat bogs

Compared with other central European middle range mountains, a distinguishing feature of the Harz is the extent of its peaty marshland. The Upper Harz alone has almost 5 sq km of moor, including the high Torfhaus Moor (also known as the Radauerborn Moor) that dates back to 8300 BC. Although much damage was caused by large-scale peat cutting in the 18th century, the sites are now protected.

Pollen analysis has enabled a general understanding of the development of the peatlands, and it is now known that the isolation of the Harz has allowed the preservation of species over thousands of years. The Brocken anemone, wolf's foot, dwarf birches, alpine hawkweed, emerald dragonflies and ring ouzels are amongst Ice Age relics that flourish here.

Wildlife

The woods give ample shelter for red, fallow and roe deer, along with foxes, pine martens and wildcats. A bird sanctuary in Osterode allows a chance to see some of over fifty species from the area in spacious aviaries, particularly interesting in the spring when black grouse, capercaillies and ptarmigans put on their courtship displays.

Picturesque towns

Sankt Andreasberg, nestling in the centre of the Harz National Park, has steep streets and bright wooden houses. The Samson and Catharina Neufang mines are open to the public as museums, showing old mine shafts and still-operational winch systems dating from the 1830s. In contrast, Wernigerode to the east is a medieval town with curious old buildings such as the Kleinste Haus, a terraced house barely 3m wide, and the Schiefe Haus, an old, leaning mill, its foundations having been eroded by water.

The old imperial city of Goslar, with fascinating medieval alleyways, numerous churches and Germany's oldest surviving Romanesque palace, lies just to the north-east of the parks. Along with its silver mine in Rammelsberg Hill, it is now a UNESCO world heritage site.

ⓘ CONTACT INFORMATION

Harz and Hochharz National Parks
Nationalparkhaus Altenau-Torfhaus
Torfhaus 21
38667 Torfhaus
Germany
Tel: (00 49) 5320 263
Fax: (00 49) 5320 266
E-mail: Torfhaus@t-online.de

m 0 ———— 6
km 0 ———— 10

Goslar

Bad Harzburg

SACHSEN-ANHALT

LOWER SAXONY

Wernigerode

Brocken

UPPER HARZ NATIONAL PARK

HARZ NATIONAL PARK

Thale →

Sankt Andreasberg

Herzberg

The Bavarian Forest National Park

Majestic forests covering the oldest mountain range in central Europe exude a magical, primeval atmosphere.

Imagine being dwarfed by gigantic trees, shafts of sunlight enlivening their sombre green, and the fresh smell of damp grass and moss in the air. Such is the overriding impression of Germany's first national park, which lies at the heart of the much larger Bavarian Forest Nature Park. Created in 1970, the national park became a UNESCO reserve in 1981, and now covers 240 sq km of mountainous forests, running parallel with Šumava National Park in the Czech Republic.

The forests

Dominated by spruce, over 95% of the park is covered by woodlands, the altitude determining the type. The valleys are damp and bleak from the cold mountain air that sweeps down into them at night. With ground frosts possible even in summer, only the hardy spruce and mountain birch grow here. On the mountain slopes between 650m and 1,200m, however, the air is warmer and the soil richer, harbouring a mixed forest of white fir, beech, spruce, sycamore and even a few yew. In particularly warm areas, the rare mountain elm, broad-leaved lime and ash are also found. Above 1,200m, the climate once more becomes harsh, with only the spruce and a few mountain ash sufficiently resistant to the cold to survive.

Unfortunately, air pollution, acid rain, and a proliferation of bark beetles in warm summers has destroyed many of the old mountain spruce, but nature's ability to restore itself is clearly visible. Fallen trees protect the new-sprouting spruce, birch and rowan, while rotting branches and bark provide vital nutrients that the thin soil lacks. The central protected forest lets nature rule, undisturbed by axes, chainsaws or guns. The awe-inspiring tranquillity of the primeval forest is broken only by rustling leaves, rushing brooks or belling stags.

Colourful blooms

Ferns, bilberries, reed grass and crinkled hair grass provide a thick carpet for the mountain spruce forest, while around peat bogs in mountain hollows and along the valley bottoms cotton grass, cranberries, and bog rosemary flourish. In the mixed mountain forest, sweet woodruff, various ferns, the yellow archangel – less poetically known as the yellow deadnettle – and the rarer martagon lily spread amongst the trees. In early summer, the banks of the clear streams are awash with the colours of the blue alpine sowthistle, delicate white goat's beard, and the yellow of the ironically-named leopard's bane, an innocuous daisy-like species.

Regrowth on old roots in the forest

Life of the forests

The long winter from October to May, and the generally cool climate, make life in the woods hard. Little food is available, so deer and therefore wolves and lynx are scarce. However, the park authorities set up feeding places during the snowy season to help the deer and allow visitors to see the animals in the wild. Birds have adapted better – the hazel grouse, capercaillie, pygmy and Tengmalm's owls, woodpeckers and stock doves are amongst over fifty species that breed regularly in the park.

Near the park's information office in Neuschönau is a *Tier-Freigelände* where native forest creatures and birds live in their natural habitats. Neither a zoo nor a wildlife park, the terrain simply offers visitors a chance to see rare or indigenous animals such as bears, lynx, and otters. The trails through this area are well-kept, and are suitable for pushchairs and wheelchairs.

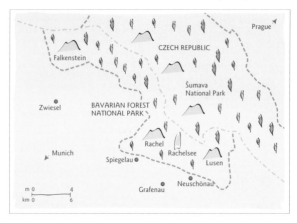

Zwiesel in the Bavarian forest

Mountains

There are more than sixty mountains over 1,000m within the national park. Views from the peaks can stretch as far as the Salzburg Alps. The best-known mountains are the Falkenstein (1,315m), Lusen (1,373m) and the Rachel, at 1,453m the highest peak in the park. On the slopes of the Rachel is the Rachelsee; created by a glacier, it is the only natural lake in the park – the others were made by dams in the 19th century. By the Rachelsee lies a much-photographed little chapel. To the south of the park there is also a cliff area that can be explored with the help of stone steps.

Sights and seasons

One of the most popular times to visit the Bavarian forest is in autumn, when the trees glow gold and bronze. Another bonus of an autumn visit is the chance to experience the Oktoberfest in Munich, about 160km away. This world-famous beer festival, despite its name, runs for the last fortnight in September, only just making it into October. Situated as it is between Austria, Germany and the Czech Republic, the forest is also an ideal central point for day trips to Prague, Salzburg, Vienna or Passau, the 'Bavarian Venice' at the confluence of the Danube, Inn and Ilz.

Closer at hand are the pretty towns of Grafenau and Zwiesel, famous for its crystal glass production.

i CONTACT INFORMATION

Bavarian Forest National Park
Freyunger Strasse 2
94481 Grafenau
Germany
Tel: (00 49) 8552 96000
Fax: (00 49) 8552 1394

Zwiesel Tourist Office
Stadtplatz 27
94227 Zwiesel
Germany
Tel: (00 49) 9922 1308
Fax: (00 49) 9922 5655

ℹ CONTACT INFORMATION

Austrian National Tourist Office
PO Box 2363
London W1A 2QB
Tel: 020 7629 0461
Fax: 020 7499 6038
E-mail: info@anto.co.uk
Web: http://austria-tourism.at/

Maison de la France
178 Piccadilly
London W1V 0AL
Tel: 0891 244123
Fax: 020 7493 6594
E-mail: info@mdlf.co.uk
Web: www.franceguide.com

German National Tourist Office
PO Box 2695
London W1A 3TN
Tel: 020 7317 0908
Fax: 020 7995 6129
E-mail: German_National_Tourist_Office@compuserve.com
Web: www.germany-tourism.de

Italian State Tourist Board
1 Princes Street
London W1R 8AY
Tel: 020 7408 1254
Fax: 020 7493 6695
E-mail: enitlond@globalnet.co.uk
Web: www.enit.it

Liechtenstein Tourism
Postfach 139
FL-9490 Vaduz
Liechtenstein

Tel: (00 423) 232 1443
Fax: (00 423) 392 1618
E-mail: touristinfo@lie-net.li

Slovenia Pursuits
New Barn Farm
Tadlow Road
Tadlow
Royston SG8 0EP
Tel: 01767 631144
Fax: 01767 631166
E-mail: angela.rennie@virgin.net

Switzerland Travel Centre Ltd
Swiss Centre
Swiss Court
London W1V 8EE
Tel: 0800 100 20030
Fax: 0800 100 20031
E-mail: stc@stlondon.com
Web: www.MySwitzerland.com

FRANCE

Les Ecrins National Park

Whilst the mountain peaks of Les Ecrins are renowned, its varied meadows and woodland yield unexpected pleasures in the French Alps.

The appeal of Les Ecrins lies in its integral variety. Some come for the unruly peaks and off-piste skiing, whilst others wish to tread the well-maintained paths, to visit the gîtes, museums and libraries run by the park's authorities, or to enjoy exhibitions, fêtes and processions.

La Meije Lever

Landscape

Les Ecrins is the largest of France's national parks. Across the 911 sq km of its central protected zone there is a sufficient range of altitudes, colours, landscapes and shapes to hold the interest of most. The land can be dramatic and wild, or hospitable and soft around the edges. There are 170 sq km of glaciers, 300 sq km of forests and 368 sq km of alpine meadows to explore. In the south-east of the park soft chalk, schist, shale and sandstone predominate, whilst in the north and west hard gneiss and granite resist the grinding of glaciers. The parkland climbs from altitudes of 800m to 4,102m, culminating in the peak of the Barre des Ecrins, a focal point for climbing enthusiasts.

Wildlife and plantlife

The diversity of the landscape in Les Ecrins fosters ibex, chamois, ermine, vole, marten, squirrel, fox, hare, golden eagle, sandpiper and plover. As the park lies across the north–south axis of the Alps and the east–west axis of the Vercors, Cevennes and Pyrennees, it is also traversed by many other wandering species.

Variety is also the major feature of Les Ecrins' botanic attractions. Around 1,800 species, from boreal to mediterranean, have found their place here. Most strikingly, white narcissus, blue gentian, blue thistle, orange lily and yellow buttercup light up the countryside in spring and early summer. Lichens also add colour to the mountainsides, growing on the scree and staining the land in many shades. Across the alpine meadows and tucked away in humid corners, rare and threatened types of plant are given particular attention by the authorities. 800 species are protected and forty of these that are especially unusual or endangered are systematically monitored in such areas as the Lauvitel Nature Reserve.

Woodland

Despite the fir plantations which climb up the west of the park in the Valbonnais, and the Scots pine, beech and oak groves, it is the larch woodland that remains most representative of the area. The larch, which populates so many of the Alpine mountainsides, blushes and bronzes with the seasons, fills out with pine needles in the summer months and releases them in the winter, continuously changing the hue of the flanks of the mountains.

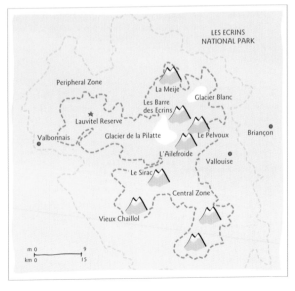

LES ECRINS
NATIONAL PARK

Peripheral Zone

La Meije

Glacier Blanc

Les Barre
des Ecrins

Lauvitel Reserve

Valbonnais

Glacier de la Pilatte

Le Pelvoux

Briançon

L'Ailefroide

Vallouise

Le Sirac

Central Zone

Vieux Chaillol

m 0   9
km 0   15

La Barre des Ecrins

Dynamic glaciers

The glaciers of Les Ecrins can be enjoyed either as a wild landscape to be tackled, or as a breathtaking backdrop. Glaciers are moulded in valleys and crevices. Some emerge pristine and white but others are black with the morainic layers that are laid over them. Some, like Glacier Blanc and Glacier de la Pilatte, stretch through valleys whilst others occupy rocky arenas, like those by the Pelvoux. Some, like the glaciers on the north face of the Ailefroide, cling to rock walls and spill over cliff-faces.

History and heritage

The lands of Les Ecrins have offered up relics, shards of ornaments and ancient objects, testifying that people have been trying to survive in this unpredictable environment from the Bronze Age. Pioneers were driven to pockets of land that had been spared by rockfalls, avalanches and floods. Traces of these ancient inhabitants are now chiselled into the mountain slopes, and their routes through the rocks are trodden by modern visitors. The area's agricultural productivity peaked towards the end of the 19th century, coinciding with the arrival of the first recreational climbers. This fresh interest in the region, in the mountains of Oisans, Vallouise and Briançonnais, could not prevent the decline of a rural culture. The park exists, in many ways, to continue to cultivate the interest of visitors, whilst protecting the pastoral heritage of the area, and the way of life and diversity of the alpine communities.

Discovering Les Ecrins

For those choosing to visit Les Ecrins today, the routes around the mountains – the Meije, the Barre des Ecrins, the Pelvoux, the Agneaux, the Ailefroide and the Olan – present spectacular views and challenging approaches. Hidden coombs and wide prairies, whilst less dramatic and less demanding, offer no less scope for discovery.

Independent journeys require careful consideration of the weather and possible routes. Nevertheless, throughout the park, the land is marked with clear trails. Guides are available for consultation, and can provide much of the necessary advice. The authorities are also able to supply background information, educational and scientific material, and maps. In a landscape that shelters many discreet types of plant and animal, binoculars, cameras, sketchbooks and nature guides may be of use to the inquisitive visitor.

ℹ CONTACT INFORMATION

Les Ecrins National Park Office
Domaine de Charance
F 05000 Gap
France
Tel: (00 33) 4 9240 2010
Fax: (00 33) 4 9252 3834

Gentians colour the alpine meadows

Regional Nature Parks in the French Alps

France's network of regional nature parks has ensured that cherished landscapes are protected, local heritage is respected, the use of land is scrutinised and the visiting public is educated.

Since 1967, France has chartered regional nature parks as a way to safeguard its countryside. Although the country has a high proportion of rural landscapes, threats have stacked up over the years: a growth in urban environments, a boom in tourism numbers and several large infrastructure projects.

The scale of these developments dwarfs the attempts of the nature parks to stabilise the pace of change. Nevertheless, the job of preservation is treated with determination. A park's charter consists of a ten year agreement between departmental officials, elected representatives and the national government to uphold particular principals.

The existence of the parks allows for progress in scientific research and in government policy. Of more immediate concern to the visitor to the French Alps, the region's natural wealth, cultural heritage and historical sites are made safely accessible.

MASSIF DES BAUGES
REGIONAL NATURE PARK

Grenoble

Briançon   ITALY

QUEYRAS REGIONAL
NATURE PARK

VERDON REGIONAL
NATURE PARK

Massif des Bauges

The area around Massif des Bauges juggles its dependence on commercial investment and tourist spending with its stunning, rugged environment. The cities on the park's periphery, Chambéry, Annecy and Aix-les-Bains, are well established and heavily developed. Broad roads carry streams of traffic over the Alps. In contrast, the distinctive landscapes of the Bauges mountains and the Chéran gorge, together with the area's hefty rivers and thermal springs are in their own way established, stubborn and resilient.

An enduring landscape

The peak of Les Bauges towers in the heart of the countryside, climbing up in a stark landscape of cliffs. The great valleys of the Chéran basin cut through the thick of the massif, and the waters teem, drawing many with their reputation for fine trout fishing. Likewise, the gorges and tunnels dig deep into the earth and are a popular destination for spelunkers.

Towards the west of the park, forests harbour healthy populations of deer and wild boar. The lands of the Game Reserve, which stretch over the Alpine prairies, are home to chamois, moufflon, capercaillies and grouse.

The trails in Queyras offer an accessible introduction to alpine walking

The stone farmhouses of Queyras

Where the grandeur of nature's shapes and sizes is coupled with the efforts of local communities to make a mark on the landscape, the results can be strange to behold, but quite spectacular: the Pont de l'Abîme wobbles at a height of 96m as it bridges the Chéran valley.

Changes in history

The lands around the Massif des Bauges are by no means unacquainted with change. Centuries ago they were cleared for farming by religious orders – the Benedictines, Carthusians and Cistercians – heralding a new intensity in the agricultural economy.

More recently, the development of tourism prompted a transformation of lifestyle and work that is arguably of equal significance. The spas of Aix-les-Bains drew considerable numbers of people in the 1880s, and following the opening of the first winter resort in 1905, its reputation was set in place as a base for cross country skiing and winter holidays.

The regional nature park holds on to its past, shielding small pockets of history. These range from the well maintained, idiosyncratic Baujue houses, with their odd angles, asymmetry and painted facades, through to the intriguing Paccard foundry bell museum.

Le Verdon

The Regional Nature Park of Verdon was only established in 1997. The inhuman scale of the area's gorges, riven by massive structural movements and centuries of gradual erosion, provide a deep sense of

geological perspective. The grandeur of the landscape is coupled with an abundant and diverse gathering of flora and fauna, as plant species from Alpine and Mediterranean origins clash on the floor of the gorges. The parkland offers a lot of activities for the energetic visitor, and the stories of people and communities which continue to unfold on these striking landscapes make an impression.

Experiencing Le Verdon

Over 1,000km of trails cross the expanse of Le Verdon. Whilst some are not particularly well waymarked, the paths are a fine way of stepping into the rhythm of the park. The trails are remnants of rural paths, once walked by the mountain farmers of the area. The Martel footpath, which can take up an entire day's walking, is named after the first person to explore the canyon in 1905.

Many of the activities that are organised for visitors take advantage of the area's rivers and lakeland. The River Verdon runs quite wild but manages to settle peaceably down as it empties into still lakes. Sailing, windsurfing and pedal-boating are popular on the lakes of Sainte Croix,

Quinson and Esparron de Verdon. Again, an indication of the complex relationship between nature's safe keeping and development is the fact that five of the Verdon's lakes are the result of damming by the French National Electrical Utility between 1949 and 1974.

An agricultural heritage

Other lands of the Verdon speak clearly of the attempts men and women have made to live on the land. Verdon continues to bear the marks of a disappearing rural culture.

The Valensole plateau is still being farmed intensively. However, where the limestone hills of the Varois high country used to be terraced into fields for the cultivation of olives, grapes and vegetables, brush and forest have grown over them. Agricultural communities and activities fade away across the region.

Although peripheral traditions such as apiculture endure, the substantial sheep raising and wool working sectors, which were once staples of agricultural life in the pre-Alpine massifs, are now the stuff of guide book asides and craft museums.

Queyras

The Regional Nature Park of Queyras was chartered in 1977. In keeping with the present tensions and dilemmas concerning development and preservation, the townships of the Queyras also boast a complex political and social history.

Awkward relationships between townships and cantons, along with the power politics of monarchs and governments, have long been a feature of the area. As a result, the land's history has been a complicated and troubled one.

Archaeology has unearthed engraved stones at Les Escoyères – evidence of Roman occupation. In the Middle Ages, although many valleys came to be settled, the poor quality of the soil eventually drove people away again. Then in 1685, much of the land was abandoned owing to the religious pressure which followed the revocation of the Edict of Nantes.

Hiking

Over a relatively small area, the lands of Queyras offer great diversity. Celebrated routes include the hikes in the Cristillan valley, up to the 16th century Church of Saint Sebastian; well-travelled paths through the green marble quarries; walks in the lakeland of St Anne of Moror; and treks across the barren rocks of the Casse.

With the exception of some steep and rocky slopes, the hiking trails, themed walking tours and discovery paths of Queyras have acquired a reputation as a relatively gentle introduction to alpine walking. Networks of paths are well maintained and signposted, and the sunny climate ensures more predictable conditions than the uppity weather of the more northerly massifs.

Things preserved

Perhaps in response to the pace of development, and in recognition of the fragility both of the natural treasures of the park and its heritage,

there is a culture of conservation and remembrance in the Queyras. A war memorial stands in Ange-Gardien, remembering the solidarity of the townships of the canton of Aiguilles. In Château Queyras, an ancient church crypt is the location for a exhibition of the region's geology. The Soum museum, housed in the oldest house in the village of Saint Véran, shows something of domestic life of times past.

The craft museum in Ville-Veille, the steel house in Aiguilles, bizarrely built in the Eiffel tradition, and the splendid rural architecture of Arvieux valley, all give interesting glimpses into the history of the park.

Sundials are also a common feature alongside the walks of the Queyras, with sober 18th century designs, and elaborately decorated 19th century

relics. Fittingly for a region so preoccupied with keeping hold of the past in the face of urbanisation, the sundials are often decorated with engravings waxing lyrical on the subject of how time chases.

CONTACT INFORMATION

Regional Nature Park of Massif des Bauges
Maison du Parc
73630 Le Châtelard
France
Tel: (00 33) 4 7954 8640

Queyras Regional Nature Park
BP 3
05600 Guillestre
France
Tel: (00 33) 4 9245 0623

Verdon Regional Nature Park
BP 14
04360 Moustiers Sainte Marie
France
Tel: (00 33) 4 9274 6395

Queyras Nature Park

Parc Jurassien de la Combe-Grède / Chasseral

*Gentle green hills, open vistas and malleable landscapes,
give another face to Switzerland and its protected areas.*

The Parc Jurassien de la Combe-Grède / Chasseral is a protected natural reserve situated in the Bernese Jura canton in Switzerland. The canton itself forms part of the north-western region of the country known as the Jura.

The Jura

This region is based around the mountain range of the same name which stretches for approximately 150km through Switzerland and into France. The area is distinct from the rest of Switzerland both geographically and culturally Its inhabitants are predominantly French-speaking and the mountains of the Jura are low and rolling, without the drama of the Alps.

The Jura is one of the less visited parts of Switzerland, which makes it a desirable destination in the summer and the snowy months when the south of the country becomes overrun. The Jura's relative lack of industry and its green and forested areas also make it an ideal location for relaxed and exploratory walking.

Young mountains

Switzerland is divided into three distinct geographical areas: the Alps, the central plateau or Mittelland, and the Jura. The Jura is sub-alpine, with peaks averaging 750m in altitude, and covers approximately 10% of the country. The Jura mountains were formed by the same process of continental plate movement which pushed up the Alps to the south, but are much younger and consist mainly of marine deposits of limestone, sandstone and marl. This rock is porous and prone to erosion, with the area's high rainfall being quickly absorbed to carve subterranean lakes, streams and caverns. The land is thickly forested, with some of the higher peaks covered to the summit with trees, while the lower slopes and valleys are cleared for farming.

Looking towards the park over a meadow of spring daffodils

Jurassic park

Within the Jura are many places where limestone formed in the Jurassic period (213–144 million years ago) has been pushed, contorted and

Autumn leaves across a path

eroded into spectacular cliffs and gorges. Although the Parc Jurassien only covers a 3 sq km section of the main mountain chain between the valley of St Imier in the north and the land bordering Lake Bienne in the south, it does contain one of the finest gorges – the Combe-Grède.

The Combe-Grède is a popular and dramatic entrance gate to the park. With steep walls of over 300m, the gorge rises abruptly from the villages of Villeret and St Imier at its mouth. The stream which runs along its bottom seems rather diminutive for having cut such a swathe.

Walkways have been built high on the gorge's walls to enable visitors to climb into the main area of the park. This ascent is very steep and in places uses iron ladders and roped supports cut into the cliffs. The path gives an impression of how water has shaped the landscape, passing by waterfalls and pools to reach the higher plains.

Le Chasseral

The majority of the park consists of
the forests and pastured slopes of
Le Chasseral, which at 1,609m is the
highest peak in the Bernese Jura.
The summit of Le Chasseral is an open
limestone plateau giving unhindered
views into the Jura, and across the
Swiss Mittelland to the Alps.

The forests which characterise much
of the region grow further down the
mountain's slopes. The name Jura is
derived from the Celtic word for
wood, and Le Chasseral is one of the
few mountains in the Jura chain
which rises above the tree line.
The northern part of the park
incorporates la Forêt de l'Envers,
home to foxes, hares, ferrets and
marmots, as well as a herd of
chamois, the result of a successful
reintroduction scheme.

Although the park is peaceful and
pleasant when clad in its summer
green, it transforms in winter to a
wilderness with a stark beauty of its
own. The Jura experiences extremely
cold winters with a thick coating
of snow blanketing the slopes of
Le Chasseral and hanging heavily
from the fir trees. Icicles grow in the
Combe-Grède, but at the first sign of
the thaw, meltwaters funnel down
the gorge, swelling the stream to a
torrent.

The Combe-Grède in summer

Chemin des Crêtes du Jura

In addition to local walking trails,
the Chemin des Crêtes du Jura, or Jura
High Route, passes through the park.
Extending for 180km through the Jura
from Geneva to Basel, the route is
itself part of a European Long

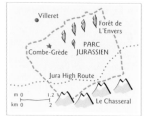

Distance Path. The E4, or
Mediterranean Arc, sweeps from
Gibraltar around to Crete, presenting
interesting options for visitors to
extend their expeditions further into
the Jura, or even beyond.

Other possibilities exist closer to
hand in nearby nature reserves.
St Peter's is a long thin island that
sits at the western end of Lake
Bienne and is joined to the shore by
a natural causeway which emerged
as the lake's water level dropped.
Historically, the island was home to
a monastery of Clunic monks, visited
by, amongst others, Napoleon,
the Empress Joséphine and
Jean-Jacques Rousseau. Today it is a
reserve for animals and birds, as its
rush-lined shores make it an ideal
breeding place.

There are several other reserves worth
visiting in the wider region, and
Fribourg, Neuchâtel and Porrentruy
all have botanical gardens, the latter
focusing on plants specific to the Jura.

ℹ CONTACT INFORMATION

**Parc Jurassien de la
Combe-Grède / Chasseral**
Case Postale 192
CH-2610 Saint-Imier
Switzerland

Bernese Jura Tourism
Avenue de la Liberté 26
CH-2740 Moutier
Switzerland
Tel: (00 41) 32 493 6466
Fax: (00 41) 32 493 6156
E-mail: information@ jurabernois.ch
Web: www.jurabernois.ch

The high plateau in the Jura

Glaciers and Gardens in the Canton of Valais

The mountainous southern canton of Valais enables visitors to experience both the vastness and the fragility of its creeping ice rivers, the glaciers.

Valais spreads along the south-western border of Switzerland following the path of the Rhône river. With its dry and sunny climate, low rainfall and areas of rocky steppe, it is often described as Switzerland's most arid canton. This description does not do justice to the area's appeal. With fifty one mountains over 4,000m, and 8,000km of marked walking trails, Valais has long been a popular Alpine holiday destination.

The Matterhorn, its celebrated mountain, straddles the border with Italy, with a well-developed tourist infrastructure spreading around it. For visitors seeking areas of natural interest however, the canton's glaciers, nature reserves and gardens may prove most appealing.

The glaciers

The sheared mountains and moraine valleys of Switzerland were revealed when the glaciers of the last Ice Age receded. Today the Swiss Alps remained heavily glaciated with over 650 glaciers occurring within Valais alone. Ranging from small in-feeding

Walking on the Aletschgletscher

glaciers to the vast Grosser Aletschgletscher, glaciers have always posed a menace to the Swiss. Many lives have been lost through ice and rock falls, and glacially-caused flooding, but now it is the glaciers which are at risk, with global warming causing them to steadily retreat. This, together with the impact of tourism, has caused concern among environmentalists and prompted discussion of creating a second Swiss national park.

Rhônegletscher

The Rhône river snakes through the middle of Valais and, together with its tributaries, creates the canton's form. The majority of the area's inhabitants live in the river's fertile valley, and most farming occurs here. Side valleys lead up towards the peaks with their resorts; the Pennine Alps in the south, the Bernese Alps in the north.

In the far east of the canton lies the Rhône's source, the Rhônegletscher (Rhône glacier). Once commanding the entire valley, the glacier now stretches for 10km and is accessible by road or on foot from the village of Gletsch. A path leads alongside the glacier from its snout to its head, enabling visitors to get a good impression of its expanse. At the nearby Fiesch glacier, an interesting section of path leads through the substantial moraine deposits left by the meltwaters as the glacier retreated.

Aletschgletscher

Europe's longest glacier, Grosser Aletschgletscher (Great Aletsch glacier), is also in eastern Valais. Stretching to 25km, the glacier's head is at Jungfraujoch in the Bernese Oberland. There are numerous ways of approaching it from Valais. The Fiesch cableway up the Eggishorn offers an easily accessible summit viewpoint. Circular walks leading off from the cableway pass down the side of the glacier, via lakes and ridges, and through the Aletschwald Nature Preservation Centre.

Aletschwald is a reserve for glacial plants, such as purple saxifrage, and for Swiss pine forests. The latter includes ancient Arolla pines whose knarled branches yield edible nuts. Beneath the trees grow twinflowers, their delicate pink flowers hoisted on slender stalks. From Belalp village, near the glacier's snout, guides lead treks, the safest way for the inexperienced to walk on the icy surface.

The Matterhorn

Alpine gardens

Other areas of botanical interest lie scattered throughout the canton. At Anzere, an alpine botanical trail leads walkers at a height of over 2,000m. Accessible in the summer months, the trail gives a chance to see familiar flowers, such as gentians, growing in their natural habitat. In Conthey, a research centre for plants with medicinal properties is open to the public by appointment. Results from tests undertaken here are entered onto a database, shared by similar research centres worldwide.

Further west there are more opportunities for both gardens and glaciers in the area around the Grand St Bernard pass. The massif is the most glaciated area of the Swiss Alps and historically the pass has served as a trade route. The village of Bourg St Pierre boasts La Linnea, the canton's highest alpine garden at 1,554m.

Another garden, Jardin alpin Floralpe is further down the Val d'Entremont at Champex. A cable-car from the village leads to a circular walk via the glaciers d'Orny and Saleina. The Trient glacier, close to the French border, is also worth visiting. The walk to the bottom of the glacier can be easily completed in a morning and passes through the spectacular Trient gorge, where wooden walkways overhang the narrowly confined river.

Lake Champex

The Matterhorn

Most visitors to Valais will want to visit the Matterhorn area. Whether or not they are interested in the resort culture, the Matterhorn still forms an enduring symbol of both the canton and Switzerland itself. Zermatt, the area's main resort, lies 1,620m above sea level at the mountain's base, and is a car-free town. Totally geared to alpine tourism, Zermatt offers high-altitude restaurants, helicopter rides, summer skiing on glacial snow, cable-cars, gondolas and alpine railways to reach higher areas, as well as package health, fitness and relaxation holidays. Encircled by thirty six mountains over 4,000m and with

400km of paths running out from it, the town is a haven for both walkers and mountaineers. Those wishing to climb the Matterhorn should be prepared, both for the extreme physical challenge and for the hefty charges that can be incurred for guides and hut accommodation.

ⓘ CONTACT INFORMATION

**Valais Tourism /
Wallis Tourism**
6, rue Pré-Fleuri
1951 Sion
Switzerland
Tel: (00 41) 27 327 3570
Fax: (00 41) 27 327 3571
E-mail: uvt@wallis.ch
Web: www.valaistourism.ch

Trient gorge

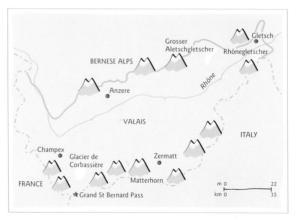

Swiss National Park

*Switzerland's only national park is a testimony to the
foresight of environmentalists and the resilience of nature.*

The Swiss National Park is located in
the Engadine valley in the eastern
canton of Graubünden. The canton is
Switzerland's largest, but despite its
size is only sparsely populated, largely
due to its mountainous and rocky
terrain. The inhabitants are dependent
on tourism, hydroelectricity and
agriculture for their livelihoods, and
speak one of three languages.

German is most common, but entire
valleys can be either Italian or
Romansch speaking, reflecting the
isolation which historically enabled
these languages to persist in the area.
As a result the canton is known by
several names: Graubünden in
German, Grischun in Romansch and
Grigioni in Italian, although rather
confusingly it is frequently referred to
by its French name, Grisons.

Walkers on the route to Margunet

The Engadine runs on a slant across
the east of the canton following the
valley of the En river. It is divided
into two distinct parts. The Upper
Engadine is fringed by the Bernina
massif. It contains several resorts,
including chic St Moritz, and its high
alpine passes lead to Italy. The Lower
Engadine is narrower and wilder, and
contains some of the best walking in
the country. It is in the southern part
of the Lower Engadine, bridging the
Ofenpass route to Italy, that the
Swiss National Park lies.

Conserving history

The area now covered by the park
would have seemed, initially, an
unusual candidate for protection, as
it had been heavily scarred by man.
Evidence that people lived in this
region dates from 3000 BC, although
the number of settlements increased
around 400 BC. The Romans invaded
in 15 BC and it is from Latin that the
Romansch language has evolved.
Until the 19th century, mining,
forestry and farming were the main
occupations, marking the land and
stripping away vegetation.

It is due to the resolve of a few
individuals that the park exists today.
The original impetus came from abroad
with the foundation of Yellowstone
National Park in America in 1872.
Hoping to emulate this, a group of
Swiss conservationists obtained a
private lease of the Cluozza valley in
1909 for the purpose of forming a
park. In 1914 the park was formally
established and over the years has
grown by a process of gradual
accretion to its current size.

Recent discussions have focused on
further, large-scale expansion. As the
only national park in Switzerland it is
felt that a wider area is needed to
fully protect the flora and fauna, and
to bring currently excluded
environments within its ambit.

The purpose of the park

The Swiss National Park is a strict
natural reserve. Many activities which
might normally be allowed within a
park are banned and no human
intervention is permitted 'that does
not serve the purpose of protection
itself'. As a result, the park has
become Switzerland's wildest region,
although it remains challenged by
hydroelectricity schemes and by the

Marmots in the park

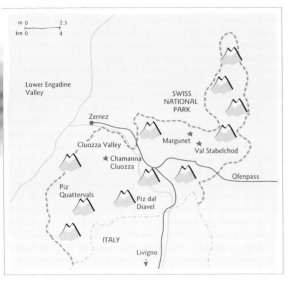

in August. For walkers, the snow can come as early as September and several of the higher level paths do not clear until July. Huts are generally open from May until October although they are not always manned.

June and July are the best times for bird-watching, and there are over one hundred species in the park. For visitors hoping to spot game birds, such as ptarmigan, capercaillie and black and hazel grouse, October, when the larch trees begin to glow ochre and gold, is a good time to see them in their forest habitat. October is also best for spotting ibex, chamois and deer, all of which come down the slopes for the winter, whilst stags can be heard belling in the valleys.

Rocks, forests & grasslands

The high rocks are predominately dolomite, which weathers in the harsh winters into strangely shaped rocky protrusions. The gradual creeping of scree slopes causes solifluction, a characteristic sight in the park, when the thin vegetative layer is carried downward with the rock to create lacy scalloped patterns on the hillsides. Beneath the peaks are the many valleys down which water flows into the River En and from there eastwards to eventually reach the Black Sea. These valleys are narrow, their slopes covered with blankets of mountain pine, a legacy from the days of

busy Ofenpass road which cuts through it. Camping, lighting fires, picnics and parking are all strictly prohibited beyond designated areas. Similarly, walkers are forbidden to leave the marked paths, of which there are twenty colour-coded routes.

Escaping the snow

Due to protective measures, many areas are totally inaccessible to visitors and the park is closed completely from November until May.

Winter begins in earnest in October with heavy snowfalls raising the risks of avalanches. During the other seasons though, the climate is generally warm and dry. The park's inter-alpine location means it enjoys low rainfall and humidity, and high sunshine hours. When visitors choose to visit the park will depend upon their interests. Its alpine nature means that spring plant growth does not start until mid-May, although by June and July the flora will be at its best, with autumn colours beginning

Margunet saddle, Val Stabelchod

forestry. In places though, twisted Cembra or Arolla pines are gradually re-establishing, as is larch. Above the forests, stunted shrubs give way to alpine grasslands and plateaux where the pervasive edelweiss and spurred pansies grow. Higher still is the rock and scree of the permanent snow zones. From here views stretch south into the Bernina massif and east into the Ortler mountains in the Italian Stelvio National Park which abuts the Swiss Park at Livigno.

Margunet

A walk from Ofenpass to Margunet combines areas of animal, botanical and geological interest. The path

Evening shadows from larch trees in the Swiss National Park

passes through forests once planted for making charcoal. In accordance with the park's non-interventionist policies these forests are now being allowed to die and naturally regenerate. Beyond the forest, the path crosses meadows before entering the rocky gorge of the Val Stabelchod, with its massive banks of scree.

A viewpoint at the base of an avalanche slope is a favoured spot for watching bearded vultures, which were reintroduced to the park in 1991. Their release was part of a sustained programme across Austria, France, Italy and Switzerland to reinstate the birds in the Alps. Within the park young vultures can often be spotted making their maiden flights. From the viewpoint the path climbs to the Margunet saddle where fingers of dolomite rock poke their way through

the sparse grass. This is a grazing area for herds of chamois, and walkers are most likely to spot them at dusk when they feed. Marmots are a more common sight during the day with the path passing a colony which has made its home in a pile of debris left by a scree slope.

Chamanna Cluozza

The village of Zernez, at the entrance to the park, is home to the main headquarters and information centre. From here an interesting walk leads to the Chamanna Cluozza, near to where footprints of some of the park's oldest residents, dinosaurs, were found in the Üerts da Diavel (Devil's Gardens). The footprints are thought to have been left by two different types of dinosaur, the herbivorous prosauropods and the dangerous

three-fingered theropods, and date from the Triassic period. They are imprinted in a huge limestone slab, acutely balanced at 2,450m on the side of the Piz dal Diavel. While the slab is too perilous to be accessible to visitors, the footprints can be seen via binoculars from Chamanna Cluozza. There is also a large hut here, allowing walkers to break the route into two days and to enjoy a night at altitude.

From Chamanna Cluozza, a route leads upwards to Piz Quattervals. This is the only peak within the park which it is permitted to climb. Unlike most of the park's routes, it is only scantily marked and is a strenuous ascent for which climbing experience is needed. In spring, hard snow can cover most of the route, while in summer there is danger of rock falls.

If, however, these challenges are broached the views from the 3,165m summit are rewarding. Walkers will also find hardy Swiss androsace, its pale flowers scattered on a water-retaining green cushion. Golden eagles, of which there are six nesting pairs in the park, can be seen circling, or, on the way down, a skylark may be startled from its nest.

ⓘ CONTACT INFORMATION

Swiss National Park
National Park House
CH-7530 Zernez
Switzerland
Tel: (00 41) 81 856 1378
Fax: (00 41) 81 856 1740
Web: www.nationalpark.ch

Hang-gliding at Tarap

ITALY

Valle d'Aosta and Gran Paradiso National Park

Italy's smallest and possibly quietest region is home to the country's highest mountain, Monte Gran Paradiso, which soars above the national park of the same name.

Tucked in Italy's north-west corner, Valle d'Aosta is generally overlooked as a tourist destination. Cloistered by mountains, the region is obscured by the larger, cosmopolitan resorts that are strung along the Alps.

However, for centuries the valley formed a crossroads at the base of the Alps for travellers between northern and southern Europe. Ringed by Monte Rosa, Mont Blanc, the Matterhorn and Gran Paradiso, the region's capital Aosta was founded in 25 BC by the Emperor Augustus. This past importance and current seclusion make the Valle d'Aosta a satisfying area to visit. Combining space and natural beauty with history, small scale attractions and local celebrations, it has something to offer at all times of year.

A beginning

Gran Paradiso National Park spans the boundaries of Valle d'Aosta and Piemonte, shared equally between the two regions. It also shares a boundary and a raison d'etre with La Vanoise Natural Park in France. The area was once used for hunting by the House of Savoy, but in 1856 King Vittorio Emanuele II declared part of it a hunting reserve, in order to protect the ibex. In 1922 the national park was established following a donation of land from a later king. However, the ibex remained at risk when they migrated to France. Accordingly, in 1963 the French established La Vanoise Natural Park which borders Gran Paradiso. There are now sufficient ibex in the park to enable them to be repopulated elsewhere.

Two views

The ibex is the first of two dominant images associated with the park. This solid, pale haired mountain goat can grow up to a metre tall. Despite its stature and its heavy crown of curved horns, the ibex treads nimbly over the rocks and slopes. Visitors will often see a flash of horn or tail as the ibex disappears up the passes but the best view occurs in the evening when ibex stop to feed on alpine grasses.

The park's second trademark is the Gran Paradiso massif. Lying mainly within the Valle d'Aosta, Monte Gran Paradiso (4,061m) is the highest mountain to fall wholly within Italy. Surrounded by the other peaks of the massif, the summits are perpetually ice-capped. In winter the entire area is under a blanket of snow and many paths do not clear until May.

The ascent

Monte Gran Paradiso was first climbed in 1860 and is a comparatively accessible and popular challenge. Well-placed refuges on the slopes mean that the ascent can be split over two or three days, but it is a mountaineering not a walking route. Proper equipment is required as the trail crosses glaciers and crevasses.

Visitors need not be climbers to enjoy the park's routes. Rising from the valleys, walkers pass through woods of fir and larch, before reaching the alpine pastures. In June and July, the meadow grass is wreathed in flowers, butterflies dancing attendance. Higher still are the tablelands, such as Piano del Nivolet, where water settles in rocks, lakes and peat bogs, and white cotton grasses wave tufted heads. The altitude is now 2,500m but these areas are easily reached, as are many of the park's glaciers. The Lavassey, Fond and Tsantelèina glaciers are all an easy climb from Val di Rhêmes, with their rocky moraines providing a sufficient feel of the high alps.

Cogne with the Gran Paradiso massif behind

Cascate di Lillaz on the border of the Gran Paradiso National Park

The freeze

With walkers, climbers and families all converging on the park for the warmer months its paths can become crowded. Autumn and winter will give a quieter view. Lodging at Cogne, Valsavarenche, Rhêmes-Notre-Dame or any of the villages which lie in the northern valleys makes the park accessible for lower level expeditions or cross-country skiing, and affords easy retreat when the weather closes in. The region also has ski resorts on its other three major mountains.

Festivities and culture

An end of year visit provides an opportunity to enjoy some of the Valle d'Aosta's culture. Once the bustle of catering to summer tourists has subsided, the valley can indulge in its own activities. In August the inhabitants of Val Soana on the park's eastern border climb to hold a party at the sanctuary of San Besso, sustaining an ancient ritual. So begins the cycle of festivities. In September there is the grape festival in Chambave, in October the apple festival at Gressan and the finals of the Bataille de Reines at Aosta where the region's best milk cow is crowned. Pageants and carnivals culminate with the snow carnival in Pila in March.

The Valle d'Aosta can also be explored for its craft and art. Most of the village churches hold beautiful examples of sculpture in wood and marble. Elsewhere in the valley small craft museums focus on textiles. Jute, bobbin lace and thick drap woven from wool are all materials traditionally made in the valley and each has a local museum dedicated to it. Folk costume is also on display at Lillianes, where it can be made to order as a colourful souvenir.

ℹ CONTACT INFORMATION

Gran Paradiso National Park
Via della Rocca, 47
10123 Torino
Italy
Tel: (00 39) 0118 606211
Fax: (00 39) 0118 121305
E-mail: comunica.pngp@
interbusiness.it

Aosta Tourist Information Office
Piazza Chanoux, 8
11100 Aosta
Italy
Tel: (00 39) 0165 236627
Fax: (00 39) 0165 34657

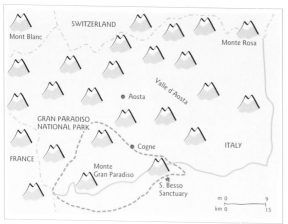

Val Grande National Park

*Space, silence and beauty in its raw form create
an atmosphere of sanctuary in Val Grande.*

Lying just south of the Swiss border,
in the Piemonte province of Italy,
is Val Grande National Park.
Only protected since 1992, the area,
given its inhospitable nature, had
been altered to a surprising extent by
humans. It is this contrast, between
the natural wildness and the evidence
of communities which have struggled
to survive here, that makes the park
so interesting.

With most of the park authority's
improvement plans still to be
implemented, Val Grande is not
somewhere where visitors will find
carefully marked paths and manicured
picnic areas. It is, however, a park
where the sense of desolation which
surrounds an abandoned stone
cottage is echoed in the harsh
mountains, and visitors will truly
feel that they are in a wild place.

The reasons for establishing the park
bear an equal duality. Accompanying
the need to preserve the area from
further intrusion was the desire to
encourage economic regeneration.
Depopulation and decline, which had
peaked in Val Grande in the mid 20th
century, were continuing in the
surrounding area due to the lack of
employment and poverty.

Corona de Ghina

Geological histories

The park is centred around two main
valleys, Val Pogallo and Val Grande,
and incorporates the Pedum mountain
range which has been a reserve since
1967. It has a complex geological
past, with magmatic, sedimentary and
metamorphic rocks as its base.

Although glaciers still cap the Alps to
the north, the steep gorges in which
streams pool and run predate the ice
ages. However, the valleys are the
landscapes the glaciers left behind.

Valley dwellers

The valleys were historically home to
an alpine economy based around
forestry and agriculture. It was a hard,
subsistence-based way of life, totally
dependent on the land and climate.
Change only came with the intrusion
of world events in 1914.

In the First World War, fears of an
attack by Germany over the neutral
Swiss border led to the construction
of the Cadorna Line through the park.
A huge undertaking of trenches and
forts, its remains can still be seen,
although it was never used.

The park was not so fortunate in the
Second World War. During the Nazi
occupation most of the pastures were
burned and many partisan soldiers
executed. While the process of
abandonment had begun earlier,
this was really the crux for Val
Grande's peoples. Most inhabitants
fled and never returned.

Modern inhabitants

Today few people live within the
park's boundaries and nature has
rapidly reclaimed the area. Many of
the woods are impenetrable due to
the spread of nettles, wild raspberry
bushes and thick scrub.

Abandoned stone cottages in Val Grande

The composition of the woods varies with altitude, although the legacy of commercial forestry has also affected what grows. Larch, which was once quite common on the higher slopes, is now sparsely represented, but beech, chestnut and various conifers are still found in abundance. In summer, in the cleared areas of the higher mountain pastures, the delicate bonnet-shaped columbine flowers, whilst laburnum blooms and ivy weaves around the crumbling stone shells of old cottages and wells.

The network of springs which thread the valleys provide opportunities to spot some of the park's wildlife. Frogs and salamanders are common, as are vipers, although they are seldom seen. Other animals, such as foxes, beech martens, voles and shrews are more likely to be found in the woods, which also has its share of reclusive residents, in owls and badgers.

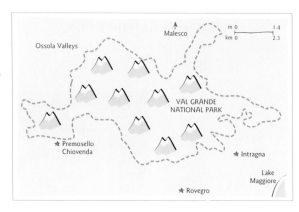

Walking

Val Grande has a wealth of paths, including longer ones which link with Switzerland or cross the park from the Ossola valleys in the west to Lake Maggiore. A popular shorter route runs through woods adjacent to a stream that tumbles down Val Pogallo. The valley was once well populated, as can be seen from the old cottages, some of which are now being restored.

Caution needs to be exercised as many of the paths are overgrown and in need of repair and reinforcement. This does not mean that walking is not possible, only that visitors need to remember that this is a wild, and in places inaccessible, park and should be approached with respect.

Visitor centres

The park has three themed visitor centres. At Rovegro the focus is on man and the woods; at Intragna it is nocturnal animals; and at Premosello Chiovenda it is the rocks and the uses people have made of them over time.

Nearby in the Ossola valleys is the Natural Park dell'Alpe Veglia e dell'Alpe Devero with its waterfalls,

blueberries, mineral springs and winter skiing. To the south-east is Lake Maggiore. Visible from Val Grande, its Mediterranean climate, bright waters and bustling tourism contrasts with the silence of the park.

$\boxed{i}$ CONTACT INFORMATION

Val Grande National Park
Villa San Remigio
28048 Verbania Pallanza (V.C.O.)
Italy
Tel: (00 39) 0323 557960
Fax: (00 39) 0323 556397

Natural Park dell'Alpe Veglia and dell'Alpe Devero
Viale Castelli, 2
28868 Varzo
Italy
Tel: (00 39) 0324 72572
Fax: (00 39) 0324 72790

Val Pogallo

Adamello Brenta Nature Park

A bridge between earth and sky, the Alps of the Adamello Brenta Nature Park bear witness to the glacial forces which formed them.

Spanning both the Brenta and the Adamello-Presanella mountain ranges, the Adamello Brenta Nature Park dominates the western side of Trentino province in northern Italy. The park's dual nature is evident throughout: from its fertile valleys to the scoured peaks of Presanella; from areas inaccessible in winter to those where civilisation has left its mark, whether by agriculture or by war.

Covering an area of 618 sq km, this duality occurs even in the rocks from which the park is formed. Adamello is volcanic granite, while Brenta is dolomitic. Likewise the soil differs, and as a result the park has a huge variety of habitats and flora.

The feature which serves to unite the park is water. With more than fifty lakes, as well as glaciers, rivers and waterfalls, the park has an abundance of it. It is fitting that in Val Meledrio, where the feet of the ranges touch, a torrent runs to divide the two.

Lakes and grottoes

Although water may be a theme of the park, the effect it has on the landscape differs depending on where it falls. In Adamello, the hard crystalline strata means that the water pools, forming the lakes and glaciers for which the park is famous. In Brenta, the water erodes the calcareous rock creating distinctive formations and dramatic skylines. It also burrows, leaving vast grottoes

and labyrinths in its wake. When the water recedes in summer these can be explored. The largest is the Collalto grotto which is nearly 5km in length and begins in the Val d'Ambiéz.

Valle di Tóvel

The impenetrability of the mountain ranges is challenged by the many valleys which score their flanks. These valleys not only provide an entrance for experienced climbers wishing to scale the peaks, but also create walking opportunities and excursions in the park for the less ambitious.

The Valle di Tóvel is among the most beautiful of these valleys, with its lake nesting in a circle of rock in the middle of the Brenta range. Now its water is clear, clean blue, but in the past, due to the presence of algae, it was known to turn red.

Walks of all levels ring the lake and a keen eye may spot a marmot, chamois, capercaillie or black grouse. The area is also a strict reserve for the scattering of brown bears in the park.

Rendena and Genova

Valle Rendena, the main valley which splits the park, is scattered with villages for rest and refreshment and serves as a congregation point for visitors to Adamello Brenta. Here restaurants offer the park's speciality foods, freshwater char and thick rinded spressa cheese.

Val Genova is 'the valley of the waterfalls'. The name is thought to derive from *zènua*, meaning a land rich in water, and as such is an appropriate introduction to the western half of the park. The walks up the valley, which is itself a branch of Valle Rendena, are not difficult. Val Genova boasts numerous waterfalls and climbs between thick forests and bare cliffs. At its close its alpine nature is revealed in a knot of rock faces and glaciers.

Lake Tóvel

Providing hospitality in the Trentino province for travellers in the Alps dates from the 13th century when the first refuges were provided by monks. The real 'boom' started in the 19th century when aristocrats came to take the waters of the multitude of mineral rich springs which flow from the slopes and valleys of the area.

Leached from the mountain rock, the waters are arsenic-ferruginous or carbon and sulphur laden depending on their source. Clinics offer cures for complaints of the skin, respiratory system and blood, or simply relaxation and beauty therapies.

CONTACT INFORMATION

Adamello Brenta Nature Park
Via Nazionale, 12
38080 Strembo
Italy
Tel: (00 39) 0465 804637
Fax: (00 39) 0465 804649
E-mail: info@parcoadamello
brenta.tn.it

Facilities

The park has a visitor centre on the shores of Lake Tóvel and two wildlife enclosures at San Romedio and Spormaggiore. All three focus on the park's most scrutinised inhabitant, the brown bear.

The visitor centre also covers other aspects of the park such as its less coveted flora. Visitors in spring and summer will be treated to displays of delicate flowers such as the lady's-slipper orchid, but at other times of year the trees are equally impressive. Due to the range of altitudes within the nature park, the vegetation is diverse. In autumn oak and maple flame the slopes, while in winter fir and spruce catch the snow.

Both the visitor centre and San Romedio sanctuary are accessible to wheelchair users. The park also runs a shuttle bus service making many of the more remote valleys accessible to those who do not arrive by car.

Glaciers and spas

Alpine guides operating from local villages lead walks onto the glaciers, of which there are over thirty in the park, including the vast Mandron glacier which is the second largest in Italy. Mountain refuges providing accommodation are dotted throughout the park, enabling walkers and climbers to watch the sunset from on high after their day's efforts.

The Brenta mountains

Paneveggio–Pale di San Martino Nature Park

There is no escaping the history which pervades the Paneveggio–Pale di San Martino: the atmosphere of the ageless mountains is coupled with a sense of the inhabitants and travellers who have passed this way before.

The move to establish natural parks in Trentino province in northern Italy began in the early 20th century, when members of local touring and climbing clubs discussed protecting this area of extraordinary beauty. It was not until 1967 however, that an area in the east was declared as the Paneveggio–Pale di San Martino Nature Park.

Initially the approach was strictly one of preservation and exclusion. Today the rules have been relaxed to recognise that it is possible to balance tourism with protection. Visitors are free to wander and stay in the park and enjoy its wealth of wildlife and plants. However, there remain areas of strict reserve where entry is forbidden, except for study purposes.

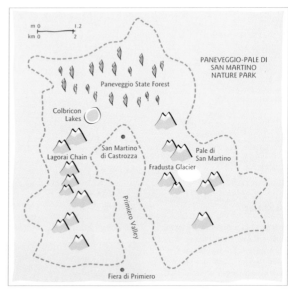

Three branches

The park curves around the Primiero valley, a bustling tourist centre throughout the year. Within the park's boundaries there are three differing areas. The dolomitic cluster of the Pale di San Martino, whose peaks jag the skyline like teeth, is the remains of a coral reef over 250 million years old. Once submerged beneath the sea, its mountains now soar to 3,192m. They rise from a wide plateau, cleft by deep fissures, which is home to the Fradusta glacier.

The second distinct area is the Lagorai mountain chain. Volcanic in origin, its slopes appear dense and sombre compared to the cream and pearl of the Pale. Here visitors come to find solitude and enjoy the peace imbued in this ancient place. On the shores of the Colbricon lakes, Mesolithic peoples camped as they hunted for food around 10,000 BC.

Game can still be seen: red deer were reintroduced in the 1960s and now flourish, whilst chamois, the target of the prehistoric hunters, have never left. Marked routes for walkers follow the probable paths of these earliest inhabitants – one takes the pass towards Paneveggio state forest, the park's third area.

Forest music

Paneveggio forest covers almost a quarter of the park. Predominantly spruce, the forest forms a blanket of green beauty even in winter. But it is its age which makes it so ecologically important. Some trees are over one hundred years old and stand 40m tall.

Alternatively known as 'The Forest of the Violins', the trees which grow here are famed for their resonant qualities. Generations of instrument makers have come to Paneveggio to choose their wood, the most famous being Stradivari in the 1700s. Culture can still be found here, with literary readings in the summer months.

Pale di San Martino rising above Lake Welsberg

Pietra castle in the Primiero valley

Peace and war

After the First World War, Paneveggio required intensive reforestation. The park was the site of prolonged fighting on the Austrian–Italian front line. Some of the most harrowing fighting occurred in treacherous conditions on the peaks of the Pale and Lagorai. Today the signs can still be seen in forts and trenches.

In the 1980s construction started on the 'Path of Peace'. In Trentino, it follows the front line for 400km, where it crossed the province. Sections of the path within the park are difficult, but other parts cover easy terrain and are accessible. In Spiazzo Rendena, in western Trentino, a small war museum displays relics, including those which the province's glaciers still occasionally reveal.

The Primiero valley year

At the head of the Primiero valley is San Martino di Castrozza. Originally a medieval community of monks, the town has been a thriving tourist centre since the 19th century. Busy in both winter and summer it provides a perfect base from which to explore.

San Martino's alpine guides led some of the original explorations of the Dolomites. They continue to lead expeditions into the Pale and can advise on the fixed rope climbs. Strictly for the adventurous, these routes include aerial ladders and exposed ascents. On a gentler level, trained astronomers hold stargazing evenings in summer or visitors can help for a day on research projects.

When the snow falls, San Martino really comes alive as a resort. It is centrally placed for the skiing for which the region is famous, but visitors need not head for the slopes. Cross-country ski-loops wind from the town into the park, crossing frozen lakes. Guides give training in snow shoe use and take treks. The walking routes are all the more beautiful for their coat of snow and the absence of other tourists. The Val Venegia, which is awash with wildflowers in spring, offers uninterrupted views of the Pale in winter. Back in town there is après-snow. Thick slices of the local toséla cheese, fried in butter and washed down with Marzemino wine or herb infused grappas.

[i] CONTACT INFORMATION

Paneveggio–Pale di San Martino Nature Park
Villa Welsperg
Via Castelpietra
38054 Tonadico
Italy
Tel: (00 39) 439 64854
Fax: (00 39) 439 762419
E-mail: info@parcopan.org
Web: www.parcopan.org

The Colbricon lakes are a popular destination for walkers

Trentino's Nature Reserves

Dotted throughout the province, the nature reserves of Trentino provide pockets of interest. Viewed together they enable a picture to be formed of this historically and ecologically diverse region.

The province of Trentino lies in the north of Italy close to the borders of both Austria and Switzerland. It is an area dominated by the Alps, with parts of the Adamello-Presanella, Brenta, Pale di San Martino, Lagorai and Ortles-Cevedale mountain ranges all falling within its boundaries. However, with 297 lakes and 177 glaciers, it is also a land of water.

Both animals and plants abound here and for good reason: just under one-fifth of the entire province is designated as a protected natural area. As well as a national park and two nature parks, Trentino boasts five nature reserves and 287 biotopes, the latter being small areas which, by virtue of their unspoilt nature, are considered worthy of protection.

People and nature

This wealth of reserves is the result of conscious environmental policy. In 1967 Trentino became the first area in Italy to create natural parks. Its aims then were strictly protectionist but over time these have evolved to an ethos which sees a place for both people and nature. As a result, visitors can choose their experience; one associated with the international resorts of the Dolomites; or a more low key, possibly more varied break, focused on the many small pockets of interest the province affords.

Tre Cime del Monte Bondone

The oldest of Trentino's reserves, Tre Cime del Monte Bondone is a 'total reserve'. All of the reserves are graded in a progressive scale denoting which human activities are allowed within them. 'Total' limits interventions to research and study. Close by are the Tridentine Museum of Natural Sciences, the Alpine Ecological Centre and the Viote Botanical Gardens. The latter has over 2,000 species of high altitude plants and flowers.

North of the reserve, visitors can enjoy plants of a different kind. Piana Rotaliana is home to the vineyards producing most of the province's wines. Delicate Riesling and smoky southern reds can be sampled here.

Laghestèl di Pine

To the north-east of Trento in a basin carved by glaciers lies the Laghestèl di Pine reserve. The glaciers have long since been replaced by damp, marshy meadows, and peat bog. In the last century the reserve's lake has been reduced to a quarter of its original size by the bog's encroachment. The lake and reedbeds are home to many wading birds and amphibians. Underneath the water's surface lurks the insectivorous *Utricularia vulgaris*, not a fish but a plant, which in summer blossoms a delicate yellow.

The reserve forms a small part of the Pine highlands, a peaceful expanse of fir forests, lakes and villages. Pilgrims have come to the area for over 250 years, since the Virgin Mary is said to have appeared to a shepherdess here. There is a mountain sanctuary at the place of the visitation.

Scanuppia-Monte Vigolana

Further to the south is the high altitude reserve of Scanuppia-Monte Vigolana. A mixture of woods and pastures, the area was until recently the hunting grounds of the Trapp family whose castle lies nearby. The reserve's current inhabitants reflect this past purpose, with capercaillie, mountain partridge, snow grouse and black grouse nesting here, and red deer roaming across the land.

The mixed woods of beech, larch, silver fir and mountain pine mean that the reserve is worth visiting at any time of year, but in winter visitors may have a better chance of spotting wildlife against the snow that banks on the ground.

Close by are the hamlets of Folgaria and Lavarone. Both are now resorts, and the latter, which claims to have the cleanest lake in Italy, was the holiday destination of Sigmund Freud. Nearby are remnants of trenches and forts, scars from the First World War.

Bès Cornapiana

The smallest reserve, Bès Cornapiana, incorporates both plateau and pasture at an average altitude of 1,600m. Lying on the slopes of Monte Baldo, the reserve has plants that did not survive glacial expansion elsewhere. The unique flora has been studied by botanists for centuries and includes species such as bedstraw, silky wormwood and yellow bear's ear. The rocks are also rich in fossils.

Campobrun

Campobrun reserve is flanked by mountains and more than two-thirds of its terrain is high and rugged. This sparseness has an appeal of its own, especially for walkers, and there are some interesting alpine plants worth searching for, such as squill lilies with their startling cobalt flowers. Campobrun is also one of the few areas in which the Bajuvara dialect, of Germanic origin, is still spoken.

Human flux

From the Mesolithic peoples who crossed the mountains in search of food around 10,000 years ago, to the current tourists, Trentino has always witnessed a flow of peoples. The alpine passes have historically been a link between northern Europe and the Mediterranean. They were strategically important in the spread of the Roman Empire, and were fought over in the First World War, after which the province became Italian territory. This history of flux is reflected in the culture of the region: in its languages, architecture, customs and food, and in the emphasis which is placed on protecting its contrasting landscapes.

i CONTACT INFORMATION

Trentino Tourist Agency
Via Romagnosi, 11
38100 Trento
Italy
Tel: (00 39) 0461 497353
Fax: (00 39) 0461 260277
Web: www.trentino.to

Trentino Park and Forest Service
Vie G.B. Trener, 3
38100 Trento
Italy
Tel: (00 39) 0461 495833
Fax: (00 39) 0461 495918

Tre Cime del Monte Bondone Nature Reserve

Exploring Liechtenstein

Natural history and cultural heritage are both accessible in Liechtenstein.
Alpine features are close to hand, to be enjoyed at a comfortable pace.

Liechtenstein is a tiny but polished country. Barely noticeable on a map, a blip between Switzerland and Austria, the principality occupies only 160 sq km on the Rhine flood-plain and the nearby forested high country. Over the border, the Swiss National Park alone covers about the same area.

Liechtenstein enjoys one of the highest standards of living anywhere. The country counts more companies than people and its prince is one of the richest men in the world. Settled in economic, customs and security agreements with Switzerland, and taking the Swiss franc as its currency, Liechtenstein can get on with the business of being prosperous and preening its pleasant lands.

Warm winds

The weather in Liechtenstein is unlikely to sway the prospective visitor one way or the other. It is influenced a great deal by the *föhn*, a warm dry wind that prevails along the sheltered edge of the country's mountains. Annual rainfall ranges from 1,050 to 1,200mm. Conditions are never extreme, with winter temperatures unlikely to drop any lower than -15°C even in its Alpine regions. In the summer months, temperatures range from 20 to 28°C.

Industry and nature

Liechtenstein's achievement lies in the fact that, in spite of a phenomenal economic boom, it remains a fresh, unobtrusive and picturesque Alpine niche. A country 25km long and 6km wide could be forgiven for showing some of the grubbier marks of industrial development after fifty years in which there has been a threefold population increase. However, each person manages to find 5,333 sq metres of personal space, and the impact of development is muted with discreet architecture and dispersion between the country's meadows and forests. It is clear that Liechtenstein's economic ambition and the pride it takes in its natural resources seem to go hand in hand.

The size of the country makes the idea of a national park unrealistic, but if national parks are understood to take care of the natural and cultural heritage of their countries, then perhaps Liechtenstein as a whole is fulfilling the role. If so, then the country does seem to carry it off with its own peculiar twist. Rather than being laden with nostalgia, the aims of preservation are wrapped up with industrial progress. Whilst certain monuments are carefully kept as pieces of historical importance, there is not the sense of mutual exclusivity between modernisation and environmentalism as elsewhere.

Conservation areas

Throughout Liechtenstein there are carefully maintained gardens, parks, sanctuaries and small nature reserves such as those in Aeulehåg, St Katharinenbrunnen and Elltal, around the town of Balzers. Beside the road that runs between Mauren and Schaanwald, in the area known as 'the village of the seven hills', and alongside the plush residential area of Eschnerberg, the Birka reserve incorporates a bird sanctuary, and makes for a pleasant recreation area with a children's playground.

The hunting lodge at Sass

The Valüna valley

Forest trails

In addition to the sanctuaries and reserves that offer quite a static observation of Liechtenstein's natural treasures, there are a number of walking trails and forest rambles that offer a slightly different perspective.

Weaving through Eschnerberg, a network of footpaths provides a tour of local history and natural features. Rock formations and springs, as well as the flora and fauna in woodlands and meadows, are mapped out for the visitor with a series of signposts and information boards. The forest nature trail in Matteltiwald begins in Rossboda and ends at the junction of the forest road from Wangerberg to Lavadina. About thirty species of shrub and tree are gathered together in the woodland. Carved wooden notice boards have been placed along the length of the walk to highlight the various species. The local forest trail, or *Waldlehrpfad*, in Schaanwald is similarly signposted with plaques incorporating diagrams and drawings.

Villages and towns

Villages and municipalities are also carefully looked after in Liechtenstein. They provide a sense of perspective in the face of dizzying economic statistics. Balzers, for example, can be accounted for by historians from documents from as early as AD 842.

Gutenberg castle stands over the town as a statuesque landmark, and a number of other significant cultural monuments are also maintained in the area, such as St Peter's chapel with its late Gothic winged altar. The village of Ruggell is a celebrated location for cycling lazily along the paths of the Ruggeller Riet where the blue iris flowers in the first weeks of summer. The village pivots around the Church of St Fridolin, designed in the late 19th century by the Viennese architect Gustav von Neumann. The village of Gamprin is home to the Schwurplatz presbytery and the symbolic Unterländer fountain, while the town of Bendern has long drawn pilgrims to its Marist grotto.

ℹ CONTACT INFORMATION

Liechtenstein Tourism
Postfach 139
FL-9490 Vaduz
Liechtenstein
Tel: (00 423) 232 1443
Fax: (00 423) 392 1618
E-mail: touristinfo@lie-net.li

 **GERMANY**

Berchtesgaden National Park

The eagle forms a potent symbol for the Berchtesgaden National Park –
both of destruction in the past and preservation in the present.

The Berchtesgadener Land forms the south-east corner of the Bavarian Alps, and is shaped like an arrowhead which protrudes into Austria. The Bavarian Alps form part of the mountain chain which stretches along the German–Austrian border.

Bavaria was an independent kingdom from 1806 to 1918 and Berchtesgaden was the preferred holiday destination of the second monarch, King Ludwig I. Since then the village has remained an important Alpine resort. It is popular with skiers and is also a good base from which to explore Salzburg, which lies 23km over the border. Although the area's name was tainted during the Second World War, when it was the 'playground' of the Nazis, this aspect of its history is now a feature of interest for visitors.

Berchtesgaden

The Berchtesgaden National Park was founded in 1978 and spreads over 210 sq km of the Berchtesgadener Land's southern tip. It contains five main mountain ranges and the scenic expanse of the Königssee, Germany's highest (602m), deepest (190m) and cleanest lake. One third of the park is rocky and glaciated, with a further third covered in mixed woodlands of spruce, beech, fir and other conifers. Elsewhere are alpine pastures and expanses of low scrub.

The Alps within the park are formed largely of Dachstein-type Triassic limestone. These rocks are particularly hard and resist folding, and as a result

Berchtesgaden village with the Watzmann behind

were pushed up, in slabs up to 2,000m thick, to form the highest peaks. Glaciers and water then set to work to create typical limestone landscapes of steep summits, slopes covered in rock debris, karst ridges and pavements, and corrie lakes. The Watzmann, Germany's second highest mountain, is within the park and its pyramidical, 2,714m summit is a classic example of glacial carving.

Keeping track

The Berchtesgaden National Park was declared a UNESCO biosphere reserve in 1990 and is graded as a 'nearly natural terrestrial ecosystem' by the German government for the purposes of their Environmental Specimen Bank, a data collection programme for environmental monitoring. Within the park spruce, beech, roe deer, earthworms and soil are routinely tested. The park authorities also run monitoring programmes, which make use of telemetry systems to track chamois, Eurasian griffon vultures, woodpeckers, red foxes, ibex and

deer. The systems monitor altitude, activity, heart rate, body temperature and head position, and have proved invaluable in understanding the habitat of the protected golden eagle.

The golden eagle is not the only bird to have been driven from the Bavarian Alps by human intervention. Before the park's formation, the landscape had been cleared and altered, and griffon vultures, bearded vultures, rock swallows and snow finches are all now rare. There are however, over one hundred species of bird in Berchtesgaden, with an additional thirty species migrating or wintering in the area. As the environment re-establishes itself, tracking the park's songbirds is another important task.

The calcified king

The Königssee was originally designated as a plant reserve in 1910 due to the variety of flora surrounding it. The lake curls around the mighty Watzmann range, with the peak of the Jenner (1,874m) at its end.

Salzburg

Berchtesgaden · Eagle's Nest

Watzmann · Königssee

BERCHTESGADEN NATIONAL PARK

AUSTRIA

m 0 ___ 4
km 0 ___ 7

Although there are over 240km of walking routes within the park, it is not possible to walk around the Königssee. Other than a short path to a lookout point, the shores are rendered inaccessible by the precipitous forest-clad mountains which rise from the water. The lake is snow-fed and its depth and steep surroundings colour it a deep bottle green. Since 1909 only electric boats have been allowed on the lake to preserve its purity, and the ferry which carries visitors from one end of the lake to the other is the best means of viewing the serrated Watzmann crags.

Königssee means 'King's lake', and local legend states that the mountains were once a cruel royal family, who as punishment for their tyranny were turned to stone while hunting. The highest peak is the king and the lesser ones his family, and it is easy to imagine from the dark rock that the mountains entomb embittered souls. From the end of the lake, visitors can walk to the smaller Obersee or head along the shore to the St Bartholomä pilgrimage chapel. The ochre onion-domed roofs of the building are a peaceful sight, especially in the early mornings when low mists are suspended between the mountains and hover above the lake.

The Führer's eyrie

Kehlstein mountain (1,837m) which rises on the park's northern border, was the site of the Obersalzberg – a complex of buildings, underground bunkers and tunnels for the Nazi elite. Hitler wrote *Mein Kampf* at Obersalzberg in 1924 and later returned to establish his *Berghof* or mountain house which he used as a recreational and political base.

Today, visitors can explore the celebrated Eagle's Nest house. Perched at 1,834m on the peak of Kehlstein, it was built for Hitler's fiftieth birthday in 1939. Five tunnels and a road were blasted from the rock, enabling an elevator to rise 124m through the mountain's core. The Eagle's Nest was to be used for entertaining foreign dignitaries but because of a fear of heights and claustrophobia Hitler seldom visited. The building is now a restaurant and views from the balcony take in the nearby mountains, the Königssee and the barren waste of Obersalzberg.

[i] CONTACT INFORMATION

Berchtesgaden National Park
National Park House
Franziskanerplatz 7
83471 Berchtesgaden
Germany
Tel: (00 49) 8652 64343
Fax: (00 49) 8652 69434
Web: www.nationalpark-
berchtesgaden.de/

**Berchtesgaden Local
Tourist Office**
Kurdirektion
Königseer Strasse 2
83741 Berchtesgaden
Germany
Tel: (00 49) 8652 9670
Fax: (00 49) 8652 967400
E-mail: info@berchtesgadener-
land.com
Web: www.berchtesgadener-
land.com

St Bartholomä on the shores of the Königssee

AUSTRIA

Hohe Tauern National Park

The deadening grip of the ice caps which used to cover Hohe Tauern has left an interesting geological legacy in an area now rich with nature.

Covering a swathe of the Austrian Alps where the *Bundesländer* (federal states) of Salzburg, Carinthia and Tirol meet, is Hohe Tauern National Park. With an area of approximately 1,800 sq km, it is the largest nature reserve in central Europe and has been established in stages since the 1980s. Interest in the area's preservation predates this to 1913 when the Austrian Alpine Club began acquiring the land around Grossglockner (3,798m), Austria's highest peak and the geographical centre of the park. In the 1950s, locals prevented the exploitation of the Krimml river for energy generation, leading to the entire area being declared a conservation zone.

Austria is a member of the International Union for the Conservation of Nature and Natural Resources, an organisation drawing members from 140 countries. The IUCN monitors over 2,000 national parks worldwide and uses a United Nations' categorisation system to rank them. Because of the degree of human intervention in the park, Hohe Tauern is classed as a category V 'Protected Landscape'.

Frozen lands

Approximately 65% of Austria's territory is covered by the Alps, and within Hohe Tauern itself there are more than 300 mountains over 3,000m. One tenth of the park is covered in glacial ice and winters of eight months are not uncommon.

Summer cottage, Tirol

Glaciers are known as *kees* in Salzburg and Carinthia, and *ferner* in Tirol, and the highest zones of the mountains where the glaciers form are called *nivale stufe*, or snow and ice zones. With the end of the last Ice Age these areas were left barren and have only been gradually repopulated by hardy plants. Now mosses and lichens grow here, as well as the glacier crowfoot. The highest alpine flower, the crowfoot puts out its diminutive pink and white flowers only briefly in July and August, but can be found at altitudes up to 4,200m.

As a glacier makes its infinitely slow passage downwards it scours the mountain rock and carries debris in its wake. The finest particles, known as 'glacier flour', are released in the meltwaters which flow from the glacier's snout and create the milky glacial streams characteristic of the park. These streams flow at their peak from June to August, but during the winter can be frozen. Below the glacial zones, exposed rock gives way to sparse coverings of alpine grasses and herbs, where in summer visitors may catch a strong waft of perfume from the rare black vanilla orchid.

Animals such as Pinzgau cattle were specifically bred in the 1800s to be able to graze the pastures of Hohe Tauern. The fresh air and water, and the herbaceous diet of the cattle, is reputed to have a positive effect on the flavour of their milk, with Pinzgau mountain cheese a local delicacy.

Below the high pastures the first stunted trees appear. Rhododendron, dwarf mountain pine and blueberry give way to larch and Arolla pine, although the latter is scarce because of extensive clearing for pasture. This is the realm of the chamois. November and December is their rutting season, when competing males fight using their lethal horns, occasionally to the death. Thicker spruce, beech and fir forests cover the montane region where the placid earth toad lives. To survive winter weather, the toads dig underground quarters, where they stay until spring when, after mating and spawning, they return to summer homes that are often up to 2km away.

The predominance of glaciers within the park has served to model the landscape. Cirques, U-shaped valleys, and glacial lakes are common, as are high moors formed in the glacial

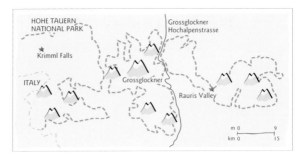

basins, where mud and beaked sedges, and cotton grasses thrive. The Rotmoos, a particularly important example, is located in the Fusch valley to the north of Hohe Tauern. It is the largest moor in the area and its chalk rather than peat base makes it a rarity in Europe. The moor can be reached by an easy hour's walk from the road, and draws many visitors due to the proliferation of orchid varieties which bloom here.

Passages

The earth toad is not the only inhabitant of Hohe Tauern to shift between its winter and summer homes. This practice is shared by

many of the humans who live on the park's boundaries and spend the summer months in cottages above the tree line, returning to their villages and farms in the valleys for the winter.

There are numerous villages surrounding the park and two toll roads and a railway traverse it. One of these roads, the Grossglockner Hochalpenstrasse, markets itself as an integral part of the park experience, emphasising its environmentally aware road-building policies. However, recession, not conservation, was the original impetus for the road's construction. It was built by 3,000 labourers over five years during the depression of the 1930s.

Walking by a lake in Hohe Tauern National Park

The village of Heiligenblut with Grossglockner behind

The summit of Grossglockner was first climbed in 1800 and since then it has proved an increasingly popular, at times congested, ascent. There are several routes up the mountain, all of which involve glacier crossings and the use of specialised equipment, and the route is commonly completed over two days.

If this seems rather difficult, a byroad of the Hochalpenstrasse leads to a viewpoint at Kaiser-Franz-Josefs-Höhe, the saddle above the Pasterze glacier. From here it is possible to catch a funicular to the glacier's edge or follow a hiking trail along its side. Pasterze extends for 9km over a surface area of approximately 20 sq km. Impressive as this sounds, the glacier is retreating to such an extent that the World Wildlife Fund for Nature has classed it as a protected area at risk. The retreat, attributed to global warming, is the largest in 5,000 years and could have potentially devastating implications for the environment.

A small chapel at Fuschertörl commemorates the workers who lost their lives to the task. In parts, the road follows the routes of the Romans, as well as the traders who crossed Hohe Tauern as they went north with their Venetian wares. Neck chains found at Hexenküche (the Witches' Kitchen), were used in the 17th century to marshal prisoners to Venice where they were to serve sentences of hard labour on the galleys.

The Hochalpenstrasse runs at the base of the Grossglockner peak and provides views of the park's most spectacular scenery at average altitudes over 2,200m. It has been extensively developed for motor-powered tourists and incorporates numerous view and information points along its 6km length. On summer days it can become so crammed that cyclists are often officially advised not to use the road. However, the Hochalpenstrasse does enable enjoyment of the park by those not physically able to hike into it and occupies only a very small part of a vast area.

Geological giants

There are many walking routes within Hohe Tauern National Park and the authorities produce helpful maps and pamphlets detailing over eighty destinations of special interest. For visitors who only have time to see the highlights, the park boasts several impressive geological giants. In addition to Grossglockner at 3,798m, there is Pasterze, the longest glacier in both Austria and the eastern Alps, and Krimml falls, claimed as the highest waterfall in Europe.

The Krimml falls are in the far west of the park in the Salzburg area. The waters plunge from the River Krimml in three stages each over 100m – a total drop of 380m. A path with lookout points leads up the fall's side

In the east of the park, in the Rauris valley, are the Geierschlafwände, the sleeping quarters of a colony of bearded vultures. The droppings below the nests encourage growth of bright red lichens which give the cliffs their local name of Rotwände, or Red Walls Rising at the head of the valley is the 3,105m Sonnblick peak, topped by the Sonnblick observatory. Built in 1886, it was for many years the highest meteorological station in the world. The observatory is still operating and, for visitors wanting a closer look, an alpine hut on Sonnblick's flank provides overnight accommodation.

[*i*] **CONTACT INFORMATION**

Hohe Tauern National Park
Nationalparkrat
Rauterplatz 1
A-9971 Matrei i. O.
Austria
Tel: (00 43) 4875 5112
Fax: (00 43) 4875 511221
E-mail: nprt@netway.at
Web: www.npht.sbg.ac.at/npht

Trekking with Haflinger ponies

A climber surveys Hohe Tauern

Donau-auen National Park

The flux and flow of the 'king of rivers' forms the setting for this ecologically important national park.

Also known as the Danube flood-plain or the Danube Riverine National Park, Donau-auen National Park lies in the Austrian federal states of Vienna and Niederösterreich. The park stretches east from the suburbs of Vienna to the international border between Hainburg in Austria and Bratislava in Slovakia. It follows the Danube (Donau in German) for 47km as it crosses the Viennese basin, incorporating the flood-plains, tributaries and forests along its banks.

Trees fringe a backwater in the park.

Niederösterreich

Covering the north-eastern corner of Austria, Niederösterreich is the country's largest province. It includes the Northern Limestone Alps, part of the Alps' foothills; the forested Waldviertel; the vineyard-covered Weinviertel and Wachau; and Marchfeld, an expansive plain which lies between the Danube and March rivers.

The climate is typically continental, with large temperature variations and low rainfall, and the province's main industries are agriculture, viticulture, and oil and natural gas extraction. Because of its capital, Vienna, the province has always attracted visitors, with tourism recently becoming more important outside the city bounds.

The Danube

Vaunted by Herodotus in his *Histories* as 'the greatest of rivers' and by Napoleon as the 'king', the Danube justifies these titles by its size alone. The second longest river in Europe, it runs for 2,820km from the Black Forest in Germany to its delta in Romania where it drains into the Black Sea. The Danube enters Austria in the north-west, running the breadth of Oberösterreich province before crossing into Niederösterreich. Here it cuts through the Dunkelsteiner forest and the eastern pre-Alps before heading to the capital and beyond to the national park.

The campaign

Beginning in 1973, plans were mooted and intermediate steps taken to establish a park around the last free-flowing basin stretch of the Danube. In 1984 a commercial venture to construct a hydroelectric power station near Hainburg was proposed. Public protest and the World Wide Fund for Nature (WWF) succeeded both in stopping the project and obtaining an agreement to establish a park. Donau-auen was finally established in 1996 and now covers an area of approximately 93 sq km lying mainly on the Danube's northern banks.

Donau-auen

The area where the park lies was historically occupied by Illyrians and Celts before the Romans arrived in the 1st century BC. They treated the Danube as a natural frontier, erecting a military camp in AD 35 on its banks at Carnuntum. Their occupation was succeeded by the Bavarians, Slavs, Avars, Hungarians and Turks.

The 19th century saw severe regulation of the Danube to control flooding. Tributaries and flood-plains were isolated from the river, resulting in siltation and a general lowering of the groundwater level. Important riverine habitats were endangered, as the cycle of flood and drainage was crucial to their ecosystems. Many animals – lynx, wolves, otters, beavers, fish, and birds of prey – were driven away or became extinct, exacerbating a reduction of wildlife which had begun when the area was a hunting ground of the Habsburgs.

Since the 1970s, conservation measures have sought to reverse this trend and work is ongoing to reconnect the Danube with its backwaters. Marshland trees are re-establishing in previously damaged areas, as the river is left to erode naturally in parts and rebuild gravel banks and islands in others.

Kingfisher

oday the Donau-auen is one of the argest ecologically intact flood-plains n central Europe, with over 700 pecies of ferns and flowering plants rowing in its forests and meadows.

More than fifty native species of fish nhabit the waters of Donau-auen, mong them the dogfish, which had een thought extinct in Austria until ediscovered in 1992. The schrätzer, teber and zingel perches are found only in the Danube and are dependent n the bank structures formed by a ree-flowing river for their survival. he recent discovery of the previously xtinct European mutminnow within he park was another reassuring find.

n the interests of regeneration, zones ave been established within the park where no human impact is allowed. However, a network of trails enables isitors to explore other areas. A cycle path follows a dyke through the verine forests and affords a view ver the flood-plains; iris, flowering ush, purple loosestrife and other wetland plants appear all the more ivid for their lush green setting. Walking tracks lead both through the lains and along the Danube's banks.

he river's ecosystem has been ompared to that of a rainforest. Visually the effect is similar, with quiet pools of verdant river life, and willows, alders, poplars, elms and ash vershadowing and trailing the water. Kingfishers nest in the steep banks, are European mud turtles bask in the hallows, while lizards sun themselves on rocks. The last beaver of the Vienna basin was killed in 1863 out since its reintroduction in 1976 he animal has spread once more hroughout its old habitat. Even if beavers are not seen their activity is isible in the form of gnawed trees nd deep waterside burrows.

Along the banks, riverine forests offer more opportunities for spotting wildlife and some of the park's 282 species of birds. Spotted woodpeckers, hedgehogs, dormice, squirrels and deer are all common amongst the trees, whilst frogs claim the ponds. The park runs guided tours, by foot or boat, including nature walks and trails for children.

Carnuntum and Eckartsau

History, as well as nature, provides a source of interest in the Donau-auen region. An archaeological park has been established at the site of the Roman military camp at Carnuntum. There were over 6,000 soldiers at the camp, with a civilian settlement later swelling the population to 50,000. A related religious site is centred around a natural hot spring, with temples dedicated to Mithras, the Persian god of light, and the goddess Kybele. Visitors can tour the ruins or, during the art festival, attend a play in the amphitheatre, which originally seated 13,000 spectators.

On the opposite side of the river is Eckartsau castle. From the 12th century the Barons of Eckartsau were feudal tenants of the Holy Roman Empire. The original fortress was incorporated into a larger Baroque-style castle in the 18th century and it was from here that the Habsburgs enjoyed their hunting grounds. At the end of the 19th century, Archduke Franz Ferdinand – heir to the Austrian throne, his assassination precipitated the First World War – laid the gardens here. In 1919 the last Austrian Emperor and Habsburg monarch, Karl I, stayed at Eckartsau with his family before fleeing to exile in Switzerland. The castle now houses the park's information centre and is open to the public.

White-tailed eagle

Thayatal

A park experience of another kind can be had in the north of Niederösterreich at Thayatal – Austria's newest and smallest national park. Thayatal abuts the Podyji National Park in the Czech Republic and plans are being made to link the two. The Thayatal section covers a mere 13 sq km and follows the course of the River Thaya. In places the banks of the river are steep and forest covered, whilst in others they become valley meadows where orchids grow. Both the rare black stork and the eagle owl live here, as well as bats and insectivorous shrews. From the park, the Thaya wends its way eastwards, eventually meeting the River March to form the Austrian–Slovakian border before joining the Danube at Donau-auen.

$\boxed{i}$ CONTACT INFORMATION

Donau-auen National Park
Fadenbachstrase 17
A-2304 Orth an der Donau
Austria
Tel: (00 43) 2212 345013
Fax: (00 43) 2212 345017
E-mail: nationalpark@donauauen.at
Web: www.donauauen.at

Niederösterreich Information
Postfach 10.000
A-1010 Wien
Austria
Tel: (00 43) 1536 106200
Fax: (00 43) 1536 106060
E-mail: tourismus@noe.co.at
Web: www.tiscover.com/noe

DONAU-AUEN
NATIONAL PARK

Vienna

March

Eckartsau

Hainburg

Danou

Fischamend

Carnuntum

m 0   3
km 0   5

Neusiedler See–Seewinkel National Park

A landscape of level vistas, prairies and shallow salt-rimmed pools creates an uncharacteristic national park in a country that is mainly dominated by the Alps.

Migrating geese gathering on one of the saline lakes in the park

Lake Neusiedl and the Neusiedler See–Seewinkel National Park lie in the north of Burgenland on the eastern flank of Austria. The province of Burgenland runs in a narrow strip from below Vienna to the orchard, vineyard and forest-covered hills in the south. Like much of Austria, Burgenland has a turbulent political past – exacerbated by its location on a border. After centuries of shifting between Austrian and Hungarian rule, the 1919 Treaty of St Germain passed the territory to Austria. In 1921 however, Sopron, the capital, voted to return to Hungary, taking a chunk out of the middle of the province.

Compared to the rest of Austria, Burgenland is low lying with a highest point of only 884m. It is relatively sparsely populated and receives fewer foreign visitors than other parts of the country. Lake Neusiedl makes up for this however, as it has always been a popular destination with the Viennese for water sports in summer, and year round for walking and cycling.

Spanning the Austrian–Hungarian border, Lake Neusiedl covers 320 sq km. It is uniformly shallow, with an average depth of just 1.1m, and has no natural outlet, making the water slightly saline and quick to warm in summer. It is the latter characteristic which makes the lake so popular and in summer its northern shores soon become crowded. Neusiedl is the largest steppe lake in Europe and more than half its surface is covered in thick reedbeds, making it an important habitat for birds.

Genesis

The area along the eastern shore of Lake Neusiedl is called the Seewinkel, or lake corner, and is the lowest region in Austria. The Seewinkel is an extension of the Hungarian lowlands which were formed between 12 and 16 million years ago when the ocean

that covered the area receded and vegetation began to appear. The water level varied with wet and dry seasons and although there is evidence of human habitation in the Seewinkel from 7000 BC, this too fluctuated as pastures reverted to swamp or lake, then dried again. Lake Neusiedl itself was formed by tectonic plate movements which created a basin at the end of the last Ice Age. Since then its surface area has varied over the

NEUSIEDLER SEE–
SEEWINKEL
NATIONAL PARK

Lake Neusiedl

AUSTRIA

Illmitz
Apetlon

Seewinkel

m 0   3
km 0   5

HUNGARY

Bearded tit in the reedbeds

eat white egret

to the endangered great bustard, a thick-set relative of the crane. Other birds of interest include merlins, harriers, sea and golden eagles, and occasionally in summer, a solitary spotted eagle. In the villages, man-made roof platforms encourage storks to breed.

Although birds dominate Neusiedler See–Seewinkel, they are not the park's only inhabitants. Hamsters, susliks (ground squirrels) and steppe polecats live in the meadow areas around Apetlon, while the south Russian tarantula can be found creeping along the salted banks of Lake Stinkersee.

The park is on a boundary between alpine and continental climatic regions, with a corresponding mix of plant species, several of which are unique in Europe. The shallowness of the lake means it thaws early in spring, and the reedbeds act to regulate fluctuations in temperature, creating a long period of vegetative growth. In the wetlands, marsh helleborines blossom in summer next to scraggy grey wormwood, while in drier areas rare feather grasses and dwarf irises can be found amongst the pastures.

enturies, from a maximum of 550 km when full, to periods of omplete dryness. The Seewinkel emained marshy until the mid 19th entury when it was drained for azing, creating the current steppe ndscape. The area now consists of astures, farmland and villages.

ark history

esearch into the unique flora and una of Neusiedler See–Seewinkel urgeoned at the beginning of the 0th century on both sides of the order. Research stations were stablished on the lakeshores from e 1940s, focusing on vertebrates, rd populations, and the ecology and onservation of the reed lands. In the te 1980s an Austrian–Hungarian anning commission was established, nd in 1992 the park was formed. ngoing research focuses on fish cology and stock management; razing and its effects on vegetation; nd the wildlife of the reed belt.

eusiedler See–Seewinkel

he national park covers the southern nd and eastern side of Lake Neusiedl nd a scattering of small saltwater kes in the surrounding wetlands. It is vided equally between Austria and ungary, where it is known as Fertö anság Nemzeti Park. Within the ark there are nature reserve zones onsisting of reedbeds and marshes nmediately abutting the lakes where o human intervention is permitted. isitors are, however, allowed within e conservation areas, which are a nixture of reclaimed agricultural land, mall lakes and marshlands.

A network of walking and cycling trails criss-cross these conservation areas, leading into the Hungarian section of the park and onwards around the perimeter of the lake. Viewing platforms along the paths enable visitors to see into the entirely reserved sections.

Spring sees many of the wetlands submerged in water and the park is alive with both resident and migratory birds feeding their young. In summer many of the shallow lakes are completely dry, leaving only salty residues. The autumn rains refill them, only to be frozen for the winter. This is often the best time to visit the park, as the paths are quieter and the skies are full of flocks of geese and ducks passing between their roosts and feeding grounds.

Birds

Neusiedler See–Seewinkel's main appeal to naturalists is ornithological. Not only do the reedbeds form a crucial habitat for waders and waterfowl but the combination of lake and steppe pastures attract diverse migratory birds. On the salt-flats and shores are the waders, with greylags, coots and bitterns common. Lapwings, curlews and godwits nest on the extensive meadowlands, whilst gulls, terns and avocets circle and call above the more saline lakes.

Of particular interest is the enclave of the park situated to the east around Hanság. Hanság means moor, and refers to the Waasen, a low-lying marsh which was drained at the end of the 19th century. It is now home

Ground squirrel

CONTACT INFORMATION

Neusiedler See–Seewinkel National Park
Informationszentrum
Hauswiese
A-7142 Illmitz
Austria
Tel: (00 43) 2175 3442
Fax: (00 43) 2175 34424
E-mail: neusiedlersee.np@netway.at

Triglav National Park

In politics and in spirit, Slovenia is an independent land, and whilst Triglav National Park does not pander to tourism, its mountains and settlements are charismatic.

The benefits of national park status that are enjoyed by Triglav have been hard won. Different groups have lobbied for the full package of permanent protective legislation for the widest possible area since 1908. Time and again campaigners have had to push offers of compromise back across the negotiating table.

However, since 1981, after decades of redefinition and renaming, the 838 sq km of Triglavski Narodni Park as it stands today, have been sheltered from development and abuse. Triglav is unique amongst Slovenia's protected areas by the degree of official preservation it enjoys, and as such the sanctity of its mountains, valleys and lakeland are guarded jealously.

Bled is just to the east of the park

Tourism in the park

As increasing numbers of visitors are drawn to what were the alpine wildernesses of Central and Western Europe, Triglav has had to strike a delicate balance. Threats of development and commercialisation continue to stir heated reactions from the people, as seen in the resistance mustered against plans to install a cable-car route to the summit of Mount Triglav. Many of the towns have avoided dramatic modernisation, taking advantage of their seclusion in the Alps. Slovenia's tourist centres, such as the town of Kranjska Gora in the north-west of the park, tend to be comparatively modest resorts. Likewise, tourist attractions, such as the Alpinum Juliana botanical gardens and the Church of St Joseph in the Soča valley, are subtle and organic.

Historically, even the country's trade and tourist heartlands have grown up in thrall to the mountains. Kranjska Gora's proximity to the valleys of Sava Dolinka and Pišnica has established the town as a base for excursions up to the peaks.

This association has brought with it the humility and reverence of the Slovenian Alpine tradition, characterised by the statue of the alpinist and writer Julius Kugy which sits before the mountains in Trenta. The development of the landscape continues at an epic geological pace, rather than in a commercial rush. The water on the limestone shapes the land more than the winter resorts do.

Triglav National Park

History and tradition

Because of this measured pace of change, the history of Slovenia is particularly close at hand. Rural communities and agricultural traditions persist in the Julijske Alpe (the Julian Alps): not in preserved chalets and processions staged for the benefit of the tourist industry, but according to the rhythms and demands of mountain life.

Similarly, Slovenia's recent stability and peacefulness is resonant because of the trouble that has gone before it. The banks of the Soča river were amongst the most brutal battle fronts of the First World War. A popular route for hikers, the road which travels from Kranjska Gora by the Vršič Pass to Bovec was partially laid by Russian prisoners of war. These men were buried beneath an avalanche in 1916, and are commemorated in a chapel which has been built nearby.

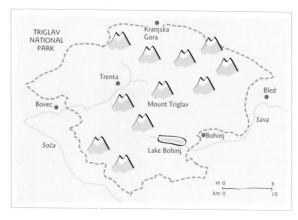

Mount Triglav

In other ways the history of Triglav National Park is the history of Mount Triglav itself. In 1778 four men from Bohinj were the first to scale the mountain's 2,864m. In spite of competition from the startling peaks of Razor (2,601m), Skrlatica (2,738m), and the geometric spectacle of Spik (2,472m), Mount Triglav has become the hub of the National Park and of the country's national imagery.

Stamped on Slovenia's national emblem, and featured in countless ancient, Romantic and nationalistic mythologies, Mount Triglav is close to the heart of the Slovenian sense of identity. The pride nurtured by organisations like the country's first Alpine society, the Triglav Friends, fed into a sense of national confidence and a will to be independent of Austro-Hungarian rule.

The same kind of societies are responsible today for the exemplary footpaths and waymarked routes that are found throughout the park, and for the upkeep of the huts and houses maintained for the benefit of walkers.

ℹ CONTACT INFORMATION

Slovenia Pursuits
New Barn Farm
Tadlow Road
Tadlow
Royston SG8 0EP
Tel: 01767 631144
Fax: 01767 631166
E-mail: angela.rennie@virgin.net

Slovenian Tourist Board
Dunajska 156
1000 Ljubljana
Slovenia
Tel: (00 386) 61 1891 840
Fax: (00 386) 61 1891 841
E-mail: lucka.letic@
cpts.tradepoint.si
Web: www.slovenia-tourism.si

Logarska Dolina Regional Park

Logarska Dolina is small and perfectly formed – a valley sprinkled with rare species, striking geology and a delicate cultural heritage.

The Slovenian Tourist Board does not mince its words. Logarska Dolina is 'indeed one of the most beautiful valleys of Slovenia'. Logarska Dolina, or the Logar valley, is situated in the expansive Štagerska province, a land of meadows and mountains practically uninterrupted by extensive urban settlements. This space, and the natural freedom that comes with it, has allowed the landscape to develop in especially idiosyncratic ways.

Official protection nurtures these unique and quirky features. Slovenia's tendency to look after 'the individual' is typified by the number of trees that have achieved renown and protected status as peculiar pieces of natural heritage. These include the 500 year old Solčava yew; Plesnik's elm with its trunk circumference of 3.7m; Logar's Lindon; and the two larches at the Klemenea caves.

Alpine conditions

As the land gradually climbs upwards towards the east of Slovenia, the climate and the conditions become noticeably more alpine. The protected area of the Logar valley runs to the foot of the Savinjske Alps. Winter in the valley stretches on, with snow settling on the mountains from November to May, before the summer months arrive, brief and hot.

The wildlife of the valley is also of an alpine bent, and flora that finds shelter includes lady's-slipper orchid, garland flower daphne, stemless trumpet gentian, auricula and edelweiss. Forests of spruce, beech, fir, larch and dwarf pine cling to the slopes that climb towards the mountain peaks.

Striking a balance

There are three players in the Logarska Dolina game: the foresters and farmers who live off the land; those who exploit, in the nicest possible way, the glory of the landscape to encourage tourism;

Rinka waterfall

and the vital, animated land itself. An example of the way that the three are moving forward in small, measured steps is the Macesnik farmstead. This exposed little building accommodates a museum which displays ways in which agricultural technology has both drawn and depended upon the movements of the land and water. Antique machinery, such as telphers, ploughs and threshing machines, is driven by a large water wheel.

The Podbreznil chapel, a recognised cultural monument, also neatly describes the way in which community, tourism and environment can nourish one another. Situated at the lower end of the Logar valley, the chapel is extravagantly decorated with typical folk designs, painted with great mastery. The artist, who remains unknown, has managed to encapsulate the tradition of a rural people that is grounded in the land. The images clearly communicate the ethos of this tradition to today's visitors.

Alternatively, the Logar Sisters Hotel can be considered. A thriving hostelry following its opening in the 1930s, the Logar Sisters rode the wave of emerging Slovenian alpine tourism. It came to be seen as a figurehead of the Logarska Dolina. Today, the exquisite timber clad and balustraded building is used as a spiritual retreat.

Lively geology

One-off features of the land include Matkov Škaf, or 'Matk's Tub'. This crater in the rock has been hollowed out by a waterfall that plummets down onto it during the spring. Igla or, 'The Needle', is another of the region's personalities: rising up above the east bank of the Savinja, it is a column of rock that has

The Savinja river is a popular place for rafting

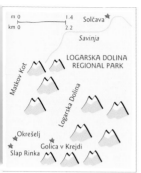

basin, full of clints and grikes, is shadowed by some of the region's great rock monuments – Turska Gora, Rinke and Mrzia Gora – making it an especially popular spot for the country's avid mountaineers. Dropped in the pine forests of the lower Logar valley are a series of erratic blocks. Out of place and quite distinctive, these boulders were gathered up by glacial movement from their native soils in amongst the rocks of the Matkov valley, and set down here as the ice receded.

Slap Rinka

All the lesser waterfalls, springs and streams which bubble under, and run around the rockscapes of the Logarska Dolina seem to feed into one another, culminating in the statuesque 90m waterfall – Slap Rinka. This sense of accumulation, which makes the Logar valley greater than the sum of its

parts, is captured in the way that streams from nearby the Slap Rinka slip through subterranean tributaries to meet the Jezera stream which swells and quickens to become the great Savinja river.

[i] CONTACT INFORMATION

Slovenia Pursuits
New Barn Farm
Tadlow Road
Tadlow
Royston SG8 0EP
Tel: 01767 631144
Fax: 01767 631166
E-mail: angela.rennie@virgin.net

Slovenian Tourist Board
Dunajska 156
1000 Ljubljana
Slovenia
Tel: (00 386) 61 1891 840
Fax: (00 386) 61 1891 841
E-mail: lucka.letic@
cpts.tradepoint.si
Web: www.slovenia-tourism.si

been chipped apart from the cliff-face. Maktovo Okro, or 'Matk's Window', is one of a number of huge carved stone arches. This rocky loop looks out from its ridge, over the valleys of Logarska Dolina on the one side and Matkov Kot on the other. The arch is easily accessed from trails which pass by it. The arena formed at the Okrešelj

Upper Savinja valley

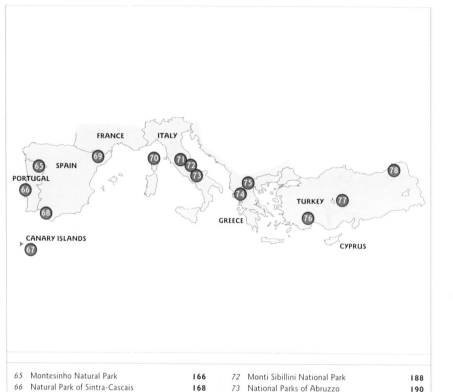

[i] CONTACT INFORMATION

Cyprus Tourist Organisation
17 Hanover Street
London WIR 0AA
Tel: 020 7569 8800
Fax: 020 7499 4935

Greek National Tourist Office
4 Conduit Street
London WIR 0DJ
Tel: 020 7734 5997
Fax: 020 7287 1369

Maison de la France
178 Piccadilly
London WIV 0AL
Tel: 0891 244123
Fax: 020 7493 6594
E-mail: info@mdlf.co.uk
Web: www.franceguide.com

Italian State Tourist Board
I Princes Street
London WIR 8AY
Tel: 020 7408 1254
Fax: 020 7493 6695
E-mail: enitlond@globalnet.co.uk
Web: www.enit.it

Portuguese National Tourist Office
22-25A Sackville Street
London WIX 2LY
Tel: 020 7494 1441
Fax: 020 7494 1868
E-mail: iceplond@dircon.co.uk

Spanish National Tourist Office
22-23 Manchester Square
London WIM 5AP
Tel: 020 7486 8077
Fax: 020 7486 8034
E-mail: info.londres@tourspain.es
Web: www.tourspain.co.uk

Turkish Tourist Office
1st Floor
170-173 Piccadilly
London WIV 9DD
Tel: 020 7629 7771
Fax: 020 7491 0773
E-mail: tto@turkishtourism.
demon.co.uk
Web: www.tourist-
offices.org.uk/turkey

Montesinho Natural Park

The forests and mountains of Montesinho Natural Park are home to rare species, as well as isolated towns and villages, where little has changed in years.

The region known as Trás-os-Montes – translated as 'behind the mountains' – is a rural, untouristed territory in one of the most rugged and remote parts of Portugal. Situated in the north-eastern corner of the country, it is a last outpost of wild landscapes and conservative tradition.

Historical monuments dating from Celtic, Roman and medieval times are evidence of the region's fascinating history and its independent spirit can still be seen in the character and traditions of the people. However, Trás-os-Montes suffers greatly from depopulation. Many small villages, nestled in valleys or perched on high plateaux, are gradually being deserted and there has been little 20th century industrial or economic growth in the area, nor in its capital, Bragança.

Agriculture is the main source of livelihood, and the isolation and lack of development in Trás-os-Montes preserves optimum conditions for wildlife in and around the Natural Park of Montesinho.

Landscape and climate

Enclosed by the Serras of Coroa and Montesinho, the region of Trás-os-Montes is said to have two sides: Terra Quente, or 'warm land' to the south, and Terra Fria, or 'cold land' to the north. The Terra Quente's softer, more prosperous landscape comprises the cultivated farmlands of the Tua and Sabor river valleys and the arterial River Douro. Originating in Spain, the Douro flows southwards for 100km along the border before turning sharply into Portugal. Carving a valley

out of the hills, its steep-sided banks are covered with terraced vineyards that define the surrounding region of Alto Douro, famous for its port wine. Terra Fria, lying north of Bragança, is far more barren and isolated than the Terra Quente, and it encompasses the rugged northern plateau of Montesinho, irrigated by the Onor, Sabor, Tuela and Rabaçal rivers.

There are several microclimates within the Terra Fria region which are mainly determined by altitude, although in general, winters are harsher, with more precipitation than elsewhere. Although the season may be short, temperatures can be extremely hot in the summer, so for cooler weather the best times to visit are during late spring or early autumn.

Montesinho Natural Park

Tucked away in the far north-east, the little-known Montesinho Natural Park is one of Portugal's largest protected areas, and one of the last refuges for the Iberian wolf. Established in 1979, the park covers 750 sq km. It provides a safe haven for a large concentration of Portugal's native wildlife species, and is an especially important reserve for those that are endangered. Here, animals can breed and hunt in the mountains and forests of Montesinho without human intervention.

Mountain streams, that form tributaries of the larger Tua, Sabor and Douro rivers, cut deep valleys through the rounded schistose hills that characterise the park. Alders, willows, hazels and poplars border the rivers, and the deciduous forests of sweet chestnut and black oak that cover the hillsides provide shelter for badgers and foxes, as well as roe deer, wild boar and their predators.

The region's geological and climatic variations have created diverse environments for a wealth of shrubs and wildflowers. Colourful cistus or rockrose species, broom, heather, French lavender and Mediterranean evergreen trees comprise the scented scrubland or *matos* of the rocky slopes. The martagon lily and bloody crane's-bill, a slender purple and yellow variety of toadflax, and delicate violets, pinks and thrift, make up a collection of wildflowers which can adapt to both woodland and scrub.

Because its natural ecology has not yet been unbalanced by modern farming and pesticide use, species which can no longer be found in other parts of Europe, such as the red-backed shrike, the tawny pipit and both the rock and ortolan bunting, still thrive in the wilderness of Montesinho. Songbirds, such as the nightingale and the red-breasted rock thrush, fill the woods and hills with their melodious calls. Birds of prey include Montagu's harriers, kites and hunting kestrels, as well as a few breeding pairs of royal eagles. The horned viper and Iberian wall lizard also inhabit the park, and streams filled with trout and barbel provide food for otters.

Bragança

The capital and main administrative centre of Trás-os-Montes, Bragança has an ancient history, and its strategic location has been the cause of many sieges and battles for its control. Populated since Celtic times, it was named after the Portuguese royal dynasty that ruled until the establishment of a republic in 1910.

The old walled citadel that dominates the town contains a medieval core of public buildings, whitewashed houses and smallholdings that have managed to survive almost unchanged to this day. There are a number of buildings of architectural note both in and outside the walls of the citadel, including a Domus Municipalis (Municipal Hall) in the Romanesque style, Renaissance and Manueline churches, and the castle's Gothic keep, which now houses a military museum. Up to recently, the town was so isolated it could only be reached by winding mountain roads or a rattling train ride. However, its university, its proximity to Spain and improved transport and communication services have given Bragança a long overdue new identity as an expanding regional centre.

The towns of Chaves, Mirandela and Miranda do Douro form a curving semicircle from west to east between Trás-os-Montes and Alto Douro. Chaves is worth visiting for its therapeutic hot springs, whilst delicacies such as cured hams and specialised local artisanal crafts, including basket work, weaving, wood carving and pottery, are to be found throughout the region.

ⓘ CONTACT INFORMATION

Montesinho Natural Park
Bairro Salvador Nunes Teixeira
Lote 5
Apart. 90
5300 Bragança
Portugal
Tel: (00 351) 273 381234
Fax: (00 351) 273 381179

Information Centre:
Delegação em Vinhais
R. de Álvaro Leite (Casa do Povo)
5320 Vinhais
Portugal
Tel: (00 351) 273 71416

The medieval castle at Bragança

Montesinho's autumn colours

Natural Park of Sintra-Cascais

The landscape of Sintra-Cascais Natural Park is punctuated both by geological and coastal features, and important cultural landmarks that are evidence of human habitation since the earliest times.

Palàcio da Pena, Sintra

Dramatically situated in the most westerly corner of mainland Europe, the Natural Park of Sintra-Cascais encompasses diverse marine, mountain and vegetated landscapes. Its territory is split by the eruptive massif of the Serra de Sintra, that lies between the beaches, dunes, cliffs and agricultural farmland of the coastal zone, and the lush greenery of the Serra's northern slopes.

The range forms part of a volcanic belt that runs parallel to the Atlantic, its granite peaks reaching their highest point at Cruz Alta (529m) in the Parque da Pena. Clouds blown inland from the sea rain on the northern side of the Serra, creating a special microclimate. The warm and moist conditions are conducive to the growth of foreign sub-tropical plants as well as rare indigenous species.

From the lively summer resort of Cascais in the south, the boundary of the natural park follows the Costa de Lisboa due north for over 40km as far as the Foz do Falcao, curving inland to the beautiful royal city of Sintra with its nearby palaces and gardens.

Sintra's cultural landscape

Sintra and its hinterland is classified as a cultural landscape under the UNESCO world heritage site scheme. Churches, chapels and hermitages of early religious settlements dot the countryside, often providing the inspiration or even the foundation for later constructions of a more secular nature. Summerhouses, chalets and palaces were built by royalty and Lisbon's nobility when Sintra was one of the main resorts for the Portuguese court during the 15th and 16th centuries. Although the court abandoned the city under the Spanish administration in the 1580s, the region's popularity resumed when Fernando II established a retreat at Palácio da Pena in the 1840s.

At the beginning of the 19th century, the Romantic movement began to find expression in music, painting, literature and architecture. In Portugal, architects and their patrons sought to reject the formality of the classical tradition and draw on design elements from the kingdom's rich architectural history. Egyptian,

Moorish, Gothic, Manueline (a later, more elaborate form of Gothic), Baroque and Italianate styles were all combined in the construction of elaborate palaces, mansions and fine houses, with their equally luxurious surrounding parks and gardens.

Monserrate Park

To the west of Sintra, the palace and park of Monserrate has had a long history of mainly foreign ownership. After visiting the Benedictine pilgrimage site of Monserrate in Spain, Friar Gaspar Petro built a commemorative chapel at this site in 1540. By 1790 it had fallen into secular use and the property was developed by an Englishman, Gerald DeVisme, who built a Neo-Gothic castle and gardens here.

Monserrate was then taken over by another Englishman, William Beckford, who, inspired by Romanticism, constructed a series of naturalistic waterfalls, now known as Beckford's falls. In 1856, a third English owner, Francis Cook, saved the estate from neglect and began an ambitious

Part of the gardens at Monserrate Park

project of exotic garden design. Enlarging DeVisme's castellated structure, Cook created a palace with an eclectic combination of mainly Moorish and Neo-Gothic influences.

In the grounds, native species of cork oak, holly and arbutus mingle with curiosities such as swamp cypresses from south-west America, 30-50m tall monkey puzzles from Australia; Mexican agaves, palms and yuccas; and Japanese bamboo, ferns, azaleas and rhododendrons. Over 2,500 species contribute to a contrasting landscape where grottoes, ruins and secluded gardens such as the fern valley, with its Australian tree ferns, are set amongst tropical waterfalls and ponds.

Palácio da Pena

The husband of Queen Dona Maria II of Portugal, Dom Fernando II, was both a nature enthusiast and a patron of the arts. In 1838 he purchased the ruins of a 15th century convent set on a hill just outside Sintra. In order to create a residence and gardens that reflected his passion for the ideals of the Romantic movement, he later added surrounding estates and a Moorish castle to his property and transformed the convent remains into the foundations of a royal palace at Pena. Already situated in rugged, vegetated territory, Dom Fernando

wished to maintain and emphasise the wildness and spirit of the location, through unstructured planting of exotic plants within the naturalistic setting of the grounds.

Ferns from Australia and New Zealand, Japanese cryptomeria, Brazilian pines, Lebanese cedars and thuja trees from North America are amongst the many foreign species that were imported and planted alongside native trees in the existing woodlands. The paths that explore the park lead to the discovery of several 'secret' locations: a colourful camellia garden and an Arab pavilion set in tranquil greenery; lakes and adjoining waterfalls that provide water for gushing fountains; and decorative architectural features such as small bowers and belvederes.

Cascais and the coast

A popular trading port since earliest times, Cascais became a favourite resort amongst the nobility during the 19th century after King Luis I converted the town's 17th century citadel to serve as his summer residence. It is still known for its lively social scene and busy nightlife.

A tour along the coast undertaken from the town exposes visitors to a different side of Portugal. At the Boca do Inferno, or Mouth of Hell, located outside Cascais, the sea pounds into gaps in the cliffs, causing a terrifying booming noise. Further up the coast, windsurfers are drawn to the beach at Guincho by the huge rollers that crash in from the Atlantic.

Sea thrift

Azenhas do Mar

North of here, the granite cliff of Cabo da Roca is the westernmost point on the continent and a prime bird-watching location. Terns, skuas, gulls and cormorants are found in abundance and many species come to breed here. Others, such as the Manx shearwater and northern gannet visit the cape as a stopping off point during migration. Sea legends of tritons and mermaids, have long been associated with this wild spot and its lighthouse which is over 200 years old.

Omphalodes kuzinskyanae

Home to a valuable ecosystem, the coastal area is increasingly under threat both from a growth in urbanisation and tourism, and insufficient government protection. The Sintra pink (*Dianthus cintranus*) and the less common Sintra thrift (*Armeria pseudoarmeria*) are found in the dunes, but a number of plant species that had become endemic to the area are now quite rare. The delicate blue eye or *Omphalodes kuzinskyanae* puts down roots amongst rocky soils and struggles to survive, but is easily stepped upon by careless walkers.

Continuing north along the coast, just south of the Praia Grande do Rodizio, is the site of the Praia Grande dinosaur tracks. Recently geologists discovered eleven trails of dinosaur footprints, possibly belonging to carnivorous megalosaurus or herbivorous iguanodons. Originally left in the mud of a swamp about 90 million years ago, the tracks were covered in layers of sediment which hardened into rock. Nearly 30 million years later, the geological processes which formed the Sintra massif raised this natural deposit into an upright position, and the tracks can now be seen set into the face of a wall.

Named after the mills that ground wheat from the surrounding countryside, the cliff top settlement of Azenhas do Mar is an attractive town. Its position affords wide sweeping views out to sea and it is the starting point for some beautiful coastal walks.

The area known generally as the agricultural zone has been farmed for centuries and extends from the coast to the western side of the Sintra massif. Dry stone walls and natural screens of canes or reeds shelter the open plains of crops from the influence of the sea.

ℹ CONTACT INFORMATION

Sintra-Cascais Natural Park
Rua General Alves Roçadas
nº 10 – 2º Esq.
2710 Sintra
Portugal
Tel: (00 351) 21 923 5142
Fax: (00 351) 21 923 5141

Mil Cores® – arte fotografica
Photographic Safaris
Jose Romao (prop.)
Apartado 648
2801-602 Almada
Portugal
Tel & Fax: (00 351) 212 959212
E-mail: direct@milcores.pt
Web: www.milcores.pt

National Parks of the Canary Islands

The Canary Islands as a whole are Spain's most protected natural area, with two fifths of the land home to four different national parks and several natural parks and reserves.

Nearer to Morocco than to mainland Spain, the Canary Islands' archipelago is made up of seven main islands, representing the tips of a subterranean zone of volcanic origin. Their explosive history and geographical location mean that there is a surprising variation of climate, topography and vegetation within the archipelago. Landscapes range from lush sub-tropical forests to arid deserts scattered with strange, sculpted forms.

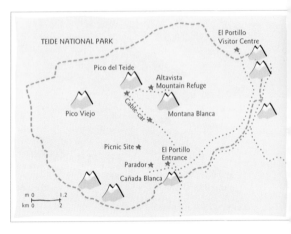

Teide National Park

The largest island in the Canaries, Tenerife is characterised by its impressive mountain range running from north-east to south-west. Located in the centre of this chain, Teide National Park is founded on a sunken natural crater, 29km in diameter. The crater forms a vast natural amphitheatre, lying at an altitude of 2,100m. It is shadowed to the north by Spain's highest

Viola palmae, La Caldera de la Taburiente

mountain, El Pico del Teide (3,717m), whose snow-capped peak soars high above the island. A series of eruptions have created channels or passages (*cañadas*) of flat volcanic soil, through which the guanche shepherds (the early inhabitants of the Canaries) drove their flocks from summer to winter pastures.

Violets and lizards

No rivers irrigate the land, and the high altitude and low temperatures would seem to create inhospitable conditions for most plant life. Despite this, the volcanic soil of the El Teide massif is fertile and a number of plant species have adapted and now thrive.

In spring, colourful clumps of Teide broom, with its pinkish white flowers, are abundant, while the park is also home to other hardy flowering shrubs. There are several endangered species, including the delicate El Teide violet. Some Canary pines have taken root and Canary cedars grow haphazardly along the cliff tops.

The few vertebrates inhabiting the dry parkland include the lagarto tizón lizard, as well as rabbits and small rodents. The latter provide meals for birds of prey such as falcons, kestrels and red kites. Shrikes are common, as well as the canary (a disappointing dull colour) and the El Teide finch with its attractive blue plumage.

Teide National Park

imanfaya National Park

Access and exploration

Although the park is open all year round, the most rewarding time to visit in terms of flowering fauna is during the spring months – the landscape being altogether less colourful and more sun scorched in the heat of summertime.

A cable-car runs from the foot of El Teide and climbs 400m to leave visitors twenty five minutes walk from the edge of the peak's crater. There is also a path leading from the base of Montana Blanca to the top of the mountain. A permit must be obtained to access El Teide on foot and walkers must be accompanied by a guide. Hikes are also organised by the park.

Conservation

There is the distinct impression that up to recently, Teide has not been properly managed from the point of view of its long term future. The overall rise in the numbers of tourists holidaying in the Canary Islands has inevitably led to a related

increase in visitors to Teide. Human pressure and environmental factors have resulted in the erosion of the landscape, putting a strain on the park's natural resources and basic services. Because there are now major

El Teide finch

concerns about Teide as a protected area, the park has been divided into different zones of control and use. Currently there are plans for even more extensive restrictions to be placed on access in an effort to enable the park to recover.

Timanfaya National Park

Situated on the island of Lanzarote, the topography of Timanfaya National Park has been shaped by periods of intense volcanic activity. Lanzarote suffered numerous eruptions during the 17th and 18th centuries (the worst took place in 1730 and lasted for six years). The pretty village of Le Geria is a good an example of how the locals made the most of the islands' violent legacy: they established their vineyards in shallow pits of volcanic soil, secured and surrounded by dry stone walls.

The park can be visited throughout the year, although the glorious arrival of the spring blooms in April injects some fresh colour and life into the landscape. Camel trips are organised at the entrance to Timanfaya, and further into the park, at El Islote de Hilario, there is an information centre and a bar-restaurant that uses the heat of the volcano to cook food.

The Route of the Volcanoes

In the south-west corner of Lanzarote, 52 sq km of land has been given over to Timanfaya National Park. The whole area resembles an eerie lunar landscape. A flat plain of solidified lava makes up the lower part of Timanfaya, with over 300 craters, volcanic cones and strange geological formations punctuating the terrain.

The 14km Route of the Volcanoes was built from volcanic material so that visitors could safely tour the southern part of the park, get close to selected craters and enjoy the

Lagarto tizón lizard

mesmerising scenery. Montaña de Timanfaya, also called La Montaña del Fuego (Mountain of Fire) is to the south; its cone can be (uncomfortably) visited on the back of a camel.

With practically no rainfall, vegetation is rare, although rushes, cactus, and broom survive. The latter is often cut, dried and burnt for practical reasons and as a spectacle for tourists. Wildlife is scarce in this part of Lanzarote, although Manx shearwater and Egyptian vultures are seen, and the haria lizard can be spotted darting between the rocks and folds of lava.

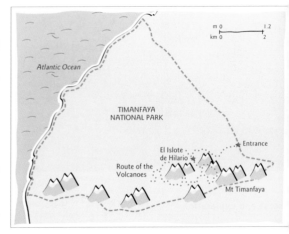

La Caldera de la Taburiente

Situated in the centre of the island of La Palma, La Caldera de la Taburiente has been a protected area since 1954. The national park covers 50 sq km,

LA CALDERA DE LA TABURIENTE
NATIONAL PARK

and is set in one of the largest craters in the world. This huge hollow lies at 800m above sea level and has a diameter of over 10km at its widest point. La Caldera's boundaries are delineated by a circle of tall summits rising up from the crater floor. La Roque de los Muchachos is the island's tallest summit at 2,423m. Forming part of the mountainous ridge at the north-eastern corner of the park, its ascent is an exhilarating challenge, with rewarding views.

Although caldera means crater, the name of the park is misleading as La Caldera de la Taburiente has not been formed by volcanic activity.

It is, rather, the result of millions of years of erosion. The forces of water have carved deep ravines in the crater walls to reveal the oldest rock types found in the Canary Islands. Innumerable springs and dramatic waterfalls gush down the sheer rock face to form rivers in the park's basin.

Plant and animal life

The best example of the archipelago's Canary pine ecosystem is preserved in La Caldera. At lower altitudes and towards the edges of the park there is a thick carpet of indigenous growth. The pine trees play a vital role in preventing erosion, as landslides are

The Route of the Volcanoes, Timanfaya National Park

Caldera de la Taburiente National Park

Canary pines of La Caldera de la Taburiente

not infrequent. At heights above 2,000m, the trees are replaced by heavily scented broom, laurel and heath. The abundant flora creates sheltered habitats for rabbits, wood pigeons and the lagarto tizón lizard. May, June and July are considered the best months to visit, when the park is in full flower.

Navigating La Caldera

To the west of the park the appropriately named Barranco de las Angustias (the Gorge of Fear) cuts a path through the crater and offers the only natural entrance to La Caldera. It is reached by main road and then must be negotiated on foot. Along the northern boundary of the park, another road skirts beneath the tall mountain ridges, eventually ending at La Roque de los Muchachos.

A natural viewing point at La Cumbrecita provides superb vistas over La Caldera. It can be approached from either side – by road from the south or by footpath from the north. Although there are several walking routes that traverse the park, it is considered dangerous to enter the ravines alone or unprepared, and visitors are recommended to make the trip with an experienced guide.

Garajonay National Park

Lying to the west of Tenerife, La Gomera is a small island with a population of about 17,000. Tourism does not thrive here as on the other islands as the climate and landscape don't promise 'sun, sea and sand'. Trade winds pile rain clouds onto the central plateau, supplying the moisture essential for its lush sub-tropical forests. Sheer cliffs dominate a rugged coastline, with the lands around the fringes of the island drier in contrast to the mountains.

Garajonay National Park

Laguna Grande

A national park since 1981 and a UNESCO world heritage site since 1986, the National Park of Garajonay is located on the main massif and is named after its highest peak, Mt Garajonay (1,500m).

The main roads of the island cross the park, with designated paths leading off into more remote areas. Numerous *miradors* or viewing points have been constructed at strategic spots. Garajonay's main information centre is located at Laguna Grande, with free guided tours organised from here.

Laurisilva forests

The park is largely protected for its wild laurel woodlands, which are also known as the Canarian laurisilva forests. This is a collective name given to a concentration of different forest types made up of perennial deciduous trees. Garajonay preserves the final examples of these forests which covered the Mediterranean coast millions of years ago and disappeared during the last period of glaciation. The continued survival of these forests depends on the island's high humidity levels and consistently mild temperatures.

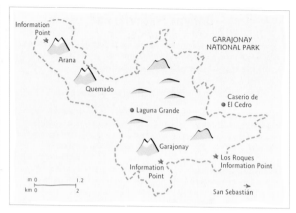

Mountain dove

Gomeran wildlife

Over 450 plant species have so far been recorded at Garajonay, thirty four of which are exclusive to La Gomera. Varying types of laurisilva forest grow in different parts of the park, corresponding to altitude and rainfall. The valleys of the park's northern slopes are prioritised in terms of protection, as their high humidity levels contribute to almost virgin areas of dense healthy growth. Further up the peaks, and in more exposed areas, the forests thin out as fewer species manage to survive.

Across the less foggy southern slopes and along the mountain ridges, large tree-like heathers cover the forest floor, their twisted branches and trunks practically smothered by a rich blanket of moss and lichen. In the south-east of the park at Los Roques, the raised crags and outcrops that jut out from the thickly covered slopes are the remains of volcanic tubes through which lava once flowed.

As well as chaffinches, warblers and falcons, Garajonay is home to two species of mountain dove found in the Canaries: the Columba trocaz bollei nests only in the highest trees and the Columba junoniae on rocky cliffs.

CONTACT INFORMATION

Teide National Park
Calle del Pillar 1
38002 Santa Cruz de Tenerife
Canary Islands
Tel: (00 34) 922 290129
Fax: (00 34) 922 290188

Timanfaya National Park
Laguneta 64
35560 Tinajo
Canary Islands
Tel: (00 34) 928 840238
Fax: (00 34) 928 840251

La Caldera de la Taburiente National Park
O'Daly 35
38700 Santa Cruz de la Palma
Canary Islands
Tel: (00 34) 922 497227

Garajonay National Park
Carretera General del Sur, no.20
38800 San Sebastián de la Gomera
Canary Islands
Tel: (00 34) 922 870105
Fax: (00 34) 922 870362

Garajonay National Park

Doñana National Park

Doñana is a haven of food and shelter for migratory birds travelling between northern Europe and Africa, especially the huge numbers of ducks and geese that make the salt marshes their winter home.

Designated a UNESCO world heritage site, Doñana National Park is situated in the province of Huelva in the Andalusian region of south-western Spain and extends over 500 sq km of coastal land.

Individual categories of legally protected land are combined in the area, with Doñana National Park, Doñana Natural Park, and a scientific / biological reserve all under different management. The natural park exists in separate zones around the national park, forming a vital interior buffer zone between the fragile ecosystem of Doñana and its surrounding areas. Doñana can be broadly divided into three different environments: salt marshes and wetlands; beaches and dunes; and wild scrubland with pine forests further inland.

History of the park

King Alfonso X was the first to officially recognise the wealth of natural resources in the Doñana area, showing his appreciation by establishing his royal hunting grounds here as early as 1262. King Alfonso's son later rewarded the Lord of Sanlúcar de Barrameda, Don Alfonso Peréz de Gúzman with further land for faithful service. Guzman's line became known as the dukedom of Medina-Sidonia, and the family was linked to the area from this time up to the last century.

The national park is named after the duchess Doña Ana de Silva, wife of the seventh duke of Medina-Sidonia. A hunting lodge was built here for her in 1595. Largely uninhabited,

Doñana was used mainly as a hunting reserve. Other activities included horse breeding, ice production (for fish preservation on ships), fishing, timber, charcoal making and salt mining.

Recognition of Doñana's ecological importance grew throughout the 20th century owing to the efforts of both hunters and naturalists. By 1964 the first 7,000 hectares had been purchased specifically for protection and preservation, and in 1969 Doñana was declared a national park. A sequence of titles, including the park's identification in 1981 as a biosphere reserve, and in 1988 as a special protection area for birds, have culminated in the 1994 declaration of Doñana National Park as a world heritage site.

Doñana's shifting dunes

Landscape and wildlife

Although Doñana is mainly classified as a humid marshy area, contrasting dry zones help to create a range of unique ecosystems within the park. Humid salt marshes and lagoons *(marismas)* are enclosed by drier areas; coastal sea dunes bordering the Atlantic on one side *(corrales)* and dense scrubland and forest on the other *(cotos)*. A thin line of evergreen vegetation *(vera)* provides relief between the marismas and the cotos.

Marismas

The topography of Doñana is determined largely by water. Its river, the Guadalquivir, rises in the Sierra de Segura mountains in the north-west of the province, and is swollen by tributaries from the Sierra de Morena as it flows through Seville, finally reaching the Atlantic and the Gulf of Cadiz at Sanlúcar de Barrameda. Here, where the mouth of the river broadens, rivulets and underground streams feed Doñana's coastal lagoons and saltwater marshlands.

In summer, the marismas dry out and flatten because of intense heat and drought. Only herbaceous plants that have adapted to the salty soil can survive. Winter brings rain and floodwaters to the delta, transforming the dry plain into a vast watery home for geese, ducks, waders and spectacular flocks of flamingoes.

When the waters recede in the spring, leaving raised sandbanks and rich alluvial deposits, a perfect shelter is created for the many species of wildfowl that come to nest and breed in the green marshy growths of rushes and aquatic plants.

Corrales

Doñana's impressive coastal dunes are made up of fine white sand. Blown by south-west winds from the sea, the dunes are constantly shifting inland towards the marshes. Only reptiles, insects and desert plants can live in these arid conditions. The last remnants of the ancient juniper forests that used to cover the coast still survive on the peaks of the dunes. Scattered copses of stone pine border the edges of the area. With time, the shifting sand-hills reach these trees and encircle them. The pine stands are eventually completely buried by the dunes, only to re-emerge once the sands have been blown relentlessly onwards.

Vera

A welcome strip of lush vera divides the exposed marshes from the dry brushland of Doñana. Grey and squacco herons, egrets, terns, storks and spoonbills nest and shelter in the cork oak aviaries. Wild boar, and fallow and red deer take advantage of the shade and graze the damp pasture that is irrigated by inland lagoons.

Flamingoes over the marismas

Cotos

The cotos are made up of a dense Mediterranean scrubland. Cork oak trees are dotted around, with a mix of rockrose, heather, rosemary, lavender and thyme contributing to a valuable habitat for some of Europe's rarest mammals. The park is a refuge for the Iberian lynx, the Egyptian mongoose and the endangered imperial eagle (fourteen breeding pairs).

Seasons in the park

Spring and autumn are generally recognised as the best times to visit, as temperatures are almost unbearable in July and August. When the winter floods subside in the spring, the exposed mudflats are teeming with flocks of breeding birds. The wildlife population in the park reaches peak numbers, and plants and trees are in full bloom at this time.

For those seeking greater solitude, and for bird-watchers with a specific interest in waterfowl, the months of November, December and January may be a more attractive time to come as there are fewer people. Individual access to Doñana is limited, and organised tours are currently the only way to visit. Separate permits, from separate bodies, are required for both the main park and the scientific reserves within it.

The scrub and forest of the cotos

Storks nesting at sunset

Under threat

Although the Doñana reserve is unique in Western Europe as the largest single area without roads or infrastructure, its isolation has become increasingly at risk.

Difficulty of access to the park begins to make more sense when the fragility of its existence and the importance of its protection and management is understood. Agricultural pesticide run-off poses a serious threat to the valuable river delta and Doñana's precious wetlands. In addition, the surrounding provinces of Huelva, Cadiz and particularly Seville are heavily populated, and contribute to the industrial pollution of the sea and the Guadalquivir river.

In recent years residential development has encroached along the outer edges of the park. Amongst other problems, this has led to increased car traffic and a rise in wildlife kills by domestic dogs and cats. Once again, the struggle for

recognition between the employment needs of the local community (in a notoriously deprived region of Spain) and the requirements of a vital natural environment is highlighted.

Proposals for a large-scale tourist development along the coast have caused a major divide between the park authorities and locals. Due to intervention from national and international organisations, expressing protest at the potential devastation such a development could cause, the plans are temporarily on hold, although an uneasy truce prevails.

Facilities for visitors

There are five visitor centres located within the park, with different information points, natural history exhibitions and audiovisual displays provided at each site. At three sites specific walking routes have been developed which pass through Doñana's various ecosystems, incorporating vantage points and observatories along the way.

El Acebuche visitor centre (Matalascañas) and La Rocina visitor centre (El Rocio) are the reservation and departure points for four-wheel drive tours through the park. These fairly tourist-orientated trips take groups along 70-80km routes.

The Sanlúcar–Guadalquivir–Doñana boat trip takes a 30km tour along the Guadalquivir and includes stops and walks through both the national and natural parks. Reservations can be made at the Ice Factory visitor centre (Sanlúcar de Barrameda). There are three designated camping grounds in the park, for which permits are required, whilst the local towns have ample accommodation facilities.

ⓘ CONTACT INFORMATION

The National Park of Doñana
Centro Administrativo El Acebuche
21760 Matalascañas
Huelva
Spain
Tel: (00 34) 959 448739
Fax: (00 34) 959 448576
E-mail: donana@mma.es

Aigüestortes-Sant Maurici National Park

Representing the characteristic glacial landscape of the High Pyrenees, this national park's stunning scenery is home to valuable indigenous plant and animal life.

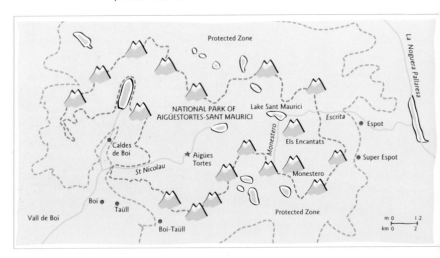

In the High Pyrenees, in the province of Lleida, Aigüestortes-Sant Maurici National Park is situated between two river valleys, the Noguera Ribagorzana and the Noguera Pallaresa. Spanning four Pyrenean counties, the park's 142 sq km is shielded by a 270 sq km buffer zone. It was established in 1955 but, at the same time, the abundant local water supplies were harnessed for hydroelectric power. As the exploitation of natural resources in a protected reserve is banned, Aigüestortes' official status as a national park has been under debate.

Winding waters

At numerous beautiful viewing points, mountains, sky, forests and lakes create a breathtaking vista. Summits of granite and slate, some reaching over 3,000m, mark the park's northern and southern boundaries. Shaped by 2 million years of glacial activity, the park is full of cirques, moraines, tarns and spectacular U-shaped and hanging valleys. The name Aigüestortes (meaning 'winding waters') is derived from the park's abundant streams and cascades.

The park is divided into east and west sections both by the regional boundary and by its two main river valleys. In the west, the valley of the Sant Nicolau river and its tributaries defines the Aigüestortes half of the park, with the Sant Maurici lake in the east marking the other part. From Sant Maurici, the Riu Escrita flows into the Vall d'Espot, eventually joining the Noguera Pallaresa valley. To the south of the lake, the twin peaks of the Els Encantats massif (Petit Encantat at 2,738m and Gran Encantat at 2,747m) tower above the lake and the Monestero river valley. Their distinctive profiles have been adopted as part of Aigüestortes' logo.

Local populations

The valleys of Aigüestortes-Sant Maurici National Park are rich in vegetation. Evergreen forests of silver fir, juniper, Scots pine and black pine cover higher slopes, while scattered deciduous woods of silver birch, beech, willow and mountain ash are found lower down. Reed marshes and lush alpine meadows are home to many plant species. Wildflowers include gentian, iris, lilies, amaryllis, buttercup and saxifrage.

Golden eagles are one of several birds of prey found in Aigüestortes

The fauna of the park is typical of the high mountains. The *isard* or Pyrenean chamois is common, staying on high ground in summer but driven downhill by harsh conditions in the winter. Wild boars, stoats, rodents and pine martens are also numerous. Woodpeckers, wallcreepers and kingfishers inhabit the green woods and riverbanks, while the elusive ptarmigan stays out of sight near the higher glaciers, and the capercaillie nests in the dense pine forests. Mountain birds of prey include golden eagles, kestrels, the solitary bearded vulture and griffon vultures.

Hydroelectric development has been cited as one of the reasons for the disappearance of the indigenous Pyrenean brown bear from its natural mountain habitat. Another rare, timid creature is the Pyrenean desman, a mole-like mammal that lives in the mountain riverbanks but is threatened by pollution and human disturbance.

Walking in the park

Aigüestortes offers the opportunity to explore both established lower level paths and challenging mountain trails. The clearly signposted GR 11 long distance path skirts Aigüestortes' northern limits. It is complemented by various waymarked, but unnumbered,

trails that traverse the park. Dams can easily be avoided as recommended tracks are located in remoter areas, with north–south routes the quieter option. There are several well-equipped shelters within the park and the buffer zone, as well as shepherds' huts. Although camping is forbidden in Aigüestortes itself, there are managed campsites at Caldes de Boí and Taüll in the west and Espot in the east.

Navigation in the park is often dependent on conditions, and rain and mist are always a possibility. Unexpected showers can occur in the mountains on a daily basis, although shifting climatic patterns show that summers are becoming warmer and drier. Spring and summer are the most rewarding times to visit – the snow melts from the alpine meadows and the valleys are awash with flowers. In the autumn, temperatures are still warm and the deciduous woods glow red, russet and gold.

Things to do

Catalunya puts a strong emphasis on tourism and there is a real diversity of attractions for the visitor. Selected routes can be followed throughout the Lleida region, exploring a theme such as folklore, castles, architecture, museums or gastronomy.

The Catalunyan Pyrenees boast many early examples of Romanesque art and architecture as it was one of the first areas in Spain to adopt the style. To the south of Aigüestortes, in the Vall de Boí, are several 11th and 12th century churches with the tall, slender bell towers characteristic of the Lombardy style. The most famous of these churches are Santa Maria and Sant Climent at Taüll.

The village of Boí hosts one of the main tourist and information offices for the national park (the other one being located at Espot). Further up the Noguera de Tor at the head of the Boí valley is the resort of Caldes de Boí; 1,150m above sea level, it has thirty seven hot springs.

CONTACT INFORMATION

Aigüestortes-Sant Maurici National Park
Information Centre
Plaça del Treio, 3
25528 Boí (Alta Ribagorça)
Spain
Tel & Fax: (00 34) 973 696189

Aigüestortes-Sant Maurici National Park
Information / Administration Centre
Prat del Guarda, 4
25597 Espot (Pallars Sobirà)
Spain
Tel & Fax: (00 34) 973 624036

Corsica

Rugged beauty and an eventful past has shaped Corsica's distinctive character and, with many of its most spectacular areas protected by UNESCO, there is much to fascinate the nature-loving visitor.

Corsica has been part of France for more than 200 years but the influence of earlier Italian and Greek occupiers remains. With a population of around 250,000, Corsicans are proud independent people who have retained a traditional Mediterranean culture despite the pressures of development and tourism. This is a land of olive and lemon groves, of bustling markets, of winding mountain roads, of granite houses clinging to precarious slopes, of perfumed air and dappled sunshine.

Kalliste

The Greeks named Corsica *Kalliste*, the most beautiful one, and it is easy to see why they found it so inspiring. Combining sandy beaches with rugged shorelines and mountainous wilderness, it is an island of contrasts with a Mediterranean climate by the coast and cooler air in the mountains. As a result of these differences, Corsica boasts 2,000 plant species, around eighty of which are specific to the island. The most notable vegetation is *maquis*, a pungent combination of low scrub such as myrtle, broom and heather. During the Second World War, resistance

fighters lay in the luxurious maquis to escape from German and Italian troops. This is how the French name for members of the resistance movement, *maquisards*, originated.

From the 15th century, the Genoese occupiers planted the beeches, Laricio pines, oaks and scented alders that now proliferate. Grapes, olives, figs, citrus fruit and chestnuts are also cultivated in the countryside.

Natural beauty

About a third of Corsica is protected by the Parc Naturel Régional de Corse, a body established in 1972 to preserve the fragile beauty of the island by keeping nature and human interests in harmony. A major problem is the threat of fires in the dry maquis – infernos in the 1980s destroyed thousands of hectares of forest. Despite such difficulties, the park has succeeded in protecting moufflon, deer, bearded vultures, ospreys and golden eagles.

GR 20

The park is developing a programme of green tourism which includes over 1,500km of walking trails, most notably the GR 20 which runs the length of the Parc Naturel Régional de Corse. Covering 177km of the mountainous terrain that forms the backbone of the island, it is one of the most demanding walks in Europe. Wandering in the wilderness for two weeks, the nightly mountain hut is the only sign of civilisation. The walk passes towering crags and granite spires, including Corsica's highest mountain, Monte Cinto (2,710m).

Bastia's old port area

Scandola Nature Reserve

Scandola is the marine heart of the Parc Naturel Régional de Corse. Located on the west coast, this mountainous peninsula is a UNESCO world heritage site. Steep cliffs plunge into the sea, the red porphyry and basalt eroded by waves to form pillars, grottoes and rocky islets. Turquoise seas lap the sandy beaches and provide a haven for marine species. The reserve can only be reached by boat, but the underwater kingdom is just as rich as the land, with boulders covered in bright corals and sponges. Fish, urchins, limpets and lobsters inhabit the clear waters.

Nearby is the Girolata peninsula, also protected by UNESCO. There are 450 types of seaweed and 125 vertebrates in the area. Although it is difficult to reach, Girolata provides a natural marina, sheltered from winds and waves. The only sign of human influence are the coastal observation towers, part of a network of 200 built in the 16th century as protection against pirates. At the first sign of danger, a warning fire would be lit and the entire island was on its guard within two hours. In these more peaceful times, many of the remaining towers are used for bird-watching.

Bastia

Bastia is the main town in northern Corsica, and was once the island's capital. The town exudes an Italian atmosphere, a legacy of the Genoese occupiers who developed the settlement. Boasting no fewer than three harbours, its labyrinthine streets reveal bustling squares shaded with plane and palm trees, gushing fountains, elegant pastel houses and sumptuous Baroque churches, chapels and monasteries.

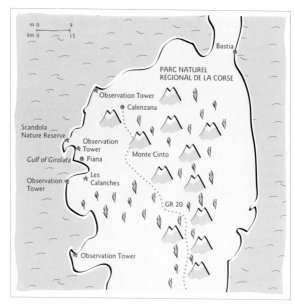

A Corsican village

Piana is a place that has preserved a typically Corsican character. It had a bloody history of rebellion and massacre during the Genoese occupation, and for 200 years the entire region was deserted. Built on a high plateau, it overlooks the lovely Gulf of Porto and is almost opposite Scandola. Piana is said to be one of the prettiest villages in France, with its ochre-coloured houses and the beautiful church of Sainte-Marie which was built in 1752 as a symbol of the resurrected community and the hope for a brighter future.

Les Calanches

Further along the coast from Scandola are the bizarre, wind-sculpted rocks called Les Calanches, resembling giant tortured forms petrified by some supernatural force. The formations have inspired artists and writers for centuries. It is said that the Devil, enraged when a pure shepherdess rejected his advances, set about making the area uninhabitable. He carved the twisted figures of those who had offended him into the red rocks nearby. The result was so frightening that it drove people away until the prayers of St Martin transformed the diabolical city to an area of great beauty. Given Corsica's tempestuous history and current tranquillity, the story could apply to the entire island.

CONTACT INFORMATION

Bastia Tourist Information
Place Saint Nicolas
20200 Bastia
Corsica
Tel: (00 33) 4 9555 9696
Fax: (00 33) 4 9531 8134

Regional Nature Park of Corsica
2, rue Major Lambroschini
BP 417
20184 Ajaccio Cedex
Corsica
Tel: (00 33) 4 9551 7910
Fax: (00 33) 4 9521 8817
E-mail: infos@parc-naturel-corse.com
Web: www.parc-naturel-corse.com

Foreste Casentinesi National Park

Beneath the ridge of the Apennines, the mixed forests of Foreste Casentinesi National Park cloak the mountainsides, providing vital shelter for animals and plants.

Surrounded by pretty towns and villages, the Foreste Casentinesi National Park is located along the Apennine ridge. Covering a territory of 360 sq km, and roughly split between the regions of Emilia-Romagna and Tuscany, the park is largely made up of ancient forests. Innumerable vein-like streams and torrents fan out from the ridge, flowing east towards the Adriatic and west to the Tyrrhenian Sea, with the source of the River Arno beginning at Mt Falterona – the park's highest mountain at 1,654m.

Red deer

A place of retreat

Often shrouded in mist and populated only by shy animals, the seemingly impenetrable Foreste Casentinesi has a silent, mystical air. This atmosphere, combined with the solitariness and natural beauty of the area, has always drawn those who have wished to escape from the secular world.

Monks and hermits came here and, along with their followers, established retreats which became popular places of pilgrimage. As well as religious sites, the park and the surrounding towns hold art and architectural treasures dating from Etruscan and Roman times through to the Middle Ages and the Renaissance.

The landscape's history

Down the centuries, the forests have undergone varying degrees of fortune under monastic, private and state ownership. Contrasting approaches often involved deforestation and clearance – for ship-building and construction – as well as preservation programmes and the introduction of red fir, Douglas fir, larch and birch.

Depopulation has been a feature of this area's countryside in the 20th century and all over the park are the remains of buildings that once housed grain or livestock, or served as mills or family dwellings. Some of the land is still cultivated by hardworking farmers who raise cattle and harvest crops of chestnuts, olives and grapes.

Although populations have fluctuated, rural traditions have remained intact here, as up until recently few smallholders were able to afford modern machinery. A healthy ecological balance has thus been maintained in the area, with fields and woods full of flowers and insects, although the songbird population has been dramatically decreased by hunting.

In an effort to raise awareness of indigenous wildlife and encourage co-operation between the farming and conservation communities, the park has collaborated with local organisations to establish agricultural and environmental programmes.

Scalandrini falls

The park's environment

Seasonal cycles bring colourful changes to the landscape. The green summer leaves of the deciduous forests turn russet and gold in the autumn. In winter, snow blankets the year-round foliage of the evergreens.

Almost a thousand species of flora can be found in the park, including cowberries, narcissus flowered anemones and the tiny tozzia. Lilies, orchids and geraniums thrive in the woodlands, whilst the fields are host to crocuses, buttercups, lady's mantle and bellflowers. Examples of many species can be seen at the Apennines Flora Garden at Valbonella, whilst the Sasso Fratino and Pietra reserves are dedicated to scientific research.

For years certain animals struggled to survive against poachers and farmers who regarded them either as a source of food or as pests. The abandonment of holdings and the reforestation of old pastures, combined with the park's recent status as an officially protected area, has meant the gradual return of a stable wildlife population. Numbers of deer (red, roe and the more common fallow); moufflon (introduced from Sardinia in the 1870s); wild boar; and even wolves have increased

Exploring the park

Foreste Casentinesi is criss-crossed with hiking and walking trails: some walks can be self-guided and are designed to reveal particular geological or ecological features. There are also mountain-biking tracks and horse-riding centres, and in winter, cross-country and downhill skiing.

To the north of the park, the 70m high Acquacheta waterfall tumbles dramatically down a sheer cliff-face. On the plateau above the falls are the remains of the hermitage of the San Benedetto in Alpe monastery, where Dante took refuge during his exile and commemorated the falls in his *Divine Comedy* (Inferno, canto XVI).

On the Emilia-Romagna side of the ridge, the town of Ridracoli is attractively situated above Lago di Ridracoli – a man-made lake, built

to provide water to the surrounding area. In the picturesque town there is an exquisite example of an arched stone bridge, originally built to serve an antique palace which now functions as a hotel. Water continues to be a theme further south at Bagno di Romagna; a spa town which has for centuries exploited the qualities of its thermal waters to attract invalids, socialites and tourists alike.

Hermitages and monasteries

According to tradition, the hermit San Romualdo (St Rumbold) first identified the special nature of Casentino when he came here in 1012. His hermitage, hidden high in the mountains, can still be visited.

The Camaldoli order have traditionally had temporal control over the region and have played an important role in the conservation of the forest. With the founding of the Camaldoli monastery in 1046 came the increased popularity of the religious retreat as a pilgrimage site. Today, the community is positively buzzing with activity due to the small café, museum and replica 16th century pharmacy run by the monks.

Perched on the edge of a rocky outcrop, the famous Franciscan monastery of La Verna sits on the southern slopes of Mt Penna. Surrounded by woods of fir, ash, elm, maple and beech, the site was donated to St Francis in 1213 by a local nobleman after the monk had come to live in the area as a hermit.

ⓘ CONTACT INFORMATION

National Park of Foreste Casentinesi, Monte Falterona and Campigna
via G. Brocchi 7 – 52015
Pratovecchio, (AR)
Italy
Tel: (00 39) 0575 50301
Fax: (00 39) 0575 504497
E-mail: parco@technet.it

Monti Sibillini National Park

Between the main Apennine ridge and the Adriatic coast, the magical Monti Sibillini National Park lies in unspoilt mountain territory, full of history, myth and legend.

Eagles over Monte Sibilla

Bordering the provinces of Umbria and Marche, Monti Sibillini National Park is located in the south-west corner of the attractive Le Marche region. Covering an area of 700 sq km, the park is made up of a central chain of over twenty limestone peaks, and the hills, valleys and villages that surround them. Myth and legend are traditionally associated with several enigmatic natural features within this beautiful landscape.

The park is an important preserve for several wildlife species, and Apennine and alpine flora. Its commercial centres are rich in examples of art, history and culture whilst medieval monuments, abbeys and hermitages are set amongst the hillside villages.

Mountain breezes

The cooler temperatures of May and June or September and October are perfect for visiting Le Marche. Light seasonal showers travelling across the mountains are only an intermittent obstacle to outdoor activities.
The early months of winter and spring bring mist and bitter winds, whilst

the deep mid-winter snow is perfect for cross-country skiing. In the warm months of high summer, the crowds of tourists that throng the infamously busy Adriatic coast rarely venture into the more isolated mountain towns, and Monti Sibillini and its refreshing breezes remain a well-kept secret amongst the privileged few.

Outdoor opera festival, Macerata

A land of sybils and demons

Fantastical stories and attributions abound in the landscape and folklore of Monti Sibillini. The region reached a peak of popularity during the Middle Ages as a source of both inspiration and fear for writers, poets and local people; the names given to some of the more unusual features within the park have remained ever since.

Monte Sibilla (2,173m), in the south-east corner of the park, christens the collection of mountains which makes up the Monti Sibillini range. Local legend tells that of one of the sybils (a prophetess of ancient mythology), hid in a cave on the side of Monti Sibillini when banished from the underworld, and subsequently made it her home.

Further south, the 'red' waters of Lago di Pilato that lap above an underlying bed of russet clay have contributed to its description as the 'demoniacal lake'. Named after the Roman procurator whose dead body was reputedly dragged here by wild buffalo, the lake lies across the high valley between Monte Vettore and Pizzo del Diavolo. Vettore is the park's tallest peak and Pizzo del Diavolo (Devil's Beard) continues the demoniacal theme.

Glacial corries (found between Monte Bove Nord / Sud and Monte Vettore), U-shaped valleys and underground caves are evidence of past glaciation, whilst rivers such as the Nera, Tenna, Ambro and Aso cut through karstic plains, creating waterfalls and deep gorges throughout the porous limestone landscape.

Le Marche

Now the location for the park's headquarters, the town of Visso in the west of the protected area was recognised as an independent city state during Roman times. Visso's surrounding valley communities were divided into five *guaite*, or districts, whose inhabitants each built their own castles as a defence against continuous Saracen raids. Towns such as Castelsantangelo and Ussita are characteristic of the fortified mountain settlements found around the park.

For a spell of quiet time by the sea, some secluded coves can still be found between the busier resorts that line the Adriatic coast north and south of Ancona. For music-lovers, an open-air opera festival is held each summer in the town of Macerata.

Further north, the small mountain town of Urbino is a celebrated Renaissance jewel in the region's crown. At its brightest during the court of Duke Federico of Montefeltro in the 15th century, the town embodied the finest characteristics of the Renaissance period in the form of enlightenment, learning and civilised government.

At the southern end of Le Marche, the busy provincial capital of Ascoli Piceno is a rival to the cultural attractions of Urbino. The travertine-paved main square is one of several architectural delights, while the character of the city has a rougher edge due to its intrepid fortunes at the hands of various rulers and its brief but significant period as a free commune from the 12th to the 15th century.

[i] CONTACT INFORMATION

Monti Sibillini National Park
l.go G. Antinori
I – 62039 Visso (MC)
Italy
Tel: (00 39) 0737 972711
Fax: (00 39) 0737 972707
E-mail: parco@sibillini.net

Le Marche Regional Tourism
Via Gentile da Fabriano, 9
60125 Ancona
Italy
Tel: (00 39) 071 806 2284
Fax: (00 39) 071 806 2154
E-mail: servizio.turismo@
regione.marche.it
Web: www.le-marche.com

Portonovo, Ancona

ITALY

National Parks of Abruzzo

Abruzzo's large network of national and regional parks, special reserves and biospheres make up a valuable structure of protected habitats where the unique environment of the Apennine range can regenerate and thrive.

Located in the heart of the Italian peninsula, the Abruzzo region is contained by high mountains to the west and the Adriatic Sea to the east. Within these boundaries, its landscape is made up of forested mountains and hills, with lowlands only occurring at the mouths of rivers as they flow into the sea.

Abruzzo boasts the tallest peaks of the Apennine range and the mountains are characterised by deep gorges and large expanses of high plateaux. Fortified medieval villages, churches and castles dot the hillsides, with fishing villages and beach resorts lining the coast.

Proudly known as the 'Region of Parks', one third of Abruzzo's territory is subject to environmental protection, including the Abruzzo, Majella and Gran Sasso-Laga national parks. There is also the recently formed Regional Park of Sirente-Velino, as well as over forty reserves and natural oases which are administered by a combination of local institutions.

The walled city of L'Aquila is the main commercial centre in the province. With a wonderful heritage of its own, including important monuments and works of art, it has remained relatively undiscovered by most tourists. Its famous 16th century citadel is now the site of the State Museum.

A region of parks

With a variety of environments existing within Abruzzo, each park shares some common characteristics in terms of topography, flora and fauna. However, each also has its own special atmosphere and distinctive features, whether they be Abruzzo's forested hills and glacial valleys, the limestone summits and vast karstic plains of Gran Sasso, or Majella's wild landscape and wealth of hermitages and chapels.

Each national park has adopted a different animal as its logo, although these species are present in varying degrees in all of the parks. Abruzzo is represented by the Marsican brown bear, Majella by the Apennine wolf, and Gran Sasso-Laga by the Abruzzo chamois.

Gradually shrugging off the perception once common in the rest of Italy that it is a backward, undeveloped region, Abruzzo is beginning to exploit its natural resources. Many more tourists are coming to the area than before, and often to explore the national parks. Certain customs still prevail however, and authentic examples of a more traditional era can be found in many of the more isolated hilltowns.

Abruzzo National Park

Abruzzo – Italy's first national park – was established in 1922 in an attempt to preserve a microcosm of the unique but rapidly diminishing environment that is typical of the Apennine chain.

Three main massifs shape the park's outline with its southern zone extending into the regions of Latium and Molise. High peaks include Monte Petroso (2,249m), Monte Marsicano (2,245m) and La Meta (2,242m). Nowadays, the park covers 500 sq km – two thirds of which are covered by forests.

Crossing the River Orfento

Abruzzo National Park

A wealth of trees

Centuries old beech woods, mixed with Turkey oaks and Austrian pines form most of the forests, with maple, mountain ash, fir, yew, laburnum, hazel, wild pear, wild cherry and apple trees also present. Species dominant in the Ice Age – silver birch and mountain pine – can also be found. Woods of black pine are at Villetta Barrea and the Camosciara Reserve, while poplars, willows and alders fringe the riverbanks.

The park's main river – the high-level Sangro – rises near the Passo del Diavolo in the north, and flows through the park to the artificial basin of Lake Barrea. Alpine flora, including gentians and edelweiss, is present above 2,000m. In spring and summer, the meadows, valleys and woodlands are carpeted by wildflowers such as violets, peonies, forget-me-nots, columbines and two endemic species – the Marsican iris and lady's-slipper.

Native species

Several successful initiatives have been undertaken to reintroduce native species that were, until recently, diminishing in numbers. This glorious landscape is home to the Marsican brown bear, Abruzzo chamois, Apennine wolves, red deer and roe deer. Rarer species such as otters, wildcats and Apennine lynx, as well as badgers, pine martens, polecats, squirrels and dormice are present in the park, but are rarely seen by visitors.

Access to Abruzzo

Only one road crosses the park, although there are over 150 different walking routes and many cycling and horse-riding tracks. The popular town of Pescasseroli in the centre of the park is perfectly situated as a base for exploring the area, while Barrea's medieval towers and churches are beautifully set against a mountain backdrop in the south-east.

Abruzzo National Park is divided into zones which are strictly monitored in order to ensure the protection both of vulnerable habitats and species, and minimise the harmful impacts of

Apennine wolf

increased human activity. As a result, the usual restrictions concerning camping and access apply. Leaflets, information on accommodation, and camping and fishing permits can be obtained from any of the fifteen visitor centres. Guided walks and horse-treks are also organised.

Majella National Park

In contrast to Abruzzo, Majella is one of Italy's newest national parks. Founded in 1993, it extends over 740 sq km between the provinces of Pescara, L'Aquila and Chieti. Larger, wilder and less 'managed' than Abruzzo, Majella offers some excellent walks in four main areas: the Morrone mountains in the north-west; the Pizzi mountains in the south-east; Monte Porrara and its surrounding area to the south; and the wide Majella massif in the centre of the park.

Majella is famous for its concentration of summits, over thirty of which reach above 2,000m. The main peak is Monte Amaro, the second tallest in the Apennines at 2,793m. It rises up out of the middle of the main massif, with its characteristic outline dominating the surrounding countryside.

Vast karstic plains stretch across wide plateaux between the peaks. The shepherds in the Abruzzo region have traditionally practiced transhumance, moving their flocks to different altitudes according to the seasons. Parts of these plains have always been grazed by sheep, but tracts are still swathed in colour when wildflowers bloom in spring and summer.

Majella's landscape

Glacial features in the form of open screes sweep down from the western side of Majella towards dense beech forests that cover the lower levels of the mountainside. Here, the Majella plateau is separated from the Morrone range by the Orta river. Swollen by its numerous tributaries, this once glaciated river cuts a broad valley through the mountains.

The park is filled with rivers and waterfalls that tumble over the rocky landscape. These watery havens offer a home to salamanders, newts and fish, which in turn provide food for bears, otters, martens and other animals that hunt along the rivers. As in Abruzzo National Park, populations of wolves, chamois, brown bear and lynx are slowly recovering after long periods of hunting and poaching.

Murelle

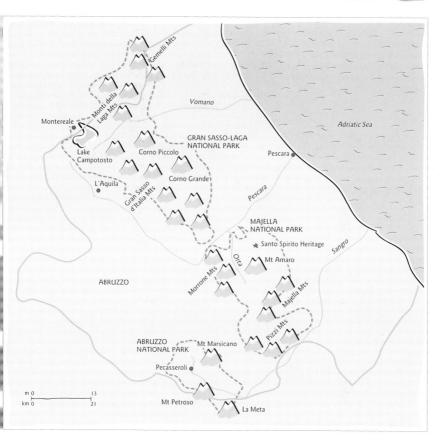

The abundance of wild herbs, alpine and meadow flowers, and blooming shrubs attracts a varied and colourful selection of butterflies to the area, including the rare apollo butterfly (Parnassius apollo), which is specially protected from capture and trade.

Since prehistoric times

Majella National Park is as valuable for its stunning cultural and historical sites as its natural environment. Archaeological finds and examples of cave art from the Palaeolithic era show that early man eked out an existence in this elemental wilderness.

Roman settlements have also been discovered and the well-preserved remains of a 1st century Roman colony can be seen at Alba Fucens, near Ovindoli. Elsewhere, the mountain villages and towns are

splendid examples of medieval strongholds, fortified to protect the inhabitants from marauders. Red-tiled dwellings cluster between narrow streets forming a tight community: a grassy perimeter surrounds the houses to safeguard sheep and livestock, and the entire population is enclosed within high walls.

Apennine gentian

During the Middle Ages, the remote landscape of Majella was favoured as a place of retreat for monks and hermits. Over forty chapels, grottoes and hermitages are hewn from the tall ridges that jut out and tower above the plains. Some teeter precariously along sheer cliff-faces, others, built into the buttery-coloured stone, are camouflaged by the rock. The most famous hermitage – Santo Spirito – is now a national monument, and is positioned high up along folds of calcareous strata above the Santo Spirito valley.

Gran Sasso National Park

The largest national park in the Abruzzo area, and one of the largest in Italy, the 1,600 sq km National Park of Gran Sasso e Monti della Laga is a truly impressive environmental preserve. Its landscape of mountains, rivers, lakes and waterfalls is enlivened – particularly in autumn – by the region's clear light and the vibrant colours of the forests and fields. With its fair share of castles, hermitages and stone villages, it is as captivating as any of the other parks, with its sheer scale and size generating an exhilarating atmosphere.

The land is divided into two zones: an interior zone which is strictly protected because of its special environmental and cultural importance; and a busier perimeter zone which has a greater number of towns and amenities.

The park's contrasting mountain formations are collectively its most characteristic feature. Three mountain groups define the area: the Monti Gemelli chain in the north of the park, and the central Monti della Laga range which connects with the vast Gran Sasso d'Italia massif, itself dominating the remainder of the territory.

Abruzzo chamois

Gran Sasso d'Italia

Stretching between the Vomano river basin to the north and the River Pescara in the extreme south, the lengthy Gran Sasso d'Italia range is home to the tallest peak in the Apennines. The jagged vertical walls of Corno Grande lead straight up to its unmistakable summit at 2,912m.

Both Corno Grande, its close neighbour Corno Piccolo (2,655m) and the other mountains of Gran Sasso d'Italia are unique in the Apennines for their limestone and dolomite composition. Atmospheric conditions, the dissolving action of water and the effects of glaciation, have formed caves, gorges, ravines, gullies, sinkholes and underground rivers and streams in the calcareous rock of the wide plateaus. Such features are very much in evidence on the southern side of the massif, where at 1,600m, the Campo Imperatore plain is spread with karstic lakes.

A glacier still exists in the park: Il Calderone (the cauldron or big pot), on the north face of Corno Grande, is the only glacier in the Apennines and the furthest south in Europe. The wide U-shaped valleys of Gran Sasso and the sweeping moraines beneath the mountains offer further evidence of the effects of glaciation.

Lake Campotosto

In contrast to Gran Sasso, the smoother summits of Monti della Laga are composed of sandstone sediments and layers of marl. Lower than the peaks of Gran Sasso, they still reach a height over 2,450m. Their geomorphology is of rounded crests with deep valleys cut by many fast flowing rivers and torrents. Defined by water, the range is also full of lakes and most particularly, a large number of spectacular high waterfalls that cascade over layers of split rock.

Lake Campotosto, with its distinctive shape, is Europe's largest artificial basin and an important reserve for the sizeable number of birds which nest, feed and breed on its shores. Surprisingly, supervised human activity is permitted here, with canoeing and windsurfing facilities available. To the west of the lake is the town of Montereale. Known for its monastery and 17th century churches, it is well positioned for access to the park and is surrounded by pretty fortified villages and a number of castles.

Gran Sasso's wildlife

Certain aspects of the vegetation, plants and insects of the Gran Sasso plateaux resemble those found in Eastern European regions of a similar topography. Large expanses of pasture sweep across the steppe-like plains, filled with swaying field grasses and

Mountain peonies

meadowland wildflowers. Endemic species, including *Androsace mathildae* and *Adonis distorta*, represent examples of the nordic and oriental origins of this post-glacial flora. The landscape is also home to grassland insects and their predators, grass snakes. Orsini's viper is found here in greater numbers than in any other part of the country.

The protective cover of the fields is also attractive to birds. Ortolan buntings, rock sparrows, crested larks, red-backed shrikes and downy pipits – species whose habitat is becoming increasingly under threat in other parts of Europe – all nest here. Other birds living at higher altitudes include alpine accentors, water and rock pipits, snow finches, rock partridges, rock thrushes and alpine choughs. They share the mountains with raptors such as goshawks, golden eagles, peregrines and eagle owls.

Gran Sasso is also host to recovering numbers of the Abruzzo chamois, reintroduced here from Abruzzo National Park. Its grasslands and rocky mountain ledges were the home of these attractive animals until they were wiped out by hunting at the beginning of the last century. They have been adopted by the park as deserving special attention and have attained a highly protected mascot-like status.

Monti della Laga

Contrasting again with the alpine and steppeland vegetation of Gran Sasso, Monti della Laga's slopes are mainly covered with forests. Low down are woods of oaks and chestnuts which date from Roman times and have always been an important resource for the mountain community. Higher up, centuries old beech forests are interspersed with yew, holly, maple, ash and elm, as well as pockets of

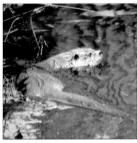

Otter

silver fir and birch. These plantations give a wonderful array of colour in the autumn time. Black bilberry bushes grow abundantly as part of the heathland between the forests and the mountain pastures. Apennine wolves, Marsican brown bears and wildcats roam the whole territory.

CONTACT INFORMATION

National Park of Abruzzo
via G. Brocchi 7 – 52015
Pratovecchio (AR)
Italy
Tel: (00 39) 0863 91955
Fax: (00 39) 0863 912132
E-mail: post@pna.it

National Park of Majella
Palazzo Di Sciascio
via Occidentale 6
Guardiagrele (CH)
Italy
Tel: (00 39) 0871 800713
Fax: (00 39) 0871 800340

National Park of Gran Sasso and Monti della Laga
Via Roio,
10/12 67100
L'Aquila
Italy
Tel: (00 39) 0862 401903
Fax: (00 39) 0862 414539
E-mail: info@gransassolagapark.it
Web: www.gransassolagapark.it

Lake Campotosto

Víkos-Aóös National Park

Located in a region of great natural beauty, rich cultural heritage and friendly people, the rivers, forests and mountains of Víkos-Aóös remain an important habitat for wildlife and a relatively undiscovered retreat.

The tall pines of the Pindhos mountains

The National Park of Víkos-Aóös is set deep in the beauty and isolation of the Píndhos mountains, in the wild Zagóri region. This remote northern territory is characterised by high, forbidding peaks, a lush, craggy landscape and a temperate climate. Fast flowing rivers tumble through steep gorges and thickly wooded ravines. Houses and farms are solidly built with local stone in an architectural style that is unique to the area. Byzantine churches, medieval monasteries and ancient stone-arched 'packhorse' bridges are scattered throughout the countryside.

Víkos-Aóös National Park

Established in 1973, the National Park of Víkos-Aóös covers a core zone of 34 sq km. An additional peripheral zone of 122 sq km also comes under state protection, although the term 'protection' must be applied loosely here. Greek government policy is not particularly enforced, in fact some

would even say that the protection of the park exists in name only, and that little is officially done to ensure the conservation of species and habitats.

Naturalists, geologists and botanists have long been aware of the wonders of Víkos-Aóös' rock and mineral deposits and its varied animal and plant life. The startling beauty and peacefulness of the park, and the clarity of its light and air, lend an almost spiritual atmosphere to the landscape. This unspoilt quality is keenly felt by visitors, who enjoy staggering views from the mountain tops and challenging but rewarding hikes through uplifting scenery.

Flora and fauna

Rare brown bears, mountain lynx and roe deer shelter amidst the thick maquis that borders rivers and ravines. Wolves, jackals and wild boar inhabit the upper forests, whilst wild goats and chamois are more

visible to humans as they teeter along steep ledges and overhanging cliffs. Otters feed on the fish that swim in the icy cold rivers, with Egyptian and griffon vultures, and golden and booted eagles patrolling their territory from above.

The park is a significant habitat for over 3,000 species of rare plants and wildflowers. In addition to many endemic species, mountain and mediterranean varieties can be found. In late spring, alpine flowers such as gentians, fritillaries and orchids appear, whilst in autumn, wild crocuses, lilies and bright cyclamen throng the woodlands. Cornflowers and violets thrive on the limestone soil with yarrow and valerian common in the damp grassy meadows.

The mixed forests consist of both deciduous and evergreen trees. Broad-leaved varieties such as hornbeam, maple, willow and oak, supplemented by elm, ash, lime and hazel, combine

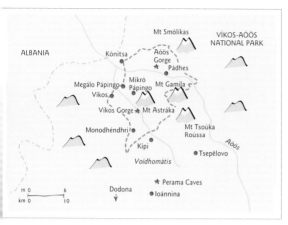

Aóös gorge

Access to the Aóös gorge is best attempted from Kónitsa; an excellent base for exploring the park and the main market town serving the mountain communities of northern Zagóri. Kayaking and whitewater rafting along the Aóös torrent are some of the exhilarating water sports offered here.

High mountain peaks tipped with snow provide a backdrop to the powerful Aóös river as its deep green waters force a wide path through the northern Píndhos. Steep slopes of rock, covered in vegetation, rise up on either side of the river, whilst the lower boughs of the trees seem to attempt to enclose it, as they dip heavily into the water.

A path follows the course of the Aóös through the high gorge with its walls of over 1,000m. On the way, it passes warm pools and refreshing springs – ideal for swimming. At its narrowest point is the interesting 18th century Stomíou monastery, perched on an lofty outcrop overlooking the torrent below. Walks south from the Aóös gorge, towards the tall peaks of Mt Gamíla (2,497m) and Mt Astráka (2,436m), join with the southern Zagóri villages and form the northern approach to the Víkos gorge via the village of Mikró Pápingo.

with vast tracts of beech trees and conifers including juniper, fir, cedar and black and Bosnian pine.

A struggle for conservation

Locals who take an interest in the preservation of the park have to contend with the fact that the very elements which give Víkos-Aóös such a unique character and atmosphere are those which also make it so difficult to protect and supervise.

The natural wildness of the region, as well as the traditional autonomy of its people, means that local hunters and poachers continue to defend their right to hunt. Their destructive activities affect roe deer, wild boar and brown bear the most, with smaller game also suffering.

On a positive note, a growing proportion of the population have become aware of the special resource that sits on their doorstep. Although reluctant to endanger the park, some local entrepreneurs have realised the necessity and even the benefits of promoting the area to outside visitors. Víkos-Aóös has become increasingly popular with walkers, and guided tours of both the park and further afield in the Píndhos range can be locally organised from the villages.

Kayaking in the park

The steep mountain ridges of Víkos-Aóös

Víkos gorge

One of the best preserved of the Zagóri villages, Monodhéndhri lies at the southern end of the park. As well as other walks, the paved path that leads down towards the Víkos gorge begins here. A tiring 12km trek, it is not for the faint-hearted or ill-shod. The path is precipitous in most places, even disintegrating in some, and it can often be washed away.

The trail winds along the thickly wooded bank of the Voïdhomátis river as it flows between steep 1,000m cliffs that loom up on either side. All efforts are rewarded by the unspoilt quality of the environment, the raw beauty of the scenery and the staggering views afforded by the path as it cuts through the gorge. Towards the end of the walk is a chance to take a left-hand detour uphill to the tiny settlement of Víkos. Otherwise, the path continues across the river and on towards the Pápingo villages.

Dodona

Situated 20km south of Ioánnina, the ruins of the Oracle of Zeus lie at the ancient site of Dodona. Somewhat off the beaten track, the site and the nearby village of Dhodhóni are one of several interesting day trips available to visitors to the Zagóri region.

Possibly the oldest site in Greece, Dodona's history is vague. Archaeological findings suggest the presence of one of the earliest Greek tribes dating from 2,500 BC. Homer refers to a later clan of priests and priestesses, who were dedicated to the worship of Zeus. Herodotus recorded that the oracle spoke to the prophets through the rustling leaves of a primeval oak tree which was sacred to the cult.

A small temple erected to the worship of Zeus in the 4th century BC became the central point for a series of larger monuments that were built on the site around that period. In the 3rd

Wild iris

century BC, there followed the construction of the vast theatre that still exists today and is often used for outdoor concerts and performances.

Perama caves

The Perama caves are found 5km to the north of Ioánnina, on the western side of Lake Pamvótis. During the Second World War, a guerrilla discovered the caves by chance whilst on the run. They extend beneath a low hill for over 2km and contain a variety of mysteriously-shaped rock formations and winding tunnels. Despite being unsympathetically adapted to squeeze in large numbers of visitors, the caves can still be recommended as an intrinsically interesting geological feature that is worth including on a tour of the area.

ℹ️ CONTACT INFORMATION

Forest Directorate of Ioánnina
6 Averof Str
45221 Ioánnina Perfecture
Greece
Tel & Fax: (00 301) 651 26591

**Ministry of Agriculture
General Directorate of Forests
and Forest Environment**
3-5 Ypokratous Str
10164 Athens
Greece
Tel: (00 301) 362 8327
Fax: (00 301) 361 2710

Préspes National Park

*Set in a landscape of lakes, wetlands, mountains and cultivated plains,
Préspes National Park is recognised as a wildlife and nature reserve of
extreme importance to the Balkan area.*

Préspes' wetlands

In the far north-west corner of Greek Macedonia, the Préspes (or Préspa) area is almost entirely made up of the Préspes National Park and its two lakes, Mikri Préspa and Mégali Préspa. Sheltered by mountains on their western and eastern sides, the lakes extend into two other countries to form natural borders between Greece, Albania and the Former Yugoslav Republic of Macedonia.

A combination of climate, geographical position and a concentration of flora and fauna has contributed to a valuable set of natural habitats for several indigenous animal and plant species – particularly bird-life. Established in 1974, Préspes' core protection zone covers merely 49 sq km of Lake Mikri Préspa (the smaller of the two lakes) and its shores. A secondary peripheral protected zone extends into the surrounding wetlands, forests and mountains, bringing the total area under protection to 256 sq km.

History

Because of its position along important military and trade routes between Italy and Byzantium, Thessaloniki (then Salonica) became an important Byzantine city during Rome's three hundred year rule over Greece. In the Byzantine period (395–1453), the remote Préspes basin became the favoured location for exiled nobility. Evidence of this can be seen in the concentration of ruined Byzantine churches and private chapels that lie scattered around Préspes' inlets and lake shores.

In the 20th century, Préspes' peace was disrupted by world wars, followed by violent local struggles which took place during the Greek Civil War of the late 1940s. After this, owing to the government's enforcement of linguistic and cultural Macedonian–Greek integration, the local population suffered persecution, resulting in a sharp rise in emigration.

Préspes' total population of about 2,000 inhabitants is now scattered between smallholdings and crumbling villages. Most make their living from stock and arable farming. The proximity of the lakes as a main source of irrigation enables the successful cultivation of a variety of crops including maize, hay, beans, clover, rye, barley, wheat and swathes of golden sunflowers.

With the general explosion of tourism in Greece in the 1970s, Préspes' lakeside residents attempted to cash in on the scenic beauty of their surroundings. However, despite a summer influx of visitors to the villages, the foreigner is only likely to experience an impression of lingering neglect and isolation rather than slick tourist development. The predominant character of the region as a largely ignored backwater has ensured the preservation of a wild environment for birds and mammals, the like of which is threatened elsewhere in Europe.

Spoonbills amidst the reedbeds

Aquatic wildlife

An important breeding, nesting and feeding site for native and visiting species, Préspes is most famous for the diversity of aquatic bird-life that populates its lakeshores and adjacent wetlands. The shallow reed-fringed waters of Lake Mikri Préspa provide the only nesting site in all of Greece for noisy groups of both white and Dalmatian pelicans.

Mixed colonies of herons, spoonbills, common and pygmy cormorants, and egrets, as well as greylag geese and goosanders, add to the park's profusion of breeding water birds. Among the smaller species, the crested grebe and the coot are particularly common, sharing the protected waters with other ducks, waders and terns.

Further down the food chain, a healthy population of fish, reptiles, amphibians and insects co-exist in this watery environment. Various species of snakes, frogs, toads, newts and waterside insects, as well as moths and butterflies, all provide sustenance for the bird-life.

The thick stems of aquatic plants, such as fool's watercress and waterlily, offer shelter and a safe place for fish to lay their eggs, while clumps of bright yellow irises bloom along the lakeshore. The activity and colour of the lakes' inhabitants may be watched from specially sited observation towers and from the reedbeds.

Wood and mountain species

Within the broader territory of the national park itself, live other protected bird and mammal species. On the mountains are white-tailed eagles, bears and wolves, with woodpeckers, doves, foxes and wild boar inhabiting the woodlands lower down. Narcissus meadows, clover, campanula, wild orchid and species of vetchling and bedstraw are amongst the sub-alpine species growing in the woods and on the heaths.

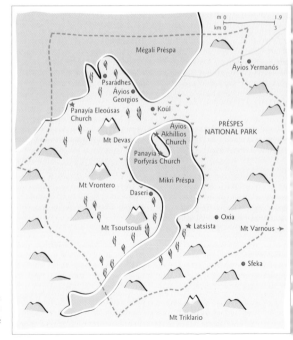

View of Prèspes' lakes across to Mt Triklario

The mountains that rise up from Lake Mikri Préspa to the east and west are thickly wooded. A mixture of Hungarian, Turkey, Macedonian, sessile and downy oak, together with hornbeam, hop-hornbeam, maple, ash, aspen and northern birch make up the lower level forests, followed by dense beech woods higher up. Tall stands of pine, fir and willow form a border between farmland and hills to the east of Mikri Préspa, with plots of juniper and box common around the western side of the lake.

Sites of interest

The best and most rewarding way to explore the park in harmony with its peaceful environment is to stay in one of the local villages and set out on foot or bicycle. A number of forest roads and unofficial walking trails link villages and sites of interest around the lakes and in the mountains further inland.

Owing to increased levels of depopulation, many villages – such as Sfeka, a mountain settlement north of Oxia; Kranies, overlooking the bay of Latsista; and Daseri, deep in the woodlands of Mikri Préspa's western shores – are now deserted. These sites still make an interesting,

if somewhat eerie stop-off, not least because of their special atmosphere, traditional architecture (now ruined), and scenic location.

Although some of the towns, particularly Psarádhes and Koúl, are now beginning to undergo haphazard development, most of the original domestic architecture, with its mixture of northern Greek and Balkan influences, is being left to fall into disrepair. Set on the river Stara, the village of Áyios Yermanós, however, still retains its traditional houses built in the local style. Apart from a park information centre, the town's main attractions are two small churches of the late Byzantine period – Áyios Athanásios and Áyios Yermanós – and their fascinating interior frescoes in the Macedonian style.

Préspes' islets

Whilst levels of tourism in the area remain small scale, increasing numbers of people are beginning to visit the park. Lake excursions can be organised with the local fishermen from Psarádhes. Sometimes accompanied by flocks of pelicans, a boat trip from the town skirts the southerly shoreline of Mégali Préspa, taking in the medieval shrines and

hermitages that are concealed in coves between the rocky headlands. Reached from the water by a steep set of steps, the spectacular 15th century church of Panayia Eleoúsas is situated atop a narrow rocky opening, and offers wonderful views to Albania's mountains and across the expanse of Mégali Préspa.

Once part of the main land mass, but now separated from it by a narrow stretch of water, the quiet little islet of Áyios Akhíllios is lovely to wander around. The ruins of the 10th century Áyios Akhíllios basilica – with its carved tombstone depicting a heron and a hawk – lie against a backdrop of reeds and the vast lake beyond.

ⓘ CONTACT INFORMATION

Préspes National Park
Region of West Macedonia
General Directorate of the Region
Forest Directorate of Florina
53100 Florina
Greece

Ministry of Agriculture
General Directorate of Forests
and Forest Environment
3-5 Ypokratous Str
10164 Athens
Greece
Tel: (00 301) 362 8327
Fax: (00 301) 361 2710

Termessos-Güllük National Park

Set in the rugged yet beautiful limestone peaks north-west of the Mediterranean resort of Antalya, this tiny park contains the wonderfully evocative remains of ancient Termessos.

Just 34km north of Antalya, but over 1,000m above sea level, the classical era remains of the Pisidian city of Termessos are the focal point of this highland area, so inaccessible that even the all-conquering Alexander the Great was forced to lift his siege of the city in 333 BC. The charm of ancient Termessos stems from its dramatic location and semi-excavated walls and columns struggling to emerge from the lush tangles of vegetation that envelop the site.

Blessed with a typical southern Mediterranean climate, the park can be visited at any time of year, although July and August can be uncomfortably hot at midday. Between November and April some rainy (and very occasionally snowy) days can be expected, leaving spring and autumn as the ideal times to explore.

History

Although most of the remains to be seen today date from the Roman era, when it was nominally a part of the Roman Empire, the city was probably founded by the Pisidian people from

Mt Kizlar in winter

Wildlife

The park is noted for its wide variety of butterflies, which can be seen in abundance in spring, and its undisturbed examples of typical Mediterranean maquis vegetation. The rare lizard orchid, found at only a handful of sites, is worth seeking out. Wild boar roam the forest, and squirrels and martens can be seen. Much rarer is the elusive wild lynx which has not been sighted for several years.

the mountains to the north in the 8th century BC. Controlling an important pass between the coast and the interior, the Termessians derived much of their income from taxing

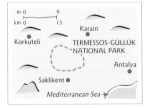

travellers. A warlike people, constantly feuding with their neighbours, it was not until the era of the Pax Romana that real stability enabled Termessos to prosper. The city was abandoned in the 5th century AD because of its remoteness and / or earthquake damage.

Termessos

From the entrance to the park, which includes a building housing a display about the local flora and fauna, a 9km long road winds up the mountain to a parking area. From here the real exploration begins, starting with a pleasant 500m walk through holly oak up a further 200m to the hilltop site.

Most spectacular is the Hellenistic Greek theatre, a wonderfully preserved semicircle of tiered stone seats, which once held in excess of 4,000 spectators, and a toppled stage building. Perched precariously above a plunging chasm and overlooked by the sheer rockface of Mt Güllük, this is arguably the most dramatically situated classical building in the world.

A footpath continues up even further to the necropolis, where a mass of stone sarcophagi, some of them elaborately carved with reliefs of the deceased and other motifs, lie strewn haphazardly amongst the encroaching vegetation. Above this stands a small watchtower on a hilltop, used to scan the surrounding forests for signs of fire. The views from here over the site, Mt Güllük, the distant Pamphylian plain around Antalya and the glittering waters of the Mediterranean are superb.

Walks

It is possible to approach Termessos from the south via a now little used path, parts of which were once an ancient way linking the city with the coast. Starting in a wooded valley cut by a crystal clear stream and ending at the theatre, the walker will be

The ancient theatre at Termessos

rewarded for the extra effort. The nearby Güver canyon, formed by a river cutting its way through the limestone escarpment, is also worth exploring, and there are picnicking facilities in the pine forests on its rim.

South-west Turkey

The Lycian peninsula to the south of the park contains some of the Mediterranean's finest coastal scenery, with dramatic cliffs, secluded coves and sandy beaches. There are numerous classical era sites, well preserved and usually wonderfully sited either on the sea (Phaselis and Olympos) or in the mountains (Arycanda and Limyra).

The Lycian Way, Turkey's first long distance footpath, is waymarked to Grande Randonnée standards and runs a spectacular course across the peaks and valleys of the peninsula. There are several mountains in the area accessible to the experienced hillwalker, including 2,366m Mt Olympos and 3,070m Mt Kizlar, both with cedar forests on their slopes.

ℹ CONTACT INFORMATION

Upcountry (Turkey) Ltd
24 St John's Road
Buxton SK17 6XQ
Tel & Fax: 01298 71050
E-mail: upcountryturkey@
hotmail.com
Web: www.upcountry.freeserve.co.uk

Upcountry (Turkey) Ltd
Antalya P.K. 528
Turkey
Tel & Fax: (00 90) 242 243 1148
E-mail: kateclow@garanti.net.tr

Antalya – the harbour in the old town

Göreme National Park and Cappadocia

A unique landscape and fascinating history combine to make Cappadocia, right in the heart of Asiatic Turkey, one of the world's most unusual and interesting regions.

In Cappadocia, a surreal landscape of rocky cones and stone capped pinnacles, deep gorges and table top mountains, overlooked by the towering peaks of Mt Erciyes (3,917m) and Mt Hasan (3,268m) provides a dramatic focal point for the vast Anatolian plateau.

Sitting astride a major east–west trade (and invasion) route, Cappadocia has had a turbulent history, and the cliff-hewn dwellings, underground cities and churches cut into the volcanic rock bear testament to the ingenuity and tenacity of the early Christian communities who built them.

Ilhara valley

Cappadocia's winters are cold and sometimes snowy, but the clarity of the air and spectacle of snow-topped fairy chimneys make it a good time to visit. Summers are hot but not unbearable, and the evenings are pleasantly cool. June is probably the best month to visit, closely followed by September.

Volcanic origins

Around 30 million years ago the volcanic mountains of the region erupted, carpeting the surrounding plateau with volcanic ash and mud. This loose conglomerate became compressed over time, forming a soft volcanic rock known as tuff. Eroded

into bizarre shapes by the combined forces of wind and water, the most striking of Cappadocia's features are the rock capped cones and pillars known as fairy chimneys, formed when a protective cap of basalt is left atop a pinnacle of easily eroded tuff.

Fertile fields

Volcanic soils and sheltered valleys make Cappadocia a very fertile region, famous for its apricots and grapes. Egyptian vultures soar above the canyon walls and birds of prey inhabit or migrate over the area, but for bird watchers the place of most interest is Sultansazligi marsh where flamingos and pelicans are the highlights.

Christian history

Cappadocia is particularly important historically as a major centre of early Christianity with over 1,000 churches and monasteries in the region. The remoteness of the valleys and the ease with which defensive cliff houses and underground cities could be constructed in the soft rock meant invading Moslem armies were often content to let the Christians alone. Despite the slow eclipse of this world by the invading Turks, Greek-speaking Christians lived here up until the 1923 exchange of populations.

Göreme National Park

Situated on the northern rim of Cappadocia, 11km from Nevşehir, this small park of 95 sq km is the best known, most visited part of the region. The park has some of Cappadocia's best examples of fairy chimneys and contains more than thirty of the most impressive rock cut churches, several of which contain the best preserved and finest frescoes in Cappadocia, mainly dating from between the 9th and 11th centuries.

Ilhara valley

Overlooked by the graceful volcanic peak of Mt Hasan, this high walled canyon of red rock in Cappadocia's south-east contains several beautiful churches and is graced by a fast running, clear river fringed by lush woodland. The cave riddled landscape of Selime, at the north-western end of the gorge, was used as a backdrop in the original *Star Wars* film.

Avanos

The small town of Avanos, just north of Göreme, is famous for the traditional pottery made from the red clay deposited by the Kizilirmak, Turkey's longest river, which flows through the town. Fine 19th century Armenian and Greek houses cling to the steep hillside above the river.

Castle rock at Ortahisar

Fairy chimneys at Ürgüp

Underground cities

The maze of tunnels and chambers in the underground cities of Derinkuyu and Kaymakli show how the locals once hid from invaders. The circular stones rolled across key tunnels to prevent enemy infiltration can be seen, as can the wine presses, the produce of which was so vital to keep the inhabitants sane in a long siege! The largest city, Derinkuyu, consists of eight floors reaching down 55m and covers an area in excess of the 1,500m which have been excavated.

Things to do

The valleys of Cappadocia are fascinating to explore on foot, but the tortuous nature of the terrain and lack of adequate maps can make route finding a problem off the beaten track.

The Ilhara canyon is one of the most enjoyable places to walk, although perhaps the best way to appreciate the landscape is on horseback, and several companies offer both day and longer trips. For a bird's-eye view, hot air balloon trips are available. Mt Erciyes makes a good target for trekkers and mountaineers, and the views from the summit are stunning. There is a small ski resort on the mountain, with good snow in winter.

ℹ CONTACT INFORMATION

Upcountry (Turkey) Ltd
24 St John's Road
Buxton SK17 6XQ
Tel & Fax: 01298 71050
E-mail: upcountryturkey@ hotmail.com
Web: www.upcountry.freeserve.co.uk

Upcountry (Turkey) Ltd
Antalya P.K. 528
Turkey
Tel & Fax: (00 90) 242 243 1148
E-mail: kateclow@garanti.net.tr

Kizilirmak
Avanos
GÖREME
NATIONAL PARK
Göreme
Üçhisar
Ürgüp
Nevşehir
Ortahisar
Ilhara Canyon
Kaymakli
CAPPADOCIA
Derinkuyu
m 0   5
km 0   8

An aerial view of the Cappadocian landscape

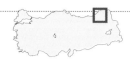

Kaçkar Mountains National Park

*Sometimes referred to as the Pontic Alps or Little Caucasus,
this remote range of spectacular peaks rises to almost 4,000m
above the south-eastern shores of the Black Sea.*

Set up in 1994 and covering an area of 515 sq km, the Kaçkar Mountains National Park encompasses a truly alpine mountain range, with glaciated valleys filled with gushing rivers and streams, high meadows, beautiful lakes, glaciers and snow choked corries. The slopes facing the Black Sea are lush and verdant, whilst those to the south and east, facing the Anatolian plateau, are more barren.

Despite their apparent remoteness, the Kaçkar have long been inhabited by man, and traces of Armenian, Georgian and Greek civilisations can all be found in or around the region. Camping is the best option in these beautiful mountains, but the trail head villages of Ayder on the Black Sea side, and Barhal on the inland side, have simple accommodation.

Summer sun – winter snow

Summer is the best time (late June to September), as the winter snows have receded sufficiently to allow access to the alpine lakes and meadows, and the nights are long and relatively warm. Particularly on the Black Sea

side, mists can rise suddenly and completely envelop the mountains, making navigation difficult even in summer. Winters are long though not especially cold and the peaks become blanketed in snow, indeed one possible meaning ascribed to the name Kaçkar is 'much snow'.

Flora and fauna

Most of Turkey's tea comes from the plantations on the lower, Black Sea facing slopes. Higher up on this side chestnut, hornbeam, beech and other deciduous trees grow, giving way to pine, until the alpine zone is reached

at 2,100m. Alpine flowers grow in abundance in the spring and summer. The blossoms of the widespread Pontic azalea are a riot of colour in spring, but the honey made from bees feeding on it is said to have hallucinogenic qualities! Bird watchers are drawn to the area in the hope of seeing the rare Caspian snow cock.

Way of life

As elsewhere in upland Turkey, spring sees the annual movement of local families to the high pastures, or *yayla*. Flocks of sheep, goats and cows graze the lush grass, and the milk from the animals is turned into butter, cheese and yoghurt. Whereas the Yörük people of southern Turkey erect tents of black goat hair at the yayla, the Kaçkar locals build wood or stone houses, a response to the colder, wetter weather of Black Sea Turkey.

Descendants of Armenians, Georgians and even Pontic Greeks are still said to inhabit these mountains, but to the casual visitor they are indistinguishable from the general population. More easily recognisable

Buyuk Çay valley

Kaçkar mountains

are the Hemsin people, whose womenfolk wear distinctive black and gold headscarves, and can be seen driving their flocks up the highland paths in spring, often spinning wool on a hand-held spindle as they go.

Trekking

There are many different trails leading through the Kaçkar. Starting from the village of Yaylalar, a beautiful walk up the valley of the Buyuk Çay stream brings walkers to the lake of Deniz Gölü. After an overnight camp here, the range's highest peak, Mt Kaçkar, can be climbed. Non-technical, the route passes under slopes holding a small glacier and clambers up scree to the summit and superb views of

Walking on a glacier high up on Mount Kaçkar

the entire range. Day walks are best undertaken from either the village of Barhal, or Ayder with its hot springs.

Beyond trekking

The Kaçkar range is also a target of mountaineers, and ski tourers in winter. Botanists will be amazed at the range of distinctive plant life, and the mountains are on the twitchers' circuit of Turkey. The mighty Çoruh river is well known to the whitewater rafting fraternity and offers a choice of moderate and difficult runs.

The Black Sea region

The port of Trabzon, once a fabled outpost of the Byzantine Empire known as Trebizond, and still boasting the magnificent 13th century church of St Sophia, is the natural gateway to the area. The Greek monastery of Sumela, clinging to sheer cliffs in a wooded valley behind Trabzon is justly famous. South-east of the Kaçkar lie the so-called Georgian valleys, visited for their attractively situated collection of distinctive medieval churches.

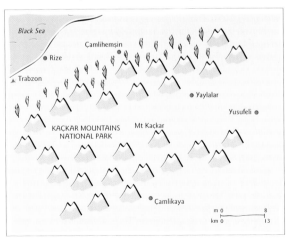

ℹ CONTACT INFORMATION

Upcountry (Turkey) Ltd
24 St John's Road
Buxton SK17 6XQ
Tel & Fax: 01298 71050
E-mail: upcountryturkey@
hotmail.com
Web: www.upcountry.freeserve.co.uk

Upcountry (Turkey) Ltd
Antalya P.K. 528
Turkey
Tel & Fax: (00 90) 242 243 1148
E-mail: kateclow@garanti.net.tr

CONTACT INFORMATION

Bulgaria –
BAAT (Bulgarian Association
for Special Interest Travel)
20-V Stamboliiski Blvd
Sofia 1000
Bulgaria
Tel: (00 359) 2 989 0538
Fax: (00 359) 2 980 3200
E-mail: odysseia@omega.bg
Web: www.newtravel.com

Croatian National Tourist Office
2 The Lanchesters
162-164 Fulham Palace Road
London W6 9ER
Tel: 020 8563 7979
Fax: 020 8563 2616
E-mail: info@cnto.freeserve.co.uk
Web: www.htz.hr

Czech Tourist Authority
Czech Centre
95 Great Portland Street
London W1N 5RA
Tel: 020 7291 9920
Fax: 020 7436 8300
Web: www.czech-tourinfo.cz

Estonian Tourist Board
Mündi 2
10146 Tallinn
Estonia
Tel: (00 372) 641 1420
Fax: (00 372) 641 1432
E-mail: info@tourism.ee
Web: www.tourism.ee

Hungarian National Tourist Office
46 Eaton Place
London SW1X 8AL
Tel: 020 7823 1032
Fax: 020 7823 1459
E-mail: htlondon@hungarytourism.hu
Web-site: www.hungarytourism.hu

Latvian Tourist Board
4 Pils Square
LV1050 Riga
Latvia
Tel & Fax: (00 371) 722 9945
E-mail: ltboard@latnet.lv
Web: www.latviatravel.com

Lithuanian State Department
of Tourism
Vilniaus g. 4/35
2600 Vilnius
Lithuania
Tel: (00 370) 2 622610
Fax: (00 370) 2 226819
E-mail: tb@tourism.lt
Web: www.tourism.lt

Polish National Tourist Office
Remo House
310-312 Regent Street
London W1R 5AY
Tel: 020 7580 8811
Fax: 020 7580 8866
E-mail: pnto@dial.pipex.com
Web: www.pnto.dial.pipex.com

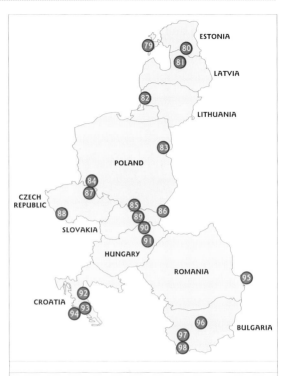

Romanian National
Tourist Office
83a Marylebone High Street
London W1M 3DE
Tel: 020 7224 3692
Fax: 020 7935 6435

Slovakia –
Czech & Slovak Tourist Centre
16 Frognal Parade
Finchley Road
London NW3 5HH
Tel: 0800 026 7943
Fax: 020 7794 3265
Web: www.czech-slovak-tourist.co.uk

Saaremaa and Vilsandi National Park

*Saaremaa is the real Estonia and Vilsandi is raw, unadulterated nature,
where the elements defy human interference but welcome visiting birds.*

Naistekivi maa, Vilsandi National Park

Vilsandi perches delicately on the edge of the island of Saaremaa and is Estonia's most westerly point. People here are only passing witnesses – there are few residents – to the powerful seas and winds which constantly mould and shape the low-lying land and its battered vegetation. The real inhabitants of Vilsandi are the thousands of seabirds and waterfowl that nest or winter in the national park as they migrate between Arctic tundra and central Europe.

Saaremaa's climate is heavily influenced by the Baltic. Winter temperatures dip to only -4°C and the sea does not freeze. Summers are bright and breezy, and the island is a popular destination with Estonians in June and July. For migrating birds, April and May see their northward passage and September and October the journey to warmer climes. To observe wintering species, just remember to wrap up against the ever present wind.

Saaremaa

It is not uncommon for a region to describe itself as having the essential essence of a country, but this is usually in the face of argument and disagreement from other areas. In Estonia however, there is a national consensus; the island of Saaremaa is thought of as the real Estonia.

Following the Soviet occupation during the Second World War, access to the island was severely restricted by military activities. Paradoxically this overt control helped preserve the lifestyles and traditions of the local agricultural communities.

Travelling towards Vilsandi

Saaremaa is sparsely populated and the typical characterisation of a flat land divided between hard-worked arable farms and expanses of juniper bushes is a true one. The journey to Vilsandi does not have to be rushed. The distances are small and there is space and time to explore along the backroads. On Muhu, the island

between Saaremaa and the mainland, is the village of Koguva with its traditional peasant cottages. A working museum, the residents continue to farm using traditional agricultural practices and implements.

Kuressaare, the main town of Saaremaa, is similarly historic. Now a small prosperous market town acting as an outlet for local produce, its charter dates from the 14th century. The Bishop's castle, a formidable, moated bastion in the Gothic style, protected the town from medieval Baltic power struggles. It now houses the Saaremaa museum. Thick-walled limestone block houses cluster in the centre of the town. They date from the 19th century when Kuressaare became a fashionable health resort. A monument to those who died in Estonia's Wars of Independence stands nearby; twice the Soviet authorities removed it and twice the locals erected a replacement.

Lake Kaali lies to the north of Kuressaare. Water collects at the bottom of this 100m wide hollow created by a meteorite strike 2,700 years ago. Further north are Saaremaa's limestone cliffs. The 20m high banks face the sea, fronted by rough pebble beaches and collapsed limestone columns which have been separated from the mainland by the Baltic's waves. Sandy beaches are found along the southern shores, the best on the Sõrve peninsula which sweeps out for over 30km into the sea. Hidden amongst the sand are the concrete remnants of Second World War military defences, whilst lighthouses stand protectively against the skyline.

The leaning lighthouse on Harilaid peninsula

Vilsandi National Park

The island of Vilsandi was first protected as a bird sanctuary as far back as 1910. Throughout the century its status has been upgraded and its scope extended until the national park was created in 1993. Unlike mountainous areas, where it is easy to imagine that landscapes of peaks and valleys are permanent, the impression of this piece of exposed coast is one of constant flux.

The whistling winds continuously transform the beach dunes, in some places creating thin spits which will eventually close off smaller bays and create coastal lakes. Waves crash onto the pebble beaches, pounding the limestone bedrock and eroding the coastline. But, as if retaliating, the actual land area continues to increase. The land is rising at a rate of 3mm per year, slowly rebounding in response to the retreat of the ice sheets at the end of the last glaciation.

Loona to Harilaid peninsula

Many of the smaller islands are strict reserves so the best way to explore the park is to walk parts of the coast. All or part of the 20km road from Loona, the manor house which acts as the park's headquarters, to Harilaid peninsula is recommended as a route.

Despite the testing conditions of wind, salt spray and sand, Vilsandi has over 500 plant species. Clumps of marram grass and sea sandwort grow on the more stable beaches, with prickly sea holly hugging the ground. Further inland begin the grasslands, busy with juniper bushes and, in early summer, the violet blooms of cornflowers. Occasionally there are orchids, with sea wormwood found only near Jaagarahu harbour.

Hundreds of thousands of ducks, geese and swans, as well as little terns and great black-headed gulls, are regular visitors to Vilsandi. For them the mild maritime climate, plentiful food supplies and undisturbed location make the park an ideal place for resting, breeding and nesting. Over 6,000 Steller's eiders winter to the north of Harilaid at Uudepanga Bay, the most significant site in the Baltic, and around 60,000 barnacle geese rest between migrations on Saaremaa in both spring and autumn. One permanent inhabitant of the park is the white-tailed eagle. Nesting in the pine stands, these birds prey on unwary ducks and geese.

ⓘ CONTACT INFORMATION

Vilsandi National Park
Kihelkonna vald
EE93401 Saare Maakond
Estonia
Tel: (00 372) 454 6880
Fax: (00 372) 454 6554

Kuusenõmme Bay

Boglands of Southern Estonia

One fifth of Estonia is wetland and Karula National Park, Soomaa National Park and Nigula Nature Reserve play an important role in protecting these fragile environments.

The seaside resort of Pärnu on the west coast and the university city of Tartu in the east are good bases from which to travel down the backroads of Estonia. Here, in the south of the country, as the towns shrink to become villages and then individual farmsteads, the undulating landscape wavers between agricultural land and wide expanses of bog.

Wet, acidic, infertile and inaccessible are all rather one-sided preconceptions that have protected the wetlands from human interference and ensured that they still remain havens of wildlife. Although the ground is never dry underfoot, late spring and summer are the best times to visit.

Pine forests, Soomaa

Karula – the land of bears

In medieval times, so the story goes, the dark forests of this area were home to brown bears and the name Karula is derived from *karu*, the Estonian for bear. A landscape reserve since 1979, Karula was made a national park in 1993. The bears have long since disappeared and it is now beavers that have gnawed their way

to the attention of visitors. The small streams that riddle the park provide these animals with an ideal habitat and their dams line the western banks of Lake Ubajärv.

Karula is a mélange of landforms resulting from the retreat of the ice sheets at the end of the last Ice Age 10,000 years ago. Glacial debris remains piled in thick ridges, whilst

eskers – long banks of sand and gravel deposited by slowing meltwater streams – stretch out across the park. The mounds of debris are separated from each other by shallow valleys. On these mounds, grassy meadows alternate with dry pine and spruce groves; in the valley bottoms, where the drainage is poor, bog pine, swamp birch and alder grow. Gently flowing brooks pool where the valleys widen to form small lakes which are often choked by reeds.

Karula also protects the traditional culture of the area. Burial mounds at Alakonni and Mähki are evidence of early occupation. Later settlers were continually threatened by the wars that have raged between various powers through the centuries.

The church at Lüllemäe, established in the 14th century, has recorded the brutal passage of armies. Rebuilt many times, it has remained a ruin since its destruction in the Second World War. Karula's scattering of isolated farms defied Soviet collectivisation but deliberate depopulation has left many of the smallholdings uninhabited.

Soomaa – the land of mires

Soomaa National Park extends over 370 sq km of marsh and forest between Pärnu and Viljandi. Even more than in Karula, it is water that shapes the physical landscape as well as the lives of the few people who still live within the park's boundaries.

The locals know five seasons – spring, summer, autumn, winter and the flood. Every year, as winter wanes, rain and melting snow raise the water levels in the the rivers by 5m. Around 40 sq km of the territory is regularly flooded, although extents of over 200 sq km have been recorded.

In the past, log boats carved from aspen were the only mode of transport during these times. The park

The lakes and forests of Karula

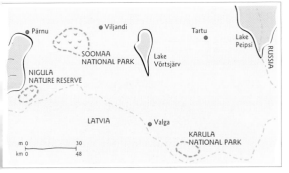

marsh andromeda. Set against this are areas of primeval forest perching on the handful of small islands, themselves only gobbets of earth rising above the bog. On Mämisaar, where there is no soil, the pine trees grow on a thick layer of moss.

Cranberry bushes favour the transitional zones around bogs, and across southern Estonia, marsh edges and riverbanks have traditionally produced excellent crops. A research centre at Nigula uses cranberries as a means of rehabilitating peatlands.

continues to keep this tradition alive with an annual boat building camp. Another popular way for visitors to tour the rivers and bogs is to take an organised canoeing trip.

Although Soomaa is based around four bogs – Kuresoo, Öördi, Kikepera and Valgeraba – and the rivers that separate them, not all of the park is wetland. On higher ground there are wooded meadows, rich in flowers including wild orchids. Isolated oak, ash and elm mix with knots of dry pine to provide a secluded habitat for lynx, wolf, elk, boar and deer. The woods are also inhabited by the rare silver-coated flying squirrel.

Nigula and the cranberry

Situated in the south-west, close to the Latvian border, the compact Nigula Nature Reserve is an accessible introduction to an Estonian mire. From afar, bogs can seem bland and monotonous, but the walkway that leads through the Nigula complex highlights their natural variety.

The central lake is fed by streams from the bog plateau. Only a few species of waterlilies prosper in the brown, acidic waters. In contrast, the bog itself often resembles a colourful meadow, with the summer blooms of cottongrass, purple heather and

ℹ CONTACT INFORMATION

Karula National Park
Ähijärve
Antsla vald
EE2723 Võrumaa
Estonia
Tel & Fax: (00 372) 785 2456

Soomaa National Park
Tõramaa
Kõpu vald
EE71211 Viljandimaa
Estonia
Tel: (00 372) 435 7164

Nigula Nature Reserve
Vana-Järve
EE86101 Tali
Estonia
Tel: (00 372) 449 1664

Valgeraba bog, Soomaa

LATVIA

Gauja National Park

The River Gauja slices through the forests and fields of northern Latvia, carving out its meandering valley. Full of nooks and crannies, the national park offers easy exploration rather than dramatic isolation.

The Gauja river in winter

Gauja National Park is situated 50km to the north-east of Riga, Latvia's attractive capital city. In the mild summer months, walking, cycling, horse-riding and boating are popular, as well as picnics at the many beauty spots that dot the countryside and visits to castles and churches. In the cold of winter, which usually lasts from November through to March, the park's paths can be followed on skis.

The River Gauja

The small town of Sigulda, which sits above the rocky bluffs overlooking the River Gauja, began to develop as a summer resort in the late 19th century. Early guidebooks tagged Sigulda as the 'Latvian Switzerland', and the general locality began to be spoken of as a national park.

In 1973 the Gauja National Park was formally established in recognition of the natural and historic importance of the area. Extending over 920 sq km, the park is named after the Gauja river which snakes its way through the central valley. Rising to the south in the Vidzeme Upland, the Gauja flows east, then north towards Estonia before swinging south-west through the park on its way to the Baltic Sea.

The Gauja is the backbone of the park; fed by numerous small tributaries, it is fast flowing after the spring melt, slowing to a stately meander in late summer. Millions of years ago, water began to erode the sandstone plateau through which the Gauja cuts, over time creating the present valley system with its stumpy outcrops and ochre riverside cliffs. One million years ago, the valley disappeared, filled with debris from shifting ice sheets. At the end of the last Ice Age, 10,000 years ago, glacial meltwater washed away the debris and the valley was reinstated.

Beyond the forests

Travelling along the river, with the closely-packed trees jostling for space at the water's edge, it is easy to presume that all of the park is forested. Nearly half of it is, with the dominant pine and spruce interspersed with broad-leaved woods of oak, lime and ash, but Gauja has a hidden diversity. There are also flower-filled meadows, green pastures, small lakes and bogs, and farmsteads with their fields of crops. It is this variety that supports 900 identified plant species, as well as lichens, mosses and 430

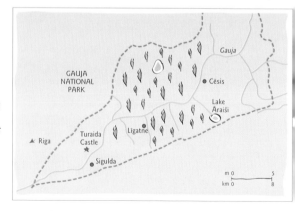

types of mushroom. Roe deer, wild boar and elk roam the forests, as well as red deer that have been recently reintroduced. Rare bird species include black storks, lesser-spotted eagles, black grouse, white-backed woodpeckers and pygmy owls. Salmon spawn in the Gauja, whilst otters hunt along its tributaries. One of these, Pērlupe, is one of the few places in Latvia where the pearl-mussel can still be found.

Outdoor activities

Close to the town of Ligatne is the park's educational and interpretative centre. A wildlife area allows visitors to see the larger mammals that still inhabit the national park, as well as the bison, lynx and bears that do not. Several short educational walks are organised. The botanical trail helps budding naturalists identify rare plant species, before encouraging them to shout their names towards the Gūdu cliffs and hear the echoes reverberate back across the river. The fairytale path weaves through the forest, the glades decorated with life-size timber carvings of Latvian folk characters.

A large tract of the river, some 210km from Vireši downstream to Sigulda, is ideal for canoeing. Beyond the park's boundaries, the Strenči rapids are probably the most scenic section, whilst still offering a gentle passage. Another good place to canoe is the Salaca river in the 400 sq km Northern Vidzeme Biosphere Reserve near the Estonian border.

Sigulda

At the turn of the previous millennium the Gauja river was an important trade route: it linked the continental interior of the east with the Scandinavian kingdoms around the Baltic, whilst also forming the border between the Liv and the Latgalian peoples. Following excavations, the latter's lake-top dwellings have been reconstructed at Lake Āraiši. From the 13th century, as German conquest of the area was followed by a series of fractious power struggles, the river again marked the territorial boundaries of different factions.

In Sigulda, the Livonian Knights built their castle on the northern edge of the town and the archbishops of Riga set theirs on the opposite bank of the river, each side confronting the other. Sigulda castle was largely destroyed in the 18th century, but the south-west corner and a tower from the central gate still survive. Turaida, the archbishops' castle, fared little better, being destroyed by fire in 1776. Parts have, however, been restored and the main tower offers excellent views over the town across the river.

Nowadays, Sigulda is a quiet, mild mannered town and acts as the main gateway to the park. As well as weaving, linen and lace craft, the town offers opera and folk festivals. Nearby Cēsis is similarly pleasant. Besides the cobbled streets of the old quarter, the Church of St John and a 13th century castle, the town is home to Latvia's oldest brewery, a status enthusiastically celebrated at an annual beer festival.

ℹ CONTACT INFORMATION

Gauja National Park
Baznīcas iela 3
LV2150 Sigulda
Latvia
Tel: (00 371) 297 4006
Fax: (00 371) 297 1344
E-mail: gaujas@nacionalais@parks.lv

The sandstone cliffs of the Gauja

Kuršių Nerija and Žemaitija National Parks

*Shifting dunes and spreading forests; the waves of the Baltic
and placid lakes; pagan rituals and Catholic pilgrimages.
All are found together in north-west Lithuania.*

Since the French National Institute of Geography recently decreed the centre of Europe to be a few kilometres from their capital city of Vilnius, Lithuanians have considered themselves to be at the core of the continent. This is as good an excuse as any to discover the who, what, where, when and whys of the country.

Kuršių Nerija and Žemaitija are excellent starting points for an active holiday, being recreational centres as well as having remits to protect their differing natural landscapes and cultural histories.

Kuršių Nerija National Park

Kuršių Nerija, which is also known as the Curonian Spit, is a sliver of land that runs parallel to the bottom half of the Lithuanian coastline. Separating the Curonian lagoon from the Baltic Sea, the thin peninsula continues south into the Russian territory of Kaliningrad. Some 264 sq km of the Lithuanian section, two thirds of which is water, was given national park status in 1991.

Kuršių Nerija is officially the sunniest place in the country, and with its long beaches is a popular destination in July and August. Fortunately, because of the strict controls on development, it is never overcrowded. Snow cover from late November to February means ice fishing on the lagoon is a popular winter pastime.

Klaipėda, the country's third largest city, is the usual departure point for a trip to the national park. Situated on the mainland, just 0.5km from the northern end of the spit, the city's history is like many of those in the Baltic States. A fortress built by the Knights of the Livonian Order; growth as a trading port (although Gdansk's merchants apparently took offence at the thought of the competition and tried to block the harbour entrance); and the resultant wealth displayed in the architecture of the old city.

Klaipėda remains a pleasant place to stop before catching the ferry, its history buoyed by a strong local economy centred on its year-round ice-free port.

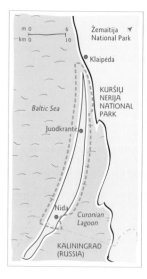

A changing landscape

The spit is a transitory landscape; it is not old in geological terms and is continually being manipulated by the sea and the wind. It is probably only the combined efforts of naturalists and engineers that have preserved the dunes in their present state, although around 10 hectares are still lost every year to erosion.

Formed about 5,500 years ago, the sand dunes were stabilised by forests of pine, oak and lime. Early inhabitants fished in the sea and hunted in the forests. By the 16th century, however, population pressure had lead to deforestation. As the trees disappeared, the winds caused havoc, burying fourteen villages beneath the shifting sand.

Remedial action was not taken for another 200 years until a man named G.D. Cuvert began a replanting programme. Since accelerated and supplemented by the building of a protective barrier, it was Cuvert's initial action that saved the spit. He is commemorated in the town of Nida.

The lakes and forests of Žemaitija

Sand and wood

The bare dunes create a beautiful landscape and, for such an empty place, the senses are continually stimulated. Sand can glitter under the summer sun or the reflected light can dazzle; the wind whistles as it whips through the shallow valleys; and the heat retained by the dunes makes them feel warmer than anticipated, especially in the autumn.

In contrast, the forests which cover nearly three quarters of the park are rich in plant and animal species. Mountain and common pine dominate, although there also areas of birch, alder, oak and ash. The shaded undergrowth is home to elk, deer, wild boar, badgers and raccoons.

However, it is the bird-life which is most impressive. Over 15 million birds pass through Kuršių Nerija each year in the spring and autumn migrations between the White Sea and the western Baltic. Wintering species include velvet scoters, long-tailed ducks, goosanders and common goldeneyes, whilst there is a mixed summer colony of 1,500 pairs of grey herons and cormorants.

Life on the spit

For such a narrow strip of land the spit has a surprising depth of human history which is reflected in the summer festivals and various museums that dot the area. The Baltic coast is a good place to find amber and pieces are often washed up on the beaches. Whilst mining a rich seam during the late 19th century, hundreds of amber figurines were found. Dated to around 4,000 years ago, these carved figures are thought to have been part of a sacrificial site at Juodkrantė.

Fishing has traditionally been an important activity at Kuršių Nerija. The fishermen's log cottages with their vertical exterior planking and daubed paintwork have been preserved. There are also examples of the flat-bottomed boats made from oak which were still being used on the lagoon up until the 1950s.

The main rhythm to life on the spit nowadays is generated by the holiday

Walkway across the dunes of Kuršių Nerija

season. As well as sunbathing, visitors can sail, windsurf, fish, horse-ride or cycle. Walking paths link the settlements, and trails through the forests are popular for mushroom and berry picking. The best places to see the dunes and wildlife is on a guided tour in the protected nature reserves.

Kuršių Nerija's status as a holiday destination is not a new phenomenon. Thomas Mann, the Nobel Prize winning German author, spent his summers here from 1930-2. His brief stays are honoured annually with a programme of readings, film, music and art exhibitions.

217

Shrove Tuesday carnival, Žemaitija

Žemaitija National Park

Žemaitija lies 60km to the north-east of Klaipėda in Lithuania's highlands. The park was established in 1991 and extends over 217 sq km, the majority of which is pine, spruce and birch forest. As well as conserving the natural and cultural landscape, the park has a recreational focus with visitors spending much of their time along the shores of Lake Plateliai.

Žemaitija's undulating landscape – the hills reach 190m which is sufficient in the lowlands of the Baltic to warrant the term 'highland' – is crossed with streams. Formed by receding glaciers

at the end of the last Ice Age, one of the notable features of the area is the large number of boulders deposited by melting ice. At Mosėdis, near to the

park, many of the rocks have been brought together to form an open air geology museum. The largest example the huge Barstyčiai Stone, was too big to move, whilst a stone with its own 'Devil's footprint' remains at Mikytai.

Lake Plateliai

The lake is usually the starting point for a visit to the park. A peaceful place, thick forests reach the edge of the calm waters, whilst the solitude of hidden bays gives rise to folk-tales of secret meetings and doomed trysts As well as eels, crawfish and marsh turtles, Plateliai contains species of salmon and lavaret that have

Looking out to the Baltic from Nagliai, Kuršių Nerija

emained isolated in the lake since the lacial retreat. Near or on the lake are ound black-throated divers, red-reasted mersangers and curlews. Organised excursions are a good ntroduction to the shy inhabitants of he forest – elk, deer, wild boar, hare, ynx and fox.

amogitians to Soviets

his north-western part of the ountry has always been connected vith the Samogitian people. Despite eing incorporated into the original tate of Lithuania in the 13th century, he Samogitians remained a separate thnic group. Protected from ssimilation by a strong unifying ulture and their own language, it is heir history that forms one of the

most interesting historical aspects of the park. Culturally isolated, the Samogitians were one of the last peoples in Europe to abandon paganism. Their acceptance of Catholicism has been ascribed to its emphasis on ritual, and the roadside crosses and shrines in the park show a mixture of religious symbols.

Žemaičių Kalvarija is a small town in the north-east of Žemaitija. It rose to prominence in the 17th century when the local bishop established an abbey. The monks built nineteen chapels illustrating Christ's journey with the cross from Jerusalem to Calvary. An annual pilgrimage follows the route every July. St John's Hill, where the town's original castle stood, has excellent views over the area.

Finally, for something a little different, there is the chance to visit a Soviet missile base. The site houses a military museum and the missile shafts are open to visitors. To complete the experience it is possible to stay overnight in the barracks.

ⓘ CONTACT INFORMATION

Kuršių Nerija National Park
Smiltynės 18
5800 Klaipėda
Lithuania
Tel: (00 370) 6 391109
Fax: (00 370) 6 391113

Žemaitija National Park
Didžioji g. 10
5655 Plateliai
Lithuania
Tel: (00 370) 18 49231
Fax: (00 370) 18 49337

Jagliai Strict Nature Reserve in Kuršių Nerija

Białowieża National Park

*This dense swathe of primeval forest is a final remnant of the sights
and sounds that dominated lowland Europe before the development
of settlements and agriculture.*

The Białowieża forest is one of the
largest surviving fragments of the
mixed forest that once spread across
Europe from the Atlantic to the Urals.
Undisturbed for thousands of years,
and then protected as a royal hunting
reserve, the Białowieża's importance
is magnified by its location on two
ecological crossroads. As well as
spanning both the Baltic and Black
Sea watersheds, the forest harbours
animal and plant species from western
and eastern Europe.

European bison

Białowieża National Park

The forest complex covers over 1,000
sq km on the Polish–Belorussian
border. After being surveyed at the
end of the First World War, the
environmental significance of the area
ensured that the core became a
forestry reserve in 1921 and was
upgraded to national park status in
1932. Now covering 105 sq km,
Białowieża National Park is the only
natural site in Poland included on the
UNESCO world heritage list.

Visiting the park

The park's roles have always been
clearly defined as being
conservational, scientific and
educational. There has been very little
development around the park and
there is no provision for holidays as
such. Visitors are encouraged to look
and learn, before leaving the area
undisturbed. Access to the strict
forest reserve is limited to small
guided tours. Close by is the bison
breeding centre, as well as the
park's headquarters and museum
which are housed in a Russian tsar's
19th century hunting lodge.

Białowieża endures a typically
continental climate, alleviated by
some oceanic influences. Snow falls
from November through to March.
A late spring and early autumn
concertina summer into July and
August when temperatures are on
average between 15 and 20°C.

Primeval forest

Over 10,000 years old, the Białowieża
primeval forest has an extremely
diverse structure and, unusually for
Europe, a two thirds / one third
deciduous / coniferous mix.
Białowieża represents the southern
limit of the naturally occurring spruce
and the north-eastern limit of the
sessile oak. Although twenty different
forest communities and twenty six
tree species have been identified,
mixed, dry-ground, hornbeam–lime–
oak forest prevails. Spruce also grows
on poorer soils, whilst ash and alder
can be found on the damp, fertile
riverbanks.

'The King of the Forest'

Białowieża boasts a staggering 10,000
animal species, but it is the bulk of
the shy European bison for which it is
best known. In the 1920s, after
centuries of deforestation and
hunting, the bison finally became
extinct across Europe except for sixty
specimens in zoos. A free range
breeding centre in Białowieża has
successfully returned 300 animals to
the forest. The largest European
mammal, the sheer size of these
placid ruminants gives them a
formidable appearance. The adult

males weigh around one tonne and
have heavily-built shoulders and front
haunches, as well as a large hump.
There is also a show reserve for the
primitive tarpan horse. Small and
sturdy with distinctive colouring,
these wild steppe horses, a forest
sub-species of which lived in
Białowieża, were hunted to extinction
in the 19th century. They have since
been reintroduced through selective
cross breeding of related species.

ⓘ CONTACT INFORMATION

Białowieża National Park
Park Pałacowy 5
17-230 Białowieża
Poland
Tel: (00 48) 835 12306

Białowieza's primeval forest

Karkonosze National Park

The Karkonosze have in the past suffered from pollution and intensive tourism. The lower slopes have been worst affected and it is only on the mountain tops that the natural ecosystems have remained unsullied.

The Karkonosze form the highest section of the Sudeten mountain chain which stretches from north-west to south-east along the Polish–Czech border. The national park, which covers 55 sq km, was established in 1959 to protect the area's glacial geomorphological features, as well as the flora and fauna associated with the peaks, peat bogs and heavily forested lower slopes. The Czech side is also protected (Krkonoše National Park) and the two meet on the central mountain ridge which acts as the international border.

Hidden treasures

After initially being lifted by tectonic activity, the granitic rock of the Sudeten belt was eroded and shaped during subsequent ice ages to form the present landscape. Underground, there are rich deposits of precious stones. The Karkonosze contain amethysts and rock crystal, whilst quartz, chrysoprase, garnets and sapphires are found nearby. Metal ores were mined in the Middle Ages and the observant prospector may still find a grain or two of gold in the rivers.

The main ridge runs between Mt Szrenica (1,362m) in the west and Mt Śnieżka (1,602m) in the east, with deep glacial cirques sitting snugly just beneath the rim on the Polish side. Now empty, apart from small lakes, the cirques were the birthplace of the local glaciers that moulded the steep valleys, cutting off side streams to form hanging valleys and waterfalls. On the ridge itself, the bare summits rise out of the blanket bogs, along with isolated rocky outcrops named by locals as 'The Pilgrims', 'The Sunflower' and 'The Beads'.

Spruce forests

Because of its harsh climate, the Karkonosze has well defined ecological zones not usually found at these relatively low altitudes. The lower slopes are heavily forested with planted spruce. A band of dwarf pine follows at 1,250m, gradually replaced by exposed moorlands and sub-alpine peat bogs interspersed with peaks.

Around 900 plant species have been documented in the park including a number of endangered endemics and relicts from glacial periods. These are supplemented by a profusion of lichens, mosses and fungi. Mammals and birds are typical of forested, mountainous areas, although the moufflon (a variety of big-horned sheep) were only introduced from Corsica in the early 20th century.

Wang Chapel

Jelenia Góra is the capital of the region and a good staging post for a trip to the Karkonosze. Founded in the 12th century, the town became an important textile centre in the 16th and 17th centuries. The old town is centred on the fine merchant houses, built in Renaissance and Baroque styles, which surround Market Square. Chojnik Hill, south-west of the town, is home to the park headquarters and a museum.

Hikers on a trail in the Karkonosze

Next to the park itself are the resort villages of Karpacz and Szklarska Poręba. The main feature of the former is the splendidly curious Wang Chapel. Shaped like an oriental temple, the timber structure was built in Norway in the late 13th century and brought to its present site in the 19th century by King Friedrich Wilhelm IV of Prussia.

Walking routes

The weather in the Karkonosze is variable at the best of times. There is a metre of snow on the higher ground for at least six months of the year and often through into April. For this reason the late spring and summer are preferable for walking, although even then be prepared for all sorts. Rain or mist can sweep in at any point without much warning.

There are several hundred kilometres of hiking routes in the park, with Karpacz and Szklarska Poręba being the starting points for most ascents into the mountains. Chairlifts operate all year and ski lifts in winter, but the

well-marked trails are what it's all about. The trek up from Szklarska Poręba to the summit of Szrenica, in the west of the park, will take between three and four hours; whilst Karpacz up to Śnieżka, at the eastern end, takes between two and three hours. At Śnieżka there is the 15th century Chapel of St Laurentius, as well a meteorological observatory built in the 1960s.

The best high route is the ridge walk between Szrenica and Śnieżka, skirting the peat bogs and overlooking six glacial cirques. Suitable for walking in either direction, it is a six to eight hour hike. Adding on the ascent and descent, the route can be completed in a long day. Alternatively it is possible to use the chairlifts at either end or to break overnight at one of the several mountain huts in the park.

Human pressures

The Karkonosze are under considerable pressure. The south-west of Poland is densely populated and the park is a popular summer and winter tourist

destination. Over 2.5 million people visit every year, mainly from Poland and Germany, and this has had a detrimental impact despite the strict controls on activity and development within the protected area.

The other problem is pollution. Acid rain from the industrial belts of southern Poland, the former East Germany and what was Czechoslovakia has damaged many of the trees. Although atmospheric emissions have fallen since the collapse of the Communist regimes, it will take many years before the forests are revived. At the moment, weakened trees killed by beetles are left standing to prevent soil erosion, a grim reminder of how human activity in one area can adversely affect the natural environment in another.

i CONTACT INFORMATION

Karkonosze National Park
ul Chalubinskiego 23
58-570 Jelenia Góra
Poland
Tel & Fax: (00 48) 75 53348

Wang Chapel at Karpacz

Tatra & Pieniny National Parks

*Lying along Poland's southern border, these contrasting parks offer
either the remoteness of steepled mountains and plunging valleys,
or the comfort of rolling hills and thick-walled castles.*

The Tatras are the highest mountains
of the Carpathians and provide the
only example of an alpine
environment in Poland. Extending for
65km along the Poland–Slovakia
border, 210 sq km were designated in
1955 as the Tatra National Park. The
park is very popular, attracting over
3 million visitors, and is an excellent
area for both hiking and skiing.

Only 25km to the east, the Pieniny
National Park offers a different
experience. Covering just 23 sq km
in the central section of the Pieniny
range, the park is compact and
accessible. As well as hiking and
rafting there are medieval castles and
picturesque timber churches to visit.

High points

Tatra National Park splits neatly into
two halves. The Western Tatras (Tatry
Zachodnie) consist primarily of
limestone and dolomite, eroded over
time to produce domed summits.
In the High Tatras, the granitic rocks
have been chiselled and gouged during
glacial periods to produce a landscape
of jagged peaks, sitting over cirques
and mountain lakes.

The main feature of Pieniny National
Park is the narrow, 10km long Dunajec
gorge. Above the river looms the
Three Crowns (Trzy Korony), the main
limestone massif of the park, of which
Mt Okraglica (982m) is the high point.

Hiking and rafting

Tatra National Park has an excellent
network of marked paths. Routes
suitable for all abilities usually start
from the town of Zakopane or at Mt
Kasprowy Wierch where the cable-car
ends. One place not to be missed,
even though it will be busy, is Morskie
Oko (Eye of the Sea). This clear, blue-
green lake is impressive, perched as it
is in the shadow of Mt Rysy (2,499m).
From there climb up to Czarny Staw
(Black Pond), where 1,000m cliffs
provide a daunting headwall.
The intrepid can continue on a very
steep climb to the summit of Mt Rysy
or turn west towards Mt Mnich.

The villages surrounding the Pieniny
are starting points for a series of
undemanding day walks up into the
mountains. The two hour climb up to

Mt Okraglica provides excellent views
of the Tatras, whilst Mt Sokolica is
the best spot to look down and along
the incised Dunajec river. A rafting trip
through the Dunajec gorge provides a
different perspective on the sheer
cliffs and the peaks above. Rafting has
developed into a tourist business,
with men garbed in traditional
costumes steering the timber crafts. At
its narrowest point the gorge shrinks
to a width of 12m and the waters are
quite fast, although for much of the
journey the river is wider and calmer.

Close to the Pieniny is the impressive
14th century Niedzica castle, built by
the Hungarians to protect their border
with Poland. A few miles upstream
on the opposite bank is the Polish
equivalent – Czorsztyn castle.
Timber churches are another notable
feature of the area. The late 14th
century Catholic church at Dębno is
the most visited example.

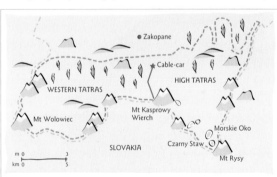

🅘 CONTACT INFORMATION

Tatra National Park
ul Chalubinskiego 42a
34-500 Zakopane
Poland
Tel: (00 48) 165 63203
Fax: (00 48) 165 63579

Pieniny National Park
ul Jagiellonska 107b
34-450 Kroscienko
Poland
Tel: (00 48) 18 262 5601
Fax: (00 48) 18 262 5603

Bieszczady National Park

*The Bieszczady mountains are an isolated, rugged sliver
in the south-eastern corner of Poland. The area's beauty is
in its silence and emptiness.*

Surrounded on three sides by Slovakia and Ukraine, Bieszczady has one of the purest natural environments in the country. The low population density has resulted in a minimal level of development, whilst poor accessibility and limited amenities mean that outdoor enthusiasts rather than groups of holidaymakers are attracted to the mountains.

Bieszczady

The national park protects 270 sq km of the western end of the Bieszczady mountains. On the lower slopes, up to 1,150m, the dominant Carpathian beech woods are interspersed with fir, sycamore and alder which follow the lines of the streams into deep ravines.

Adjoining these forests are the *poloniny* – the verdant sub-alpine pastures which cover the ridges and summits of the massifs. These meadows of tufted hairgrass and low bushes have led the Bieszczady to be called 'the grassy roof of the world'.

Outdoor activities

Winters are long and cold, although the thick, crisp snow and empty landscapes are ideal for cross-country skiing. The mild summers are suited to walking, horse-riding and sailing.

The national park is strictly protected and hiking is restricted to the 135km of marked trails. However, the main trails, which start from Wetlina, Cisna and Ustrzyki Górne, encompass the best of the peaks, including the 1,346m high Mount Tarnica, and the poloniny. Elsewhere in the mountains there are fewer restrictions and more opportunities for roaming. A network of huts provides basic accommodation.

The alternative mode of transport in the mountains is the Hucuł horse. An endemic breed, related to the primitive mountain horse, Hucuł are now specially bred at centres in the Bieszczady. Short and stocky, the horses are hardy animals, capable of surviving the harsh winter months.

The River San is the longest tributary of the Vistula which eventually reaches the Baltic Sea. The damming of the San to the north of the park has created two storage reservoirs. The largest, Lake Solińskie, is sufficiently deep to offer excellent sailing, as well as pike, trout and perch fishing. For the experienced canoeist the 300km trip from Lake Myczkowce downstream to Przemyśl is an invigorating expedition.

[i] **CONTACT INFORMATION**

Bieszczady National Park
Lutowiska 50
38-714 Ustrzyki Górne
Poland
Tel: (00 48) 90 309156

Krkonoše National Park

A panoramic view from a high ridge or the tumbling splash of a waterfall in a valley bottom are sights and sounds to savour in the Krkonoše.

The Krkonoše in summer

The Krkonoše are the Giant Mountains. With a beautiful alpine landscape and rare plant communities this should be the perfect place to hike, cycle and ski. But anyone visiting north-east Bohemia will soon see that industrial pollution has dulled the sheen of the dense forests and ancient peaks. However, to ignore the Krkonoše because they are not what they once were would be to do them an injustice.

Out of season

Choosing when to go to the Krkonoše is vital. There's much to be said for going when the chairlifts are closed in early spring and late autumn, as in the summer daytrippers are ushered effortlessly to crowd all the good spots. Beware though that the mountains may be wet. On average, it rains on 200 days of the year, which helps to produce excellent snow for the start of the skiing season in late December, but can also mean soakings in the summer months.

Don't be lulled into a false sense of security by the relatively low heights of the mountains. Although the highest point is only just over 1,600m, conditions throughout the range are comparable to those above 2,000m in the Alps. Walkers should be prepared for deteriorating conditions, especially on the ridges where there is often mist and the buffeting winds can bring temperatures down to freezing even in the summer.

Krkonoše National Park

The national park covers 360 sq km of the Krkonoše mountains to the north-east of Prague on the Czech–Polish border. It encompasses two broadly parallel ridges, running from north-west to south-east, from which the weathered massifs fall away sharply into wide, shallow valleys which carry the five rivers born in the mountains down to the lowlands. The northern ridge is the higher of the two and marks the international border.

Survival of the forests

Four fifths of the park is forested and above the valleys spruce stands rise to 1,300m. It is here that the effects of acid rain are most prominent, with the weakened trees succumbing to insects. Around one quarter of the trees have been damaged.

North-east Bohemia has no heavy industry of its own and the pollutants have all been blown in from the coal burning stacks of other regions and countries. To really see what damage can be done go to Špindlerův Mlýn, where the worst of the barren tragedy unfolds in earnest.

Above the tree line there is a remarkable diversity of environments. Beneath the rocky summits sit corries gouged out in previous ice ages. These are home to niche communities of arctic plants, whilst the peat bogs and meadows elsewhere on the slopes provide habitats for dwarf pine, rowan and rare alpine and sub-alpine flowers

The Charles Bridge, Prague

Walking and cycling

There are 1,000km of marked paths through the valleys, forests and up onto the ridges, although routes to the tops are closed in winter. Access to other areas is restricted occasionally to allow regeneration.

Pec pod Sněžkou is usually the starting point for the three hour hike up to Sněžka – the Snow Mountain. Having clambered up to 1,602m it can be disheartening to be surrounded by people who came up on the chairlift. So, weather permitting, having enjoyed the panoramic views back into the Czech Republic and across to Poland, pressing on along the ridge is a good option. 'The Path of Czech–Polish Friendship' is where Lech Walesa and Václav Havel secretly met prior to the Velvet Revolution. Along it to the east is the peak of Svorová and to the west is Slezká bouda.

The River Labe, which eventually enters the North Sea as the Elbe, flows down the main valley. The source of this mighty river can be reached from the town of Špindlerův Mlýn. After a pleasant walk along the valley and then a sharp ascent, it is an anti-climax to find that the spring rises from a rather uninspiring bog. For a better example of the latter, start from Janské Lázně and climb Černá

hora – the Black Mountain. Here, the peat bogs support a fragile community of relict glacial plants.

The Krkonoše are also part of a nationwide cycle network. The local paths that run through the foothills link up with routes that range across the region. In winter, skiing is the only mode of transport in the mountains and the favourable snow conditions make the Krkonoše a popular destination. Although the facilities are not as sophisticated as in Western resorts, they are cheaper. The snow also temporarily masks the impact of the acid rain on the trees.

The Giant of the Mountains

It is the setting that makes the towns and villages of the foothills rather than the places themselves, but there are interesting things to be found.

Harrachov was one of the first communities established when the Krkonoše were settled in the 18th century. Glassmakers were attracted to the area by the minerals and Bohemia's central position on European trade routes. The town's original 18th century glassworks still operates and there is a small museum.

The Krkonoše museum and a 16th century château, now home to the park headquarters, are in Vrchlabi. In Trutnov, an historic town to the east, there is a statue of Krakonoš – the giant said to guard the Krkonoše, rewarding the good and punishing the bad. For the mountains' sake it is about time he reawakened and came back to protect the area once again.

ⓘ CONTACT INFORMATION

Czech Tourist Authority
Czech Centre
95 Great Portland Street
London W1N 5RA
Tel: 020 7291 9920
Fax: 020 7436 8300

Czech & Slovak Tourist Centre
16 Frognal Parade
Finchley Road
London NW3 5HH
Tel: 0800 026 7943
Fax: 020 7794 3265
Web: www.czech-slovak-tourist.co.uk

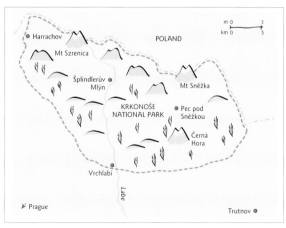

Šumava National Park

*An undisturbed and tranquil landscape of forested slopes
and ancient mountains sprawling beyond the Czech Republic
into Germany and Austria.*

Šumava National Park is an idyllic
environment with small villages
scattered along the foothills providing
pleasant bases for relaxing forays
along the many paths. The park is
large, but most parts of it are
accessible on foot and the tallest of
the mountains can still be climbed in
a good day's walk. Beware though,
that despite its peaceful exterior,
underneath Šumava is still a
wonderfully wild place.

Lake Plesné in the heart of Šumava

Summer and winter

The months of July and August offer
a typical continental summer of hot,
intense weather and high numbers of
visitors, especially from Prague and
the other cities. The quieter times of
May, June and September, with their
pleasant, comfortable days, are
preferable. Winter is long and cold,
but the solitude of skiing through
silent, empty forests is rewarding.

Šumava National Park

Šumava is the Czech Republic's
largest national park, covering
690 sq km. Originally designated a
Protected Landscape Area in the
1960s, the area was promoted to its
present status in 1991. However,
while other parts of Europe have
suffered from the pressures of people,

transport and industry, a central
reason for the preservation of the
pristine beauty of Šumava lies not
with conservationists but, ironically,
with the Cold War.

A sensitive border region following
the raising of the Iron Curtain,
Šumava was off-limits to visitors and
development was forbidden by the
authorities. The forests have also not
been particularly affected by acid rain,
although air pollution remains a
potential threat to the peat bogs.

Ancient mountains

The Šumava massif runs for 140km
along the Czech–German border.
Formed from two separate chains,
the area is one of the oldest mountain
regions in Europe, its now dulled
peaks still bearing the evidence of
glacial activity from many thousands
of years ago. These isolated, rounded
summits rise to around 1,350m,
300m above the high level plateau.
Immediately beneath the tops lie the
lakes, the crystal clear water sitting
behind dams of glacial debris.

Green lungs

The lower slopes are thickly forested
with beech, fir and spruce, which
higher up give way to spruce stands
and finally scree slopes. Where the
forest was cleared by charcoal burners
supplying the burgeoning industries of
the lowlands, there are now mountain
grasslands resplendent with the
colours of spring flowers.

The only example of virgin primeval
forest left is at Boubín, which was
first singled out for protection in the
mid 19th century. The moorland and
peat bogs of the plateau are the

Lake Lipno in winter

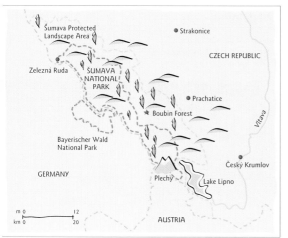

protective bulk of the castle. The town retains local cultural traditions via vibrant celebrations, seemingly regardless of whether tourists are present or not. Throughout the year there are a series of music and film festivals, as well as concerts and plays in the castle gardens, whilst local folk customs and costumes are kept alive by street processions.

$\boxed{i}$ CONTACT INFORMATION

Czech Tourist Authority
Czech Centre
95 Great Portland Street
London WIN 5RA
Tel: 020 7291 9920
Fax: 020 7436 8300

Czech & Slovak Tourist Centre
16 Frognal Parade
Finchley Road
London NW3 5HH
Tel: 0800 026 7943
Fax: 020 7794 3265
Web: www.czech-slovak-tourist.co.uk

country's most important wetland sites. These, along with the vast tracts of undisturbed forests, have provided havens for various plant species, including many glacial relicts.

The bird life is also rich, with kingfishers, woodpeckers, peregrines, eagles and capercaillie amongst the rarer species. In contrast, the larger animals are largely absent, having been hunted to extinction in the last century. Only the deer have survived, although a small population of lynx has been reintroduced.

Outdoor activities

Around 1,500km of marked hiking trails provide plenty for the walker and nature lover to enjoy. There are no designated long distance routes, but by linking the well-marked paths it is possible to explore the length and breadth of the mountains. The highest point is Plechý at 1,378m, close to Trojmezí where the Czech, Austrian and German borders meet. Mountain biking is an enjoyable alternative mode of transport.

Eight rather formidably named 'educational paths' focus on particular local areas of interest. These day walks explore the primeval forest, some of the stranger rock formations, the flora of the peat bogs, and the 15th century Schwarzenberg Canal down which timber was once floated to Prague and Vienna.

The River Vltava rises in Šumava. Its upper reaches are well populated with brown and rainbow trout and are consequently a favourite haunt of anglers. The damming of the river for a hydroelectric power station created Lake Lipno. Well-equipped with water sports facilities, it is possible to sail and windsurf here. Below the dam the river is fast flowing. The whitewater of the Devil's Current is a challenging route for canoeing enthusiasts.

Český Krumlov

The Šumava region remained predominately feudal in character up until the 19th century. The opulent splendour of the aristocratic elite's castles and town houses is intertwined with the economical simplicity of the Baroque-style village buildings and timber farmsteads.

Several small museums dotted around the towns also provide insights into mining and glass-making industries, as well as the natural history and archaeology of the Šumava. The Bagpipe Festival held in the castle at Strakonice every August brings an international flavour to the area.

The small medieval town of Český Krumlov deserves all the praise that it is given. It is one of the country's most beautiful towns, with a wealth of Renaissance and Baroque houses lining the maze of cobbled streets and alleyways, whilst nearby looms the

Český Krumlov

Spiš and the Slovenský raj

Comprising a compact plateau, the area known as the Slovenský raj (translated as 'the Slovak paradise') has become an increasingly popular destination since trails were first developed in the late 19th century.

Window waterfall, Suchá Belá gorge

Many walking trips in Slovakia begin with the impressive Tatra mountains which lie across Slovakia's northern border with Poland. After the size and might of these chiselled peaks, it can be easy to pass by the smaller treats crammed into Spiš, the region to the east of the range. In addition to the walking trails of the Slovenský raj, Spiš offers nearby towns and villages filled with fine examples of Gothic cathedrals, churches, chapels, townhouses and castles.

Slovenský raj National Park

The Slovenský raj is a karst plateau, separated from the wider limestone bedrock of central Slovakia by the meandering valley of the Hornád river in the north and the initial stages of the Hnilec river in the south. Smaller streams criss-cross the plateau carving a network of tight, twisting canyons strewn with boulders, waterfalls and rapids. Other surface features include hollows, sinkholes

and disappearing streams, whilst underground there are extensive cave systems. In recognition of its beauty, its geological and ecological importance, and the increasing pressures of development, an area of 20 sq km was granted national park status in 1988.

Nearly all of the park is covered in forest; mainly fir, beech, pine and spruce, although maple and yew can be found in the gorges. Interestingly, the way plants are distributed in the park is largely the reverse of what is found in the mountains. Sun-loving plants crowd on top of the plateau, especially on exposed rocks or open pastureland; lilies and orchids prefer the shade of the forest floors; and edelweiss, normally associated with alpine zones, grows in the darkened coolness of the canyon bottoms.

Although small populations of brown bears, wolves and lynx exist, visitors are much more likely to see the

butterflies, over 2,000 species of which have been documented. Other forest inhabitants include pine martens and foxes, whilst otters hunt along riverbanks and chamois, introduced thirty years ago, roam freely. Birds of prey are common, as are the twittering notes of finches, plovers and wagtails in spring.

Over and underground

The main attraction of the Slovenský raj is that it offers a very different terrain to the open expanses of the central European mountain ranges. Clambering through narrow gorges with the forest canopy casting dark shadows all around, the experience is more intimate and claustrophobic. There is no sweep of skyline as a reference point. Heights are accentuated by the slipperiness of the rocks and noises amplified by echoes reverberating between the walls.

There are 300km of trails across the park. Paths go into the forests and across the open plateau, but the most exciting go through the ravines. Walkers have to follow the exact routes of the streams, constrained from detours by unscalable walls. With ladders or steps used to climb beside waterfalls or cross exposed slabs, a hike can be both rewarding

The town hall in Levoča

The sites around Spišské Podhradie have been incorporated into the UNESCO list of world cultural heritage. The castle of Spišský hrad is always an impressive sight, its thick limestone walls rearing up from the surrounding plain. Perched on a rocky outcrop, the castle guaranteed the security of travelling merchants whilst deterring jealous rivals from disrupting the continuous flow of goods. Starting from a single central tower, the castle's sprawling size was extended over four centuries, with towers, palaces, entrance gates and battlements added at various stages.

The Spišská kapitula complex stands nearby in deliberate opposition to the castle's determinedly secular show of power. This fortified religious compound was the church's means of asserting its control over the population and defending itself against invaders from the east. The main building is the two towered Cathedral of St Martin.

A few kilometres south in Žehra is the Church of the Holy Ghost, a small Early Gothic building with a black-tiled, steep-pitched roof and an onion-shaped dome atop the main tower. Inside, members of the Sigray family had the walls decorated in religious frescoes – *The Tree of Life* and *The Living Cross* – their own faces recognisable in the some of the scenes.

The town of Levoča contains several hundred buildings from the Gothic period. The original Gothic town hall was rebuilt in the Renaissance period and now houses a museum. The main church, St James's, contains an amazing example of Gothic wood carving. The altar of Master Pavol is over 18m high with intricate depictions of the Last Supper and life size representations of the Virgin Mary, St James and St John.

and hair raising. Popular routes are often one-way, to reduce passing problems at critical points. Another focal point for visitors is the Dobšinská ice cave in the south-west corner of the park. Here, summer temperatures are well below 0°C, and stalactites are formed when water percolating through the limestone drips into the cave system and freezes.

Gothic Spiš

As nature can be beautiful yet daunting, so art and architecture can evoke comparable feelings with their ability to combine extraordinary detail with sheer physical size. Spiš contains some of the finest examples of Romanesque and Gothic buildings and interior decoration in central Europe.

As well as generating wealth from the gold and silver mines near Gelnica, Spiš held a dominant local position on east–west and north–south medieval trade routes across the continent. The immigration of skilled German artisans – builders, stone masons and wood carvers – in the 13th century gave feudal lords the skill base to convert their accumulated wealth into increasingly elaborate architectural forms in the Gothic style.

CONTACT INFORMATION

Slovenský raj National Park
Letecká 3
052 01 Spišská Nová Ves
Slovakia
Tel: (00 421) 965 442 2010
Fax: (00 421) 965 441 2026
E-mail: slovraj@spisnet.sk

Aggtelek National Park

*Beneath the undulating hills and valleys is hidden a
treasure trove of caves, combining echoing passageways
with intricate limestone structures.*

The Aggtelek National Park is
the Hungarian section of the
Gömör-Torna limestone plateau
which stretches across northern
Hungary and southern Slovakia.
Over 700 caves have been discovered,
some 250 of which are in Aggtelek.
Given national park status in 1985,
the area was listed as a world heritage
site ten years later in recognition of
the geological and geomorphological
importance of its caves. Above
ground, the quiet, forested landscape
is a haven for birds, butterflies,
amphibians and reptiles, as well as
the occasional brown bear or lynx.

Pasque-flower

A limestone landscape

The national park is divided into
two sections by the River Bódva.
The Aggtelek plateau to the north-
west was formed from calcareous
material deposited at the bottom of a
shallow, tropical sea which covered
the area 230 million years ago.
Subsequent uplift of the sedimentary
rock opened cracks and fissures,
which developed into the gorges that
are still etched on the surface today.

Dry stream beds show the paths of
seasonal water flows, whilst the
sudden slump of sinkholes mark
the funnels through which water
infiltrates the plateau. Where the

forest cover has been removed from
the slopes, the rock has been eroded
by wind and rain to produce uneven
limestone pavements known as the
Devil's Ploughland. Beneath this
pockmarked surface lie the caves.

Baradla's subterranean art

Baradla is the biggest and best known
of the caves. Rainwater and melted
snow penetrating the plateau, have
reacted with the calcium carbonate
present in the limestone, dissolving it.
Over the past 2 million years corrosion
and collapse has produced a network
of corridors and caverns. The complex
was largely ignored until surveyed

properly at the end of the 18th
century. As the extent and beauty of
the cave became apparent, Baradla
developed as a popular destination
for adventurous tourists.

Baradla has a breathtaking array of
dripstone formations. Visitors are
treated to a seemingly unending
display of intricate stalactites,
stalagmites, draperies and flowstones
An active imagination is all that it
takes to convert the decorations into
the Xylophone, the Dragon's Head,
the Lighthouse, the Weeping Willow,
Noah's Ark, the Yawning Crocodile,
the Butcher's Shop and the 17m high
Observatory stalagmite.

The caverns can be equally as
impressive. In the Mirror Hall the
detail of the ceiling is reflected in the
perfect calm of the underground lake,
whilst the Concert Hall hosts an
annual programme of classical music.
The stalagmites in the Black Chamber
are darkened with soot from early
tourists' torches, whilst the best
colours are the vivid whites, yellows,
reds and browns at Jósvafő.

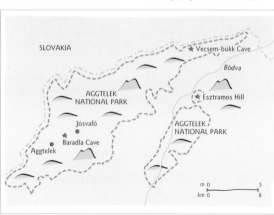

The Dragon's Head dripstone in the Baradla cave

The Aggtelek karst

Aggtelek's wildlife

Back on the surface, the park is mainly covered in beech, oak and ash, but the forest clearings, grasslands, bare hilltops and occasional watercourses provide a variety of ecological niches.

White-bibbed dippers, kingfishers and wagtails feed along the stream banks, whilst hazel grouse inhabit the oak woods. Dice snakes bask in the sun on rocks close to the streams and the rare Aesculapian snake slithers through the woods. Snake-eyed skinks scuttle across boulders and the fire salamander, with its bright orange streaks and blotches, is found near Tengerszem pond.

Bats are common; twenty one of the twenty eight European species are found in the park, including the Mediterranean horseshoe bat. Some prefer to hibernate in the constant temperatures of the caves; others prefer hollow trees or church towers.

The fauna of Aggtelek is not restricted to the surface habitats. However, despite the caves supporting around 500 species, visitors are unlikely to see many. The rarest examples – the Hungarian blind carabid beetle and the well shrimp – live only in the dark recesses of the lower levels of Baradla.

Visiting the Aggtelek karst

The surrounding mountains protect Aggtelek, sheltering the park from the climatic fluctuations which affect the Great Plains to the south. The area is wettest in spring and early summer, when the heaviest rains combine with

Red-backed shrike

the spring melt to swell the streams and flood parts of the caves. It is driest at the end of the summer, with most of the surface water disappearing.

The Baradla cave is open all year round, but access is by guided tour only. There are several ways into the cave, but the main entrance is neatly

tucked below the 50m high Baradla cliffs on the edge of Aggtelek village. Shorter tours follow the walkways and electric lights of the airy central passageway, which often breaks into larger chambers and caverns. Longer tours, including a seven hour trip, explore the smaller lateral corridors. Here visitors walk along stream beds, dry or muddy depending on the season, and carry their own torches.

Above ground, as well as nature trails and specialist walks for those interested in bird-watching, zoology, botany or photography, there are tours that explore Aggtelek's long human history. The first evidence of human habitation dates from 7,000 years ago when a Neolithic people inhabited the Baradla cave entrance, leaving behind tools and pottery.

Subsequent occupations are marked by gold jewellery and black pottery from the Bronze Age and an Iron Age burial site in the Hall of Bones, the first chamber within the Baradla cave.

ⓘ CONTACT INFORMATION

Aggtelek National Park
Tengerszem oldal 1
3758 Jósvafő
Hungary
Tel & Fax: (00 36) 48 350006
Web: www.anp.hu

Hortobágy National Park

The Great Hungarian Plains offer much more than emptiness. The land, often hailed as 'Where the sky meets the Earth', possesses a mosaic of ecosystems teeming with some of the richest bird-life in Europe.

![The annual crane migration]

The annual crane migration

The sights and sounds that greet visitors in Hortobágy today are not those of a neatly preserved environment, but rather a rescued one. The creation of the national park in 1973 was a final attempt to halt the adverse impacts of mechanised agriculture and give conservationists the time to recreate ecosystems that were on the brink of disappearing.

The most rewarding times of year for the nature lover are undoubtedly when the bird migrations take place. In spring, the skies are darkened with 200,000 white-fronted, greylag and bean geese which come to feed in the wetlands. In autumn, it is the ducks which migrate, tens of thousands resting at the Halastó ponds before continuing their long journey from

Finland down to their wintering grounds in northern Africa. However, the most spectacular event is the annual crane migration, with over 50,000 birds roosting in the shallow fish ponds before continuing elegantly south across the plains.

Whilst Hortobágy National Park covers only a fraction of the plains it does extend over almost 800 sq km of grasslands, marshes and fish ponds. The nature trails act as a good introduction to these ecosystems. They are, however, scattered around the park and accessing these can be difficult without transport. Entrance is by ticket only.

Flood-plains and forests

Hortobágy was once the flood-plain of the Tisza and Berettyó rivers. A patchwork of forests and marshes, the flood-plain was the home of peasant farmers who lived and worked on islands of fertile soil. The area was largely deforested by the destructive passage of armies throughout the Middle Ages. Now only pockets of the original forests are left, such as at

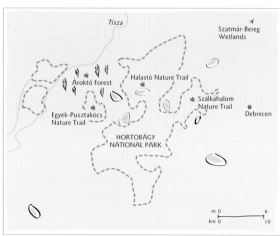

Tisza

Szatmár-Bereg
Wetlands

Arokto Forest   Halastó Nature Trail

Szálkahalom
Nature Trail

Debrecen

Egyek-Pusztakócs
Nature Trail

HORTOBÁGY
NATIONAL PARK

m 0   6
km 0   10

Ároktő, where willows line the banks and stands of oak, ash and elm grow higher up. In the mid 19th century the River Tisza was dammed, and although it still continued to flow, the yearly cycle of flooding was controlled. As the marshes dried and the soil became increasingly infertile, traditional livelihoods disappeared and were replaced by the fertilisers and machines of modern agriculture. With the loss of their habitats many bird species disappeared from Hortobágy.

Nine Hole Bridge

The main focus of the park's work has been to control access and restore the marshlands. Artificial irrigation canals begun in the 1950s have been extended, ponds and reservoirs built or revived and the whole area subject to careful wetland management. The results have been successful. Hortobágy is now protected under the international Ramsar Convention on Wetlands and over 350 breeding and migrating bird species have been recorded.

Hortobágy's puszta

The Szálkahalom trail takes visitors to the edge of the *puszta*, or grasslands. Faced with the vast sweep of land with clouds billowing across blue skies, it is easy to miss small variations in the height of the plain. But these changes in elevation are important. On the high, dry, alkaline soils grow fescue grasses interspersed with dwarf clover and sea lavender; whilst, at marginally lower altitudes where the soil has higher salt concentrations, there is artemisia, viper's grass and sea aster.

Occasionally, if the soil has been eroded, there are patches of inhospitable alkalinity in which only the hardiest plants survive. Where the land rises – in Szálkahalom at the ancient burial tombs – there are

Waterlily

pockets of more fertile loess grassland. The birds of the puszta are typically lapwings, godwits, skylarks, plovers, redshank, cranes and snipes, joined each year by migrants from the cold of the mountains.

Szatmár-Bereg's wetlands

The Szatmár-Bereg Landscape Park is to the north-east of Debrecen, further up the River Tisza and, importantly, above the dam. For visitors, the park provides a glimpse of a wetland environment in its natural state. Its small summits also offer a welcome break from Hortobágy's flat expanse.

The regular flooding of the Tisza regenerates the backwaters, marshes and wet meadows, providing new supplies of nutrients each year. Sand martins nest and kingfishers hatch their young in the collapsed riverbanks, heron colonies live noisily amongst the branches of the poplar, willow and ash groves, and otters and beavers patrol the river shore. On the higher ground there are stands of hornbeam and oak, the forest floor carpeted in the vivid colours of wood anemones, snowdrops, Carpathian crocuses and butterfly orchids.

Further back from the river in the marshes are the eerie, flooded alder groves, the water surface covered in a shimmering green occasionally stained pink with the flowering of water violets. It is in these areas that Szatmár-Bereg is under the greatest pressure. Previous flood prevention schemes have dried up much of the marshes, including Ecsed, once the biggest swamp in the whole country.

ⓘ CONTACT INFORMATION

Hortobágy National Park
Sumen u. 2
4024 Debrecen
Hungary
Tel: (00 36) 52 349922
Fax: (00 36) 52 410645
Web: www.hnp.hu

The sun setting over Hortobágy

Plitvice National Park

Plitvice – a land of lakes and forests – straddles two roles: a natural environment of immense scientific and educational importance and a place of outstanding beauty accommodating a million visitors each year.

Plitvice National Park covers over 194 sq km at the end of the Mala Kapela and Pljesevica mountain chains in continental Croatia. The area has been recognised as a site of particular importance throughout the 20th century. The first calls for Plitvice to be protected were before the First World War. In the late 1920s the area was proclaimed a temporary national park, and permanent status was granted in 1949.

The lakes

A string of sixteen terraced lakes, each connected to the other by a cascade over a limestone barrier, forms the centrepiece of the park. Fed by the Crna Rijeka (Black River), the Bijela Rijeka (White River) and a multitude of subterranean streams, the water is crystal clear, coloured blue, green and turquoise. The upper lakes sit in a wide river valley, whilst the lower ones are trapped in a narrow gorge. The height difference from the highest lake, Prosce, to the lowest, Novaković Brod is 135m, after which the lakes finish at the 72m high Sastavci waterfall.

An evolving environment

Plitvice is unusual in that karst landscapes generally have few surface water features. Normally limestone and dolomitic rocks are dissolved over thousands of years to produce a

The winter freeze in Plitvice

jagged, dry landscape, characterised by sinkholes and disappearing streams leading into a richly developed subterranean drainage network. However, in Plitvice it seems that over the past 4,000 years favourable climatic conditions have encouraged the growth of particular types of mosses in the rapids on the river, where the oxygen levels in the water are highest. The mosses retain the carbonates present in the water in their roots and, as layer builds upon layer, a marked limestone step has been established. Behind each of these barriers a lake has developed.

This process of transformation is continuous. The conditions for moss growth are actually best in the lower lakes and it is here that the barriers grow fastest. As they rise so the depth of the lake immediately behind increases, sometimes drowning previous barriers. There is evidence in Kozjak, the second largest lake, of five of these submerged steps.

The forests

As the lakes depend on the quality of the water flowing into them, the boundaries of the park have been set wide. Plitvice covers all of the surface watershed of the rivers and streams feeding into the lakes. The catchment area is thickly forested with beech, spruce, fir and pine. Because of the range in altitude there are eleven different bio-communities in the park, each with its own reserve. One such area is Corkova Uvala, an 80 hectare spread of primeval beech and fir trees up to 50m in height.

The forests also protect the lakes. Without their cover, erosion of the weak dolomite rocks on the catchment slopes would fill the lakes with debris, whilst abrasion would damage the fragile limestone steps. The forests have not always been successful – old maps indicate a lake which now no longer exists, a victim of previous centuries' deforestation.

Visitors

The authorities have worked hard at managing the varying demands on the park and continually emphasise sustainability. No cars are allowed by the lakes and entrance is by ticket only. Outside the park, development has been light and strictly controlled. It is possible to visit all year round, with the snow-topped mountains and ice-clad falls a real treat in winter.

ℹ CONTACT INFORMATION

Croatian National Tourist Office
2 The Lanchesters
162-164 Fulham Palace Road
London W6 9ER
Tel: 020 8563 7979
Fax: 020 8563 2616
Web: www.htz.hr

One of the park's lakes sitting behind its limestone barrier

Krka National Park

The Šibenik region is one of the Mediterranean's quieter corners where there is still the space and time to make discoveries in a fascinating and varied landscape.

The Krka National Park and the town of Šibenik are symbolic of the contrasts that are found in central Dalmatia. There are the rugged limestone mountains of the mainland set against the intricate archipelagos of the Adriatic Sea. And there is the diversity and natural beauty of the various parks and reserves in combination with the rich and well-preserved cultural heritage of the ancient coastal settlements.

It is a landscape that offers much to the interested visitor and which, thankfully, remains free from the concrete development of resorts.

Visovac monastery sits peacefully in the middle of the River Krka

Mediterranean summers

Šibenik and the central Dalmatian coast enjoy a pleasant Mediterranean climate with warm, dry summers coupled with cooling sea breezes and the temptations of the Adriatic. Inland, in the national park, the river and the waterfalls counteract the heat. In winter it is mild and wet, but note that much is likely to be closed.

Karst landscapes

Krka National Park shows the Croatian karst at its best. Karst environments are formed by the dissolving action of carbon dioxide and water on carbonate rock, which in Krka's case is limestone. Over thousands of years this process has resulted in the formation of a series of distinctive geomorphological features, with the Krka river fighting its way through a long gorge and plunging over rapids. Karst landscapes also feature highly developed subterranean drainage systems, making them ideal territory for those interested in exploring potholes and caves.

The area is rich in Mediterranean and sub-Mediterranean flora and fauna. The surrounding forest is mixed, with hornbeam, cypress, poplar, oak and willow represented, while over 200 bird species are found, including golden eagles, and the river is home to Visovac trout and Adriatic salmon.

The Adriatic is also the Mediterranean at its best. Elsewhere polluted and crowded, in Croatia the sea is blue and clear and clean. It also provides the rhythm of life on the coast, with time being marked in the small fishing villages with the departure and safe return of the boats.

Krka National Park

Established in 1985, the 142 sq km Krka National Park follows the line of the Krka river, from its source in the foothills of the Dinaric mountains on its short journey through the dramatic karst landscape to its finish in the Adriatic. The river flows through a limestone gorge, dropping over 220m in 50km, with eight sets of rapids.

The Krka drops over eight sets of rapids in its journey to the coast

Only two falls – Skradinski buk and Roški slap – are in the park itself, although the former is the most impressive of all with a 46m drop over seventeen limestone steps.

Šibenik

First named in royal documents in 1066, Šibenik is the country's oldest native town on the coast. Originally developing around St Michael's castle,

Šibenik grew haphazardly in medieval times, with a dense, interlocking web of houses and streets interspersed with resplendent ecclesiastical architecture. By the mid 17th century the original castle had been supplemented by three additional defensive fortresses, as the town, by then an autonomous region within the Venetian state, sought to defend itself from the encroaching Ottoman Empire.

The town's most renowned feature is the Cathedral of St James. Designed in the Decorative Gothic style by Juraj Dalmatinac in the mid 15th century, and finished fifty years later by Nikola Firentinac, the building is recognised as a masterpiece of Croatian architecture with its unique skeletal stone construction.

Today, despite the effects of time and war, Šibenik has managed to preserve its character and is now a tourist and cultural centre. For the last forty years the town has held an annual International Children's Festival, where groups from around the world perform in the streets.

Visovac and Skradin

After the noise and rush of the falls, visitors are surprised to find the tranquillity of Visovac. This small island is the site of an old Franciscan monastery, established in the 16th century. Now home to a library of books and manuscripts, the monastery is the best place for contemplating the serenity of the park in perfect peace and quiet.

At the mouth of the Krka, where the river mixes with the Adriatic to form a brackish estuary, is Skradin. Originally an Ilyrian settlement, the Romans developed it into a fortified town and remnants of the aqueduct and other municipal buildings are well preserved as a national monument.

i CONTACT INFORMATION

Croatian National Tourist Office
2 The Lanchesters
162-164 Fulham Palace Road
London W6 9ER
Tel: 020 8563 7979
Fax: 020 8563 2616
Web: www.htz.hr

St John's fortress guards the channel into Šibenik

Kornati National Park

Surrounded by the rich tones of the Adriatic, the Kornati islands are silent, undisturbed places with the intense, bleached colours typical of the rural Mediterranean.

Lying offshore from central Dalmatia the Šibenik archipelago covers 242 islands, rocks and reefs, of which some 109 are within the Kornati National Park.

Kornati's islands

The islands are characterised by sheer coastlines with cliffs plunging up to 100m into the sea in places, whilst on Kornati, the largest of the group, there is an intensely weathered limestone plateau that has developed over thousands of years.

Vegetation is sparse and hardy, with maquis, small pine forests and olive trees competing for the better soils. There are also the remains of previous times: an Illyrian fort, a Roman villa, peasants' huts and fishing shacks, and the remnants of old field systems.

Kornati National Park

Adriatic Sea

In contrast to the land, the sea is a vibrant and varied place. The coastal bed is another world of coral reefs, fissures, caverns and canyons teeming with a throng of sea life. The Adriatic is home to an estimated 365 species of fish, of which 112 are edible, as well as squid, cuttlefish, octopus, shrimp, lobster, mussels and oysters.

Sailing

The Šibenik archipelago has eight marinas and the Adriatic is a perfect place to sail. The sea is clean and transparent, with a beautiful myriad of greens, blues and yellows changing throughout the day.

The Adriatic is also safe as sea currents are generally slow, but the local wind systems bring variety to sailing. From September through to May the *buro* brings cold, dry air and bright weather, whilst the *jugo* is a warm, humid wind accompanied by rain. During the summer, the *maestral* blows fine weather and a cooling breeze in towards the shore.

Murter and Zlarin

The islands of Murter and Zlarin lie close to the shore and outside the boundaries of the national park. Now connected to the mainland by a bridge, Murter is a place of pine woods and sandy bays, the latter being rare for Croatia where rocky shorelines are more common. The landscape is shaped by the traditional activities of fishing, ship building and olive growing, although tourism is becoming increasingly important.

KORNATI NATIONAL PARK

Zlarin is the nearest island to Šibenik, the area's main town. Zlarin was first inhabited in the 13th century and in the 15th century grew famous for supplying corals from local reefs to jewellery craftsmen in far off Naples. Now, following severe population decline throughout the 20th century, the island is beginning to reinvent itself. Facilities remain limited, but Zlarin, with its absence of cars, is an ideal place to escape to.

i CONTACT INFORMATION

Croatian National Tourist Office
2 The Lanchesters
162-164 Fulham Palace Road
London W6 9ER
Tel: 020 8563 7979
Fax: 020 8563 2616
Web: www.htz.hr

The dramatic cliffs of Kornati's islands

ROMANIA

The Danube Delta

At the end of its continental journey, the Danube fragments into a multitude of watery pathways. Travelling by boat is the only way to absorb the immediacy of the sights and sounds of the delta.

The Danube is a river that can leave visitors deluged in facts before they have even seen it. Europe's second longest river curls south-east across the continent from its birthplace in Germany's Black Forest. On this 2,820km journey the river collects water from nearly 200 tributaries, eventually emptying 6,300 cubic metres of water per second into the Black Sea, and depositing about 75 million tonnes of alluvial material per year at the mouth of the delta. But to experience the Danube's might, vibrancy and life, at any point along the river, it is best to get onto the water and go with the flow.

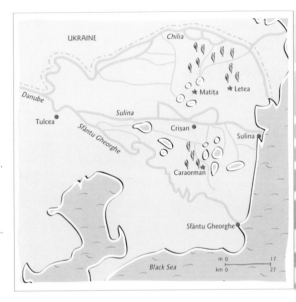

The Danube Delta

At the port of Tulcea, after nearly a 1,000km journey along the Bulgarian border and across the flat plains of southern Romania, the Danube splits into three main branches. The Chilia delineates the northern side, the Sulina forms a central spine and the Sfântu Gheorghe marks the southern edge of the delta. From these arteries branch a network of smaller channels, narrow backwaters, silted canals, lakes, marshes and sandbanks that extend over 5,600 sq km. It is this rich tapestry of ecosystems – twenty five have been documented – and the diversity of flora and fauna they support that makes the Danube Delta a site of world ecological importance.

Preserving the delta

Notwithstanding its size, the delta, like many natural environments, is powerless and fragile when exposed to the vagaries of human actions.

Fishermen on the Danube Delta

Under Communist rule, the exploitation of the delta culminated under the Ceauşescu regime with the commercial harvesting of reeds and the reclamation of land for agriculture. Drained areas were protected from flooding by the erection of dykes, identifiable nowadays by thin lines of trees planted to stabilise earth banks. What was gained for agriculture was lost to fish, especially the sturgeon that arrive each year to deposit their roe (which is harvested to produce caviar) in the sheltered waters. Forced into faster moving channels, where eggs are easily swept away, sturgeon populations have fallen and the species is now endangered.

After the revolution of 1989, the more receptive political atmosphere enabled the delta to be designated as a UNESCO biosphere reserve. Within the reserve are eighteen smaller protected areas where no activity damaging to the local ecosystem is allowed. Visitor access to these zones is regulated by permit. Continual vigilance, especially over such events as agricultural pollution or proposed hydroelectric dams, should ensure that the delta remains protected.

From Rome to the present

With much of the landscape – plains, mountains, valleys and plateaux – dating back millions of years, it is surprising to note that the delta was only formed around 6,000 years ago. Before this, the Danube ended in a simple gulf on the Black Sea but the build up of silt has gradually developed the delta. Tulcea, once on the coast, is now 80km from the sea. The northern part of the delta, fed by the Chilia channel which takes two thirds of the Danube's flow, has grown 6km since the 1830s.

In ancient times the Danube was used by the Greeks and Romans as a natural barrier against the 'barbarian' tribes who lived beyond its far shore. A Roman town called Aegyssus was built on the site of the modern Tulcea, its foundation on seven small hills mimicking Rome. Today, Tulcea is a major port and industrial centre. Heralded as 'the Gateway to the Danube Delta' it is also the starting point for the tourism of the area.

Water covers much of the delta and, as there are no roads, boats are the only option. Cruise ships tout their trade along the Sulina channel, but the best way to experience the delta is leave the main thoroughfares. Motor boats, canoes and rowing boats can all be hired and a guide is useful as the maze of backwaters can become confusing. Occasional small islands provide dry areas for camping, although mosquitoes are a nuisance from May through to July.

In the midst of the delta

Despite the scarcity of land, a huge number of plants, flowers and trees prosper in the delta. Many hectares are covered by floating reed beds, whilst open water is splattered with the crisp colours of white and yellow waterlilies. Mixed forests of poplar, ash, willow and alder grow on sandbanks, the long tendrils of lianas resembling a tropical rainforest.

The sheer variety of habitats makes the delta a birdwatcher's paradise. Over 300 species have been found, including geese, swans, ducks, cranes, herons, songbirds, seabirds, waders, falcons and eagles. Small cormorants proliferate, whilst Europe's largest colony of pelicans is located at the Matita depression. White-fronted geese are one of many species that pass across the delta from the Arctic to more temperate wintering grounds.

Although a few mammals have adapted to life on the marshes or islands, the range of habitats – fast flowing, slow moving, river, estuary and sea – supports around 160 fish species. Perch, pike, bream, zander, carp, tench, barbel, mullet, mackerel and flounder may all be caught outside the sixty days following spawning. Fish are a staple of the local diet and fish dishes can be tried in nearby restaurants.

i CONTACT INFORMATION

Romanian National Tourist Office
83a Marylebone High Street
London W1M 3DE
Tel: 020 7224 3692
Fax: 020 7935 6435

Central Balkan National Park

From forested hills to rugged peaks, the Stara Planina is the place to enjoy some of the most enchanting sunrises and sunsets to be seen anywhere in Bulgaria.

Although not as high as Bulgaria's Rila or Pirin mountains, nor boasting their dramatic alp-like terrain, the Stara Planina are, nonetheless, imposing in their own way. With a total length of over 500km, the main ridge of this range stretches west to east across the country from the Serbian border to the Black Sea.

From spring to autumn

Extending as it does across the centre of Bulgaria, the Stara Planina forms an important climatic boundary between colder northerly and warmer southerly air masses.

This means that the weather can be quite harsh, with heavy winter snows and spring rain. Summer and autumn are, however, much more settled and are good for hiking. Of course, it is this bountiful precipitation that helps to keep the range so lush and green. Thus, despite the occasional shower, in spring and early summer the area becomes a paradise for botanists.

Stara Planina

Although untouched by glaciation, the Stara Planina still possess their own rugged grandeur, particularly the limestone regions where the mighty rock massifs have been deeply carved into narrow canyons and are studded with caves and cascading streams.

The greater area of the park is covered in thick forests, and spruce, fir and a variety of pines are all represented. However, deciduous species, and in particular beech, are dominant, and these mountains are said to preserve one of the largest expanses of ancient beech woods in Europe.

The national park

Founded in 1991, the Central Balkan National Park stretches for about 80km along the main ridge of the Stara Planina. It encompasses about 732 sq km and includes nine strict nature reserves which make up over a quarter of its total area.

Brown bears

The park's territory ranges in altitude from 500m to well over 2,000m, and it is this altitudinal variation, along with its diverse relief and peculiar climate, which helps contribute to its enormous biodiversity. Visitors are well catered for with the provision of ample mountain huts interconnected by a series of marked paths, including a section of the European Rambler Association's E3 trail.

Bears and grasshoppers

The animals of the region are represented by over 200 species of vertebrates. Mammals include brown bears, wolves, wild cats and some isolated groups of chamois, whilst otters live along the rivers.

There is much of interest for ornithologists, with the forests supporting woodpeckers and both Ural and Tengmalm's owls. Above the tree line, alpine accentors,

One of the frescoes at Troyanski monastery

alpine choughs and shorelarks, as well as water pipits, ravens and golden eagles, are found. Notably conspicuous are the great numbers of grasshoppers and crickets that, during the summer months, are an ever present feature of the grassy ridges.

Troyan

Troyan, a quiet town situated at the northern foot of the Stara Planina, is the main gateway to the park. It is well worth spending some time here to visit the museum of folk arts and crafts. Troyan is best known for its ceramics, and today skilled masters still make and decorate pottery by hand. Items are produced from a locally gathered dark brown clay and, after an initial firing, are decorated with a distinctive pattern.

Not far from the town, in the valley of the Cherni Osŭm, lies the Troyanski monastery, the third largest in Bulgaria and one of the most beautiful. Founded in the 14th century, the monastery is renowned for its remarkable frescoes and icons.

Paradise

Situated on the south of Mt Botev, at an altitude between 1,500m and 1,800m, is a locality known quite simply as 'Paradise'. Here on a small grassy plateau beneath a magnificent

Walking in the vicinity of Mt Botev

garland of rocks sits a mountain hut which makes an ideal base from which to explore the region. It can be reached in about four hours from the town of Kalofer by means of a marked trail which climbs up through a thick forest of beech. Beyond the hut, the trail, aptly known as the 'Tarzan

Path', zig-zags steeply up towards the ridgeback, skirting past Raĭskoto Prŭskalo, the biggest waterfall in Bulgaria with a drop of 125m. Finally, less than three hours from the hut, is the summit of Mt Botev (2,376m) and its fine views over the rest of the Stara Planina.

CONTACT INFORMATION

BAAT (Bulgarian Association for Special Interest Travel)
Odysseia-IN Ltd (activity / special interest tour operator)
20-V Stamboliiski Blvd
Sofia 1000
Bulgaria
Tel: (00 359) 2 989 0538
Fax: (00 359) 2 980 3200
E-mail: odysseia@omega.bg
Web: www.newtravel.com

Wilderness Fund
9 Pl. Slaveikov Square
Sofia 1000
Bulgaria
E-mail: wild_fund@mbox.cit.bg

Perelik Guiding Services
31a Canterbury Road
Herne Bay
Kent CT6 5DQ
Tel: 01227 373046
Fax: 01227 373727
E-mail: perelik2000@yahoo.com

Kademliata waterfall

Rila National Park

One of Rila's most striking features is its large number of lakes.
Poetically referred to as the 'Eyes of the Rila', they stare up
brightly towards the surrounding peaks.

It is thought that the Rila mountains take their name from an ancient Thracian word meaning 'rich in water'. It is undoubtedly a fitting title, for this land of shimmering lakes and sparkling streams is the source for three of the Balkan peninsula's major rivers, the Mesta, Maritsa and Iskŭr. It is also a region of stunning alp-like peaks and includes Mt Musala (2,925m), the highest summit in south-eastern Europe.

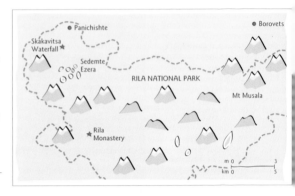

Winter snow

Lying less than 100km south of the Bulgarian capital, Sofia, the Rila mountains are easily accessible. Borovets at the northern foot of the range is one of the most popular bases, especially in winter when it becomes a vibrant ski resort.

However, for those wanting to escape the bustle of the pistes, one of the best ways to experience the Rila in all its winter beauty is to join an organised snow-shoe trek and gain access to some of the more remote and peaceful parts of the mountains.

Spring comes late to the high parts of the range, giving way imperceptibly to summer. For high-level hiking, the long days of July and August are most suitable, although autumn does see the deciduous trees change colours.

Rila National Park

The park was founded in 1992 and covers 1,079 sq km, just under half the total area of the Rila mountains. Almost one fifth of the park has now been designated as strict nature reserves, protecting a range of habitats and ecosystems which are home to a diverse assortment of unique and endangered species.

Within and around the national park are almost thirty huts and refuges linked together by a good network of well-marked paths. These include sections of the E4 and E8 trails which provide the perfect way to visit some of the most beautiful parts of Rila.

Rila monastery in winter

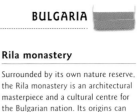

Snow-shoeing in the vicinity of Sedemte Ezera

Alpine landscapes

The Rila mountains are geologically very complex, but dominated by crystalline schists, granites and granito-gneiss. These ancient rocks have been successively folded and uplifted, and then sculpted by the power of glaciation into an alpine-type landscape of deep trough valleys, moraines and cirques.

But the park certainly isn't all rocks and scree. There are also large tracts of alpine meadows, whilst more than 60% of its area is covered by some of the most diverse and ecologically valuable forests in Bulgaria.

Wild boar

The distinctive scrapes and furrows left by wild boar are a common sight amongst the dwarf pine, though the animals themselves are much less conspicuous. Brown bears, wolves and wild cats also live here but are rarely seen. Sightings of an occasional small group of chamois bounding across rocks, or of roe deer and red squirrels are much more likely.

Several pairs of golden eagle nest within the park, as well as goshawks, and kestrels. Wallcreepers can be found in several places, as can colonies of alpine choughs. Within the forests, nutcrackers advertise their presence with their harsh scolding calls, whilst the three-toed woodpecker is a more secretive resident. Along streams, grey wagtails and dippers are much in evidence.

Sedemte Ezera

Situated in a large cirque on the northern flank of the mountains, this group of seven glacial lakes is one of the most attractive and popular places in the national park.

The lakes lie scattered down the mountainside, each with its own unique character and specific name. Dominating the cirque is Mt Haidūta which, although not the highest peak in the region, still commands attention on account of its dramatic shape and prominent position.

Rila monastery

Surrounded by its own nature reserve, the Rila monastery is an architectural masterpiece and a cultural centre for the Bulgarian nation. Its origins can be traced back to a hermit who came to Rila in the 10th century.

The monastery appears like a fortress from the outside, with high sombre stone walls. However, the interior offers a dramatic contrast with tiers of elegant whitewashed arcades and verandas surrounding a courtyard and a brightly decorated church.

ⓘ CONTACT INFORMATION

BAAT (Bulgarian Association for Special Interest Travel)
Odysseia-IN Ltd (activity / special interest tour operator)
20-V Stamboliiski Blvd
Sofia 1000
Bulgaria
Tel: (00 359) 2 989 0538
Fax: (00 359) 2 980 3200
E-mail: odysseia@omega.bg
Web: www.newtravel.com

Perelik Guiding Services
31a Canterbury Road
Herne Bay
Kent CT6 5DQ
Tel: 01227 373046
Fax: 01227 373727
E-mail: perelik2000@yahoo.com

A horse-rider rests near to Souhoto Ezero

Pirin National Park

The northern section of the Pirin mountains is particularly wild, with an array of jagged peaks and rugged knife-like ridges forming the heart of the Pirin National Park.

Rising up in the south-western part of Bulgaria between the Struma and Mesta rivers, the Pirin mountains are one of the most dramatic and spectacular ranges in the country. They are aptly named after the Slavic storm god, Perun, who was said to have ruled over this harshly beautiful region.

Pirin National Park

Originally founded in 1962, the boundaries of the Pirin National Park have been systematically expanded over the years. It now covers more than 400 sq km, a large proportion of the entire range. The park incorporates two strict reserves and a host of other protected natural sites, and has been included in the list of UNESCO world heritage sites.

With wild camping forbidden in the region, there are several huts and refuges scattered about the mountains providing convenient accommodation. These are connected by a good network of marked paths, including a section of the trans-continental E4 trail which leads right through the heart of the park.

The arrival of spring

Pirin's weather can be as severe as its landscape, particularly in winter when the mountains experience heavy snowfalls and occasional avalanches.

Spring always approaches from the south, wafted gently up the valleys of the Struma and Mesta by warm Mediterranean winds. Nature lovers can follow it as it creeps gently through the mountains, first exploring the dappled forests and sunlit glades of the lower southern slopes before venturing up to the northern peaks where even in the height of summer there are still pockets of ice, as well as splendid displays of alpine flowers.

Trees and mountains

The altitude of the park ranges from about 1,000 to almost 3,000m, including some forty or so peaks above 2,500m, with Mt Vihren (2,918m) being the highest. The lower slopes are thickly forested, and although there are beech woods in places, conifers are dominant, including interesting species such as Macedonian and Balkan pine.

One specimen of the latter, found growing in the upper reaches of the Bûnderitsa valley, ranks amongst the oldest trees in the country with an estimated age of about 1,300 years. Higher up, the forest gives way to dwarf pine and juniper, and above this is a world of alpine meadows, scree and rocks. Here, scattered amongst the crests and ridges are a score of gracefully sculpted cirques containing over 170 glacial lakes.

Pirin poppies and chamois

The majority of the park is composed of granites, gneiss and crystalline schists, but in the north-west the highest parts are formed from marble and limestone. This juxtaposition of siliceous and calcareous rocks means that the Pirin boasts a diverse flora including some hundred or so Bulgarian endemics, of which several grow nowhere else in the country. One of the most beautiful of these is the delicate yellow Pirin poppy, which can be found flowering high up on the face of Mt Vihren throughout the summer.

The fauna of the park is equally as varied, with mammals such as brown bear, wolf, wild cat, wild boar, pine marten and red deer sheltering in the forests. Beyond the tree line, on the most inaccessible peaks, walkers can catch the occasional glimpse of chamois moving fleet-footedly across the rocks. It is here too that golden eagles, peregrines, alpine choughs and wallcreepers can be spotted.

Bansko

Bansko is the gateway to the national park, a small town with a laid-back feel sitting comfortably at the north-eastern foot of the range. Despite its development into a popular resort, the place still manages to maintain its old-world character and charm.

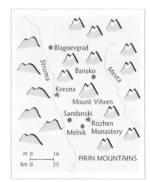

Tevno Ezero with Mt Kamenitsa in the background

The centre of the town is particularly well preserved, with numerous traditional National Revival Period houses flanking a network of narrow cobbled alleys. Partly hidden behind high walls, Bansko's houses have the appearance of little fortresses with small barred windows and solid doors. There are also a couple of beautiful churches, including one dedicated to the Holy Trinity which is possibly the finest in the region.

Tevno Ezero

Within the courtyard of the Holy Trinity church at Bansko is a statue of Peyu Yavorov, a famous Bulgarian poet and revolutionary whose activities and writings are closely connected with the Pirin. A favourite haunt of his was Tevno Ezero, a beautiful glacial lake situated up in the heart of the mountains on an expansive grassy cirque, where he wrote one of his most popular works. It is indeed an inspirational spot, with the lush meadows and shimmering water contrasting starkly with the harsh rock walls of Mt Kamenitsa (2,822m) and its neighbours.

Kazanite cirques

For nature lovers, one of the most rewarding excursions in the national park is a visit to the Kazanite cirques, tucked in beneath the north-eastern face of Mt Vihren. From the Bûnderitsa hut, a well-marked path first leads through ancient forests of Macedonian pine, before emerging into the open and climbing up through two lakeless cirques. The lower cirque is covered in lush grass, and the upper in rocks and scree, but both are bejewelled by a wealth of alpine flowers. Here, there is a good chance of seeing chamois.

ℹ CONTACT INFORMATION

BAAT (Bulgarian Association for Special Interest Travel)
Odysseia-IN Ltd (activity / special interest tour operator)
20-V Stamboliiski Blvd
Sofia 1000
Bulgaria
Tel: (00 359) 2 989 0538
Fax: (00 359) 2 980 3200
E-mail: odysseia@omega.bg
Web: www.newtravel.com

Pirin Tourism Forum
3 Stefan Milenkov str.
2700 Blagoevgrad
Bulgaria
Tel & Fax: (00 359) 73 35458
E-mail: scabrin@pop3.aubg.bg

Perelik Guiding Services
31a Canterbury Road
Herne Bay
Kent CT6 5DQ
Tel: 01227 373046
Fax: 01227 373727
E-mail: perelik2000@yahoo.com

CREDITS

Thank you to all those individuals and organisations who contributed material for the Activity Series.

■ Text credits

Julian Perry	Bulgaria
Benedikte Ranum	Norway
Terry Richardson	Turkey

■ Picture credits

Pictures are credited from top to bottom on each relevant page. Every effort has been made to ensure that these are correct. If there are any unintentional errors or omissions we would be pleased to update the information in future editions.

4a	Dawn Runnals / Cornwall Tourist Board
4b	Faroe Islands Tourist Board
4c	Photo: Joomas Trapido
4d	Bernese Oberland Tourism
4e	Circeo National Park
4f	Photo: D Maraux
8a	Seitseminen National Park
8b	Greenland Tourism, Copenhagen, ©Manfred Horender
8c	Den Norske Turistforening
8d	Seitseminen National Park
8e	Iceland Travel Group Ltd
8f	Faroe Islands Tourist Board
10a	Seitseminen National Park
10b	Seitseminen National Park
11	Seitseminen National Park
12	Finnish Tourist Board
13a	Finnish Tourist Board
13b	Timo Hentilä
14	Pyhä-Häkki National Park
15	Pyhä-Häkki National Park
16a	Seitseminen National Park
16b	Seitseminen National Park
17	Seitseminen National Park
18	Swedish Travel & Tourism Council
19	Swedish Travel & Tourism Council
20	Lonsstyrelsen Vösternorrland
21a	Lonsstyrelsen Vösternorrland
21b	Swedish Travel & Tourism Council
22	Photo: Klas Johansson, Publisher: Naturvårdsverket Förlag
23	Photo: Klas Johansson, Publisher: Naturvårdsverket Förlag
24a	Turistinformationen Gnosjö
24b	Turistinformationen Gnosjö
25	Turistinformationen Gnosjö
26	Norwegian Tourist Board
27	Bodø Regional Hiking Association
28a	Hardangervidda Natursenter Eidfjord
28b	Hardangervidda Natursenter Eidfjord
29	Hardangervidda Natursenter Eidfjord
30a	Den Norske Turistforening
30b	Den Norske Turisforening
31a	Den Norske Turisforening
31b	Den Norske Turisforening
32	Erik Bannersvej, JNA Express Foto
33	Erik Bannersvej, JNA Express Foto
34a	Danish Tourist Board
34b	Danish Tourist Board
35	Danish Tourist Board
36	Iceland Travel Group Ltd
39a	Photo: Christopher Rennie
39b	Iceland Travel Group Ltd
40a	England's North Country Tourist Board
40b	Courtesy of Yorkshire Tourist Board
40c	Paul Tomkins – Scottish Tourist Board
40d	Wales Tourist Board Photo Library
40e	Wales Tourist Board Photo Library
40f	Dawn Runnals / Cornwall Tourist Board
42	©Dúchas, The Heritage Service, 51 St. Stephen's Green, Dublin 2
43a	©Dúchas, The Heritage Service, 51 St. Stephen's Green, Dublin 2
43b	©Dúchas, The Heritage Service, 51 St. Stephen's Green, Dublin 2
44	©Dúchas, The Heritage Service, 51 St. Stephen's Green, Dublin 2
45	©Dúchas, The Heritage Service, 51 St. Stephen's Green, Dublin 2
46a	©Dúchas, The Heritage Service, 51 St. Stephen's Green, Dublin 2
46b	©Dúchas, The Heritage Service, 51 St. Stephen's Green, Dublin 2
48a	©Dúchas, The Heritage Service, 51 St. Stephen's Green, Dublin 2
48b	©Dúchas, The Heritage Service, 51 St. Stephen's Green, Dublin 2
49	©Dúchas, The Heritage Service, 51 St. Stephen's Green, Dublin 2
50a	©Dúchas, The Heritage Service, 51 St. Stephen's Green, Dublin 2
50b	©Dúchas, The Heritage Service, 51 St. Stephen's Green, Dublin 2
51	©Dúchas, The Heritage Service, 51 St. Stephen's Green, Dublin 2
52a	©Dúchas, The Heritage Service, 51 St. Stephen's Green, Dublin 2
52b	©Dúchas, The Heritage Service, 51 St. Stephen's Green, Dublin 2
53	Bord Failte – Irish Tourist Board
54	Mitchell Kane Associates
55	Bord Failte – Irish Tourist Board
56a	The Highlands of Scotland Tourist Board
56b	The Highlands of Scotland Tourist Board
57	The Highlands of Scotland Tourist Board
58a	The Highlands of Scotland Tourist Board
58b	The Highlands of Scotland Tourist Board
59	The Highlands of Scotland Tourist Board
60a	Cairngorm Ski Area
60b	Cairngorm Ski Area
61	Cairngorm Ski Area
62a	Argyll, the Isles, Loch Lomond, Stirling & Trossachs Tourist Board
62b	Argyll, the Isles, Loch Lomond, Stirling & Trossachs Tourist Board
63	Paul Tomkins – Scottish Tourist Board
64	Northumberland National Park
65a	Northumberland National Park
65b	Northumberland National Park
66a	Yorkshire Tourist Board
66b	Yorkshire Tourist Board
67	Yorkshire Tourist Board
68a	North Yorkshire Moors National Park
68b	North Yorkshire Moors National Park
69	North Yorkshire Moors National Park
70	Peak District National Park Centre
71	Peak District National Park Centre
72a	Linda Sheard
72b	Brian Pearce
73a	©ENPA
73b	West Somerset Tourism
74a	Wales Tourist Board Photo Library
74b	Wales Tourist Board Photo Library
75	Wales Tourist Board Photo Library
76	Wales Tourist Board Photo Library
77	Wales Tourist Board Photo Library
78	Wales Tourist Board Photo Library
79	Wales Tourist Board Photo Library
80	Wales Tourist Board Photo Library
81a	Wales Tourist Board Photo Library
81b	Wales Tourist Board Photo Library
82a	Cliché Jean-Pierre Gestin – Parc Naturel Regional d'Armorique
82b	Comité Régional du Tourisme de Limousin
82c	Photo: D Maraux
82d	Tourismusverband Ostbayern e.V.
82e	Touristik Nördlicher Schwarzwald e.V.
82f	Photo: Bernhard Grimm
84	Parc Naturel Régional d'Armorique
85a	Parc Naturel Régional d'Armorique
85b	Parc Naturel Régional d'Armorique
86	Parc National Régional de la Brenne
87a	Parc National Régional de la Brenne
87b	Parc National Régional de la Brenne
88a	Comité Régional du Tourisme de Limousin
88b	Comité Régional du Tourisme de Limousin
89	Comité Régional du Tourisme de Limousin
90a	Marc Sagot
90b	Photothèque PNRLF – Jaques Fournier
91	Pierre Soissons
92a	Photothèque PNRLF – Jaques Fournier
92b	Photothèque PNRLF – Serge Chaleil
93a	Photothèque PNRLF – Serge Chaleil
93b	Photothèque PNRLF – Jaques Fournier
94	Parc Naturel Régional du Morvan, Alain Millot
95a	Parc Naturel Régional du Morvan, Alain Millot
95b	Parc Naturel Régional du Morvan, Alain Millot
96	PNRGC, Serge Fenech
97a	PNRGC, Laurent Gaignerot
97b	PNRGC, Serge Fenech
98	Luxembourg National Tourist Office
99	Luxembourg National Tourist Office
100a	Luxembourg National Tourist Office
100b	Luxembourg National Tourist Office
101a	Luxembourg National Tourist Office
101b	Luxembourg National Tourist Office
102	Hautes Fagnes–Eifel National park
103a	Hautes Fagnes–Eifel National park
103b	Document OPT & A.K.
104	Biesbosch National Park
105a	Biesbosch National Park
105b	Biesbosch National Park
106	Hoge Veluwe National Park
107a	Hoge Veluwe National Park
107b	Hoge Veluwe National Park
108a	Archiv NPA/Pollmeier
108b	Archiv NPA/Pollmeier
109	Archiv NPA/Pollmeier
110	Nationalparkamt Rügen, Manfred Kutscher
111	National Park Vorpommersche Boddenlandschaft: Sporns
113a	Nationalparkamt Müritz
113b	Nationalparkamt Müritz
114a	Hans-Jörg Wilke
114b	Bernhard Grimm
115a	Hans-Jörg Wilke
115b	Hans-Jörg Wilke
116a	Hans-Jörg Wilke
116b	Bernhard Grimm
117	Hans-Jörg Wilke
118a	Nationalparkhaus Torfhaus
118b	Nationalparkhaus Torfhaus
119	Nationalparkhaus Torfhaus
120	Nationalparkverwaltung Bayerischer Wald: Pöhlmann
121a	Kurverwaltung Zweisel
121b	Kurverwaltung Zweisel
122a	Photo: Ammon
122b	Photo library: APT del Trentino. Photo: V. Banal
122c	Bernese Oberland Tourism
122d	Office du Tourisme du Jura Bernois

22e Parco Nazionale Dolomiti Bellunesi
22f ©Schweiz Tourismus / C. Sonderegger
24 Stéphane Godin
25a Photo: Chamagne
25b Parc National des Ecrins
26 Parc Naturel Régional du Queyras
27a Parc Naturel Régional du Queyras
27b Parc Naturel Régional du Queyras
28 Parc Naturel Régional du Queyras
29 Parc Naturel Régional du Queyras
30a Office du Tourism du Jura Bernois
30b Office du Tourism du Jura Bernois
31a Office du Tourism du Jura Bernois
31b Courtesy of Tourist Board, Switzerland
32a Photo: SVZ / F. Pfenniger
32b Valais Tourism
33a Valais Tourism
33b Valais Tourism
34a The Swiss National Park
34b The Swiss National Park
35 The Swiss National Park
36a The Swiss National Park
36b The Swiss National Park
37 Photo: SVZ / F. Pfenniger
38 Regione Autonoma, Valle d'Aosta
39 Regione Autonoma, Valle d'Aosta
40a Parco Nazionale Val Grande
40b Parco Nazionale Val Grande
41 Parco Nazionale Val Grande
42a Photo Library: APT del Trentino.
    Photo: Visintainer
42b Photo Library: APT del Trentino.
    Photo: Spagnolli
43 Photo Library: APT del Trentino.
    Photo: V. Banal
44 Photo Library: APT del Trentino
45a Photo Library: APT del Trentino.
    Photo: Zotta
45b Photo Library: APT del Trentino.
    Photo: G. Cauulu
46a Photo Library: APT del Trentino.
    Photo: G. Cauulu
46b Photo Library: APT del Trentino.
    Photo: G. Cauulu
47 Photo Library: APT del Trentino.
    Photo: G. Cauulu
48 Liechtenstein National Tourist Office
49 Liechtenstein National Tourist Office
50 Ammon: Kurdirektion Berchtesgaden
51a Storto: Kurdirektion Berchtesgaden
51b Ammon: Kurdirektion Berchtesgaden
52a Karnten Werburg Marketing
52b Foto-archiv Tirol Werbung
53 Karnten Werburg Marketing
54a Karnten Werburg Marketing
54b Karnten Werburg Marketing
55 Karnten Werburg Marketing
56a Donau-auen National Park
56b Donau-auen National Park
57 Donau-auen National Park
58a NeusiedlerSee–Seewinkel National Park
58b NeusiedlerSee–Seewinkel National Park
59a NeusiedlerSee–Seewinkel National Park
59b NeusiedlerSee–Seewinkel National Park
60a Slovenia Pursuits
60b Slovenia Pursuits
61 Slovenia Pursuits
62a ©Iris Kürschner
62b Slovenia Pursuits
63 ©Slovenian Tourist Board
64a Circeo National Park
64b Parque Natural de Montesinho
64c Granada Tourism Office
64d Spanish Tourist Office, London
64e Algarve Tourist Board
64f Algarve Tourist Board
66 Parque Natural de Montesinho
67a Parque Natural de Montesinho
67b Parque Natural de Montesinho
68 João Paulo (Pena Palace, Sintra)

69 Nuno Calvet (Monserrate Park, Sintra)
70 Dália Lourenço
71a JL Dória
71b Dália Lourenço
72a CENEAM – O.A. Parques Nacionales,
    España
72b CENEAM – O.A. Parques Nacionales,
    España
73a Lanzarote Tourist Office
73b CENEAM – O.A. Parques Nacionales,
    España
73c CENEAM – O.A. Parques Nacionales,
    España
74 CENEAM – O.A. Parques Nacionales,
    España
75 Spanish Tourist Office
76a CENEAM – O.A. Parques Nacionales,
    España
76b CENEAM – O.A. Parques Nacionales,
    España
77a CENEAM – O.A. Parques Nacionales,
    España
77b CENEAM – O.A. Parques Nacionales,
    España
78 Spanish Tourist Office
79 Spanish Tourist Office
80a Parque Nacional de Doñana
80b Spanish Tourist Office
81 Parque Nacional de Doñana
82 CENEAM – O.A. Parques Nacionales,
    España
83 CENEAM – O.A. Parques Nacionales,
    España
84a Office du Tourisme de
    Porto-Vecchio sud Corse
84b Office Municipal du Tourisme, Bastia
85 Office du Tourisme de
    Porto-Vecchio sud Corse
86a National Park of Foreste Casentinesi
86b National Park of Foreste Casentinesi
88a Parco Nazionale del Monti Sibillini
88b Assessorato al Turisme
    Regione Marche
89 Italian State Tourist Board
    (E.N.I.T.), London
90a Parco Nazionale della Majella
90b Parco Nazionale della Majella
91 Italian State Tourist Board
    (E.N.I.T.), London
92a Parco Nazionale della Majella
92b Parco Nazionale della Majella
93 Parco Nazionale della Majella
94a Pino Sabbatini, Parco Nazionale del
    Gran Sasso e Monti della Laga
94b Maurizio Cardelli, Parco Nazionale del
    Gran Sasso e Monti della Laga
95a Parco Nazionale della Majella
95b Alfonso Di Ottavio, Parco Nazionale
    del Gran Sasso e Monti della Laga
96 Balis
97 Global Scenes, Tunbridge Wells
98a Balis
98b Judith Gilliland
99 Global Scenes, Tunbridge Wells
200 Global Scenes, Tunbridge Wells
201 Balis
202a Terry Richardson,
    Upcountry (Turkey) Ltd
202b Terry Richardson,
    Upcountry (Turkey) Ltd
203a Terry Richardson,
    Upcountry (Turkey) Ltd
203b Terry Richardson,
    Upcountry (Turkey) Ltd
204a Terry Richardson,
    Upcountry (Turkey) Ltd
204b Terry Richardson,
    Upcountry (Turkey) Ltd
205a Terry Richardson,
    Upcountry (Turkey) Ltd

205b Terry Richardson,
    Upcountry (Turkey) Ltd
206a Terry Richardson,
    Upcountry (Turkey) Ltd
206b Terry Richardson,
    Upcountry (Turkey) Ltd
207a Terry Richardson,
    Upcountry (Turkey) Ltd
207b Terry Richardson,
    Upcountry (Turkey) Ltd
208a Photo: Joomas Trapido
208b Lubomir Popiordanov / Odyssia-in
208c Hungarian National Tourist Board
208d Hungarian National Tourist Board
208e Duna-Ipoly Nemzeti Park Igazgatóság
208f Croatian National Tourist Board
210 Vilsandi National Park
211a Vilsandi National Park
211b Vilsandi National Park
212a Soomaa National Park
212b Photo: Joomas Trapido
213 Soomaa National Park
214 Gauja National Park
215a Gauja National Park
215b Gauja National Park
216 Žemaitija National Park
217 Kuršiu Nerija National Park
218a Žemaitija National Park
218b Kuršiu Nerija National Park
219 Kuršiu Nerija National Park
220 Polish National Tourist Office
221 Polish National Tourist Office
222 Polish National Tourist Office
223 Polish National Tourist Office
225a Polish National Tourist Office
225b Polish National Tourist Office
226 Czech Tourist Authority
227 Czech Tourist Authority
228a Czech Tourist Authority
228b Czech Tourist Authority
229 Emma Gilliland
230a Slovenský raj National Park
230b Slovenský raj National Park
231 Czech and Slovak Tourist Centre
232a Aggtelek National Park Directorate
232b Aggtelek National Park Directorate
233a Aggtelek National Park Directorate
233b Aggtelek National Park Directorate
234 Hortobágy Nemzeti Park Igazgatóság
235a Hungarian National Tourist Board
235b Hungarian National Tourist Board
235c Hungarian National Tourist Board
236 Croatian National Tourist Board
237 Croatian National Tourist Board
238a Croatian National Tourist Board
238b Croatian National Tourist Board
239 Croatian National Tourist Board
240a Croatian National Tourist Board
240b Croatian National Tourist Board
241 Croatian National Tourist Board
242 Romanian National Tourist Office
243 Romanian National Tourist Office
244a Lubomir Popiordanov / Odysseia-in
244b Lubomir Popiordanov / Odysseia-in
245a Lubomir Popiordanov / Odysseia-in
245b Lubomir Popiordanov / Odysseia-in
246 Lubomir Popiordanov / Odysseia-in
247a Lubomir Popiordanov / Odysseia-in
247b Lubomir Popiordanov / Odysseia-in
248a Lubomir Popiordanov / Odysseia-in
248b Lubomir Popiordanov / Odysseia-in
249 Lubomir Popiordanov / Odysseia-in
256a Photo SVZ / W. Storto
256b The Highlands of Scotland
    Tourist Board
256c Luxembourg National Tourist Office
256d Finnish Tourist Board
256e Vilsandi National Park
256f Algarve Tourist Board

INDEX

INDEX